Lecture Notes in Artificial Intelligence   5348

Edited by R. Goebel, J. Siekmann, and W. Wahlster

Subseries of Lecture Notes in Computer Science

W0036190

Doron A. Peled
Michael J. Wooldridge (Eds.)

Model Checking and Artificial Intelligence

5th International Workshop, MoChArt 2008
Patras, Greece, July 21, 2008
Revised Selected and Invited Papers

 Springer

Series Editors

Randy Goebel, University of Alberta, Edmonton, Canada
Jörg Siekmann, University of Saarland, Saarbrücken, Germany
Wolfgang Wahlster, DFKI and University of Saarland, Saarbrücken, Germany

Volume Editors

Doron A. Peled
Bar Ilan University
Ramat Gan, 52900, Israel
E-mail: doron.peled@gmail.com

Michael J. Wooldridge
University of Liverpool
Liverpool L69 3BX, UK
E-mail: mjw@liverpool.ac.uk

Library of Congress Control Number: 2009921993

CR Subject Classification (1998): I.2.3, I.2, F.4.1, F.3, D.2.4, D.1.6

LNCS Sublibrary: SL 7 – Artificial Intelligence

ISSN   0302-9743
ISBN-10   3-642-00430-X Springer Berlin Heidelberg New York
ISBN-13   978-3-642-00430-8 Springer Berlin Heidelberg New York

springer.com

© Springer-Verlag Berlin Heidelberg 2009
Printed in Germany

Typesetting: Camera-ready by author, data conversion by Scientific Publishing Services, Chennai, India
Printed on acid-free paper   SPIN: 12623488   06/3180   5 4 3 2 1 0

Preface

Model checking is a branch of software and hardware verification that involves developing algorithms for the automatic verification of systems. Originating from mathematical logic, "model checking" stands for the process of determining whether or not a formula of some logic is satisfied by a model for the logic. Initiated two and a half decades ago, with papers that have gained their authors the 2007 Turing award, this active research area has resulted in rich theory, and the development of a number of widely used model-checking tools. These include Carnegie-Mellon's SMV, Cadence-SMV, and Bell Laboratories' SPIN. Some of the main activities in model checking involve development of expressive specification formalisms, in particular, temporal logics, the modeling of systems, and finding efficient algorithms for automatically checking that a model of a system satisfies its temporal specification.

The success of model checking in the computer-aided verification community has led to a growth of interest in the use of model checking in AI. One common interest between these two fields is verification of autonomous systems. Logics for autonomous systems can express properties that are not commonly used for reactive systems, expressing properties related to the knowledge and belief of components (agents) of the system about other components. New model-checking algorithms, for such specification properties, are challenging and useful for various applications, including online auction mechanisms, which are embedded in various Internet services, and autonomous robots.

Conversely, results in AI are applicable for model checking. The main challenge in model checking is to address the time and space complexity of analyzing realistic systems. Thus, some AI heuristic search techniques can be used as a basis for model checking. SAT-solving is another interface between these two research areas; while being the focus of AI research for many years, a new model-checking technique called "Bounded Model Checking" makes use of it as a basis for faster analysis and for analyzing bigger systems.

The MOCHART workshop brings together both researchers in AI with an interest in model checking and researchers in model checking who are interested in AI techniques.

Previous editions of the workshop were held in Riva del Garda, Italy in 2006 (as a satellite workshop of ECAI), San Francisco in 2005 (as a satellite workshop of Concur), Acapulco in 2003 (as a satellite workshop of IJCAI03), and Lyon in 2002 (as a satellite workshop of ECAI02).

MOCHART 2008 was held as a satellite workshop of the ECAI 2008 conference.

June 2008   Doron Peled
                                                           Michael Wooldridge

Workshop Organization

Co-chairs

- Doron Peled (Israel)
- Michael Wooldridge (UK)

Program Committee

- Rajeev Alur (USA)
- Massimo Benerecetti (Italy)
- Rafael Bordini (UK)
- Kousha Etessami (UK)
- Michael Fisher (UK)
- Gerard Holzmann (USA)
- Hadas Kress-Gazit (USA)
- Orna Kupferman (Israel)
- Alessio Lomuscio (UK)
- Ron van de Meyden (Australia)
- Peter Niebert (France)
- Charles Pecheur (USA)
- Wojciech Penczek (Poland)
- Franco Raimondi (UK)
- Mark Ryan (UK)
- Farn Wang (China)

Table of Contents

Verifying Time and Communication Costs of Rule-Based Reasoners

Natasha Alechina, Brian Logan, Nguyen Hoang Nga, and Abdur Rakib*

University of Nottingham, Nottingham, UK
{nza,bsl,hnn,rza}@cs.nott.ac.uk

Abstract. We present a framework for the automated verification of time and communication requirements in systems of distributed rule-based reasoning agents which allows us to determine how many rule-firing cycles are required to solve the problem, how many messages must be exchanged, and the trade-offs between the time and communication resources. We extend CTL* with belief and communication modalities to express bounds on the number of messages the agents can exchange. The resulting logic, $\mathcal{L}_{CRB}$, can be used to express both bounds on time and on communication. We provide an axiomatisation of the logic and prove that it is sound and complete. Using a synthetic but realistic example system of rule-based reasoning agents which allows the size of the problem and the distribution of knowledge among the reasoners to be varied, we show the Mocha model checker [1] can be used to encode and verify properties of systems of distributed rule-based agents. We describe the encoding and report results of model checking experiments which show that even simple systems have rich patterns of trade-offs between time and communication bounds.

1 Introduction

A key application of multi-agent systems research is distributed problem solving. Distributed approaches to problem solving allow groups of agents to collaborate to solve problems which no single agent could solve alone (e.g., because no single agent has all the information necessary to solve the problem), and/or to solve problems more effectively, e.g., in less time than a single agent. For a given problem and system of reasoning agents, many different solution strategies may be possible, each involving different commitments of computational resources and communication by each agent. For different multi-agent systems, different solution strategies will be preferred depending on the relative costs of computational and communication resources for each agent. These tradeoffs may be different for different agents (e.g., reflecting their computational capabilities or network connection) and may reflect the agent's commitment to a particular problem. For example, an agent may be unable to commit more than a given portion of its available computational resources or its available communication bandwidth to a particular problem. For a given system of agents with specified inferential abilities and resource bounds it may not be clear whether a particular problem can be solved at

---

* This work was supported by the Engineering and Physical Sciences Research Council [grant number EP/E031226].

D. Peled and M. Wooldridge (Eds.): MOCHART 2008, LNAI 5348, pp. 1–14, 2009.

all, or, if it can, what computational and communication resources must be devoted to its solution by each agent. For example, we may wish to know whether a goal can be achieved if a particular agent, perhaps possessing key information or inferential capabilities, is unable (or unwilling) to contribute more than a given portion of its available computational resources or bandwidth to the problem.

There has been considerable work in the agent literature on distributed problem solving in general (for example, [2,3,4,5]) and on distributed reasoning in particular ([6,7]). Much of this work analyses the time and communication complexity of distributed reasoning algorithms. However, while we have upper (and some lower) bounds on time requirements for reasoning in distributed systems, possible trade-offs between resources such as time and communication are less clear. In previous work, e.g., [8,9,10] we have investigated time vs. memory trade-offs for single reasoners, or just time requirements in [11], and in [12], we investigated resource requirements for time, memory and communication for systems of distributed resolution reasoners.

In this paper, we focus on a more detailed investigation of time and communication trade-offs for *rule-based reasoners*. We present a framework for the automated verification of time and communication requirements in systems of distributed rule-based reasoning agents. We extend CTL* with belief and communication modalities to express bounds on the number of messages the agents can exchange. Communication modalities are a novel logical concept (the only related work we are aware of is [13] which introduced nullary modalities for expressing the number of formulas in agent's memory), and considerably simplify the logic expressing communication bounds presented in [12]. The resulting logic, $\mathcal{L}_{CRB}$, can be used to express both bounds on time and on communication. We provide an axiomatisation of the logic and prove that it is sound and complete. Using $\mathcal{L}_{CRB}$ to specify bounds on the number of messages the agents can exchange, we can investigate trade-offs between time and communication resources, and we show how the Mocha model checker [1] can be used to encode and verify properties of such systems.

The structure of the paper is as follows. In section 2 we describe systems of communicating rule-based reasoners that we want to verify. In section 3 we introduce the epistemic logic $\mathcal{L}_{CRB}$. We describe the Mocha encoding of the transition systems which are models of the logic in section 4. Model-checking experiments are described in section 5 and we conclude in section 6.

2   Systems of Communicating Rule-Based Reasoners

In this section, we describe the systems of communicating rule-based agents which we investigate.

The system consists of n_A agents, where $n_A \geq 1$. We will assume that each agent has a number in $\{1, \ldots, n_A\}$, and use variables i and j over $\{1, \ldots, n_A\}$ to refer to agents. Each agent has a *program*, consisting of propositional Horn clause rules, and a working memory, which contains facts (propositions).[1] If an agent i has a rule $A_1, \ldots, A_n \to B$,

---

[1] The restriction to propositional rules is not a very drastic assumption: if the rules do not contain functional symbols and we can assume a fixed finite set of constant symbols, then any set of first-order Horn clauses and facts can be encoded as propositional formulas.

the facts $A_1, \ldots, A_n$ are in the agent's working memory and B is not in the agent's working memory in state s, then the agent can fire the rule which adds B to the agent's working memory in the successor state s'.

In addition to firing rules, agents can exchange messages regarding their current beliefs. We assume that there is a bound on communication for each agent i which limits agent i to at most $n_C(i)$ messages. Each agent has a communication counter, c_i, which starts at 0 and is not allowed to exceed the value $n_C(i)$. The exchange of information between agents is modelled as an abstract *Copy* operation: if a fact A is in agent i's working memory in state s, A is not in the working memory of agent j, and agent j has not exceeded its communication bound ($c_j < n_C(j)$) then in the successor state s', A can be added to agent j's working memory, and c_j incremented. Intuitively, this corresponds to the following operations rolled into one: j asking i for A, and i sending A to j. This is guaranteed to succeed and takes one tick of system time. The only agent which pays the communication cost is j. These assumptions are made for simplicity; it is straightforward to modify our definition of communication so that the 'cost' of communication is paid by both agents, communication takes more than one tick of time, and communication is non-deterministic. An agent can also perform an Idle operation (do nothing).

A problem is considered to be solved if one of the agents has derived the goal. The time taken to solve the problem is taken to be the total number of steps by the whole system (agents firing their rules or copying facts in parallel, at most one operation executed by each agent at every step). The communication cost for each agent is the value of communication counter for that agent.

As an example, consider a system of two agents, 1 and 2. The agents share the same set of rules:

RuleB1 $A_1, A_2 \rightarrow B_1$
RuleB2 $A_3, A_4 \rightarrow B_2$
RuleB3 $A_5, A_6 \rightarrow B_3$
RuleB4 $A_7, A_8 \rightarrow B_4$
RuleC1 $B_1, B_2 \rightarrow C_1$
RuleC2 $B_3, B_4 \rightarrow C_2$
RuleD1 $C_1, C_2 \rightarrow D_1$

Time	Agent 1	Agent 2
t_0	$\{A_1, A_2, A_3, A_4\}$	$\{A_5, A_6, A_7, A_8\}$
operation:	RuleB2	RuleB4
t_1	$\{A_1, A_2, A_3, A_4, B_2\}$	$\{A_5, A_6, A_7, A_8, B_4\}$
operation:	RuleB1	RuleB3
t_2	$\{A_1, A_2, A_3, A_4, B_1, B_2\}$	$\{A_5, A_6, A_7, A_8, B_3, B_4\}$
operation:	RuleC1	RuleC2
t_3	$\{A_1, A_2, A_3, A_4, B_1, B_2, C_1\}$	$\{A_5, A_6, A_7, A_8, B_3, B_4, C_2\}$
operation:	Idle	Copy (C_1 from agent 1)
t_4	$\{A_1, A_2, A_3, A_4, B_1, B_2, C_1\}$	$\{A_5, A_6, A_7, A_8, B_3, B_4, C_1, C_2\}$
operation:	Idle	RuleD1
t_5	$\{A_1, A_2, A_3, A_4, B_1, B_2, C_1\}$	$\{A_5, A_6, A_7, A_8, B_3, B_4, C_1, C_2, D_1\}$

Fig. 1. Example 1

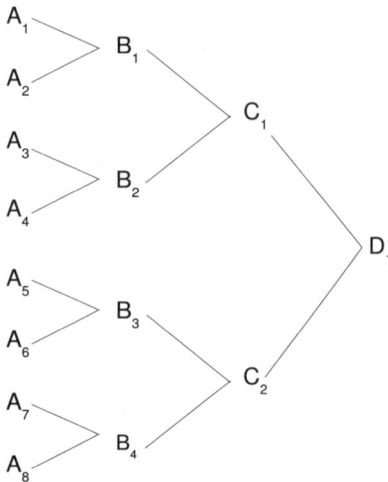

Fig. 2. Binary tree example

The goal is to derive D_1. Figure 1 gives a simple example of a run of the system starting from a state where agent 1 has A_1, A_2, A_3 and A_4 in its working memory, and agent 2 has A_5, A_6, A_7, A_8. In this example, the agents require one communication and five time steps to derive the goal. (In fact, this is an optimal use of resources for this problem, as verified using Mocha, see section 5).

Throughout the paper, we will use variations on this synthetic 'binary tree' problem, with A_is being the leaves and the goal formula being the root of the tree, as examples (see Figure 2). We vary the number of rules and the distribution of 'leaf' facts between the agents. For example, a larger system can be generated using 16 'leaf' facts $A_1, \ldots, A_{16}$, adding extra rules to derive B_5 from A_9 and A_{10}, etc., and the new goal E_1 derivable from D_1 and D_2. We will refer to it as '16 leaf example'. Similarly, we will consider systems with 32, 64, 128 etc. leaf facts. We have chosen this form of example because it is typical of distributed reasoning problems and can be easily parameterised by the number of leaf facts and the distribution of facts to the agents.

3   Extending CTL* with Belief Operators and Communication Counters

In this section we introduce the formal models of the systems informally described in the previous section. Essentially, they correspond to infinite tree structures (representing branching time), where each state consists of the states of the agents (and the state of each agent corresponds to the contents of its working memory and a record of the number of copy actions it has performed). Transitions between states correspond to all agents executing one of their possible transitions in parallel, where possible transitions include applicable rule firings, copy actions, or idling.

Such structures can be directly encoded in Mocha, by encoding the contents of each agent's memory as boolean variables and the communication counter as an enumeration type variable, as described in section 4. However, this does not give us a precise logical description of systems of distributed rule-based reasoners and an appropriate logical language to describe such systems. We have therefore developed a language in which we can express the properties of the system, including agent's beliefs and communication bounds. This language is an extension of CTL*, and contains a belief operator for each agent and communication modalities. (Although the belief operators are interpreted syntactically, we still refer to them as modalities, as is common in syntactic epistemic logics, see e.g., [14].) We provide an axiomatisation of the tree structures described above in this logical language. This gives us a precise way of reasoning about resource bounds in the resulting logic, $\mathcal{L}_{CRB}$. In particular we can reason about the interaction of temporal, belief and communication modalities, and the logical properties of communication modalities. It also provides us with a high-level specification language which can be translated in CTL* (in fact, all the properties of interest are expressible in CTL, but for technical reasons—to make the completeness proof easier—we based our axiomatisation on CTL*).

We begin by defining an internal language for each agent. This language includes all possible formulas that the agent can store in its working memory. Let $\mathcal{A} = \{1, \ldots, n_A\}$ be the set of all agents, and P a finite common alphabet of facts. Let Π be a finite set of rules of the form $p_1, \ldots, p_n \rightarrow p$, where $n \geq 0$, $p_i, p \in P$ for all $i \in \{1, \ldots, n\}$ and $p_i \neq p_j$ for all $i \neq j$. For convenience, we use the notation $pre(\rho)$ where $\rho \in \Pi$ for the set of premises of ρ and $con(\rho)$ for the conclusion of ρ. For example, if $\rho = p_1, \ldots, p_n \rightarrow p$, then $pre(\rho) = \{p_1, \ldots, p_n\}$ and $con(\rho) = p$. The internal language IL, then, includes all the facts $p \in P$ and rules $\rho \in \Pi$. We denote the set of all formulas of IL by $\Omega = P \cup \Pi$. Note that Ω is finite.

The syntax of $\mathcal{L}_{CRB}$ includes the temporal operators of CTL^* and is defined inductively as follows:

- $\top$ (tautology) and $start$ (a propositional variable which is only true at the initial moment of time) are well-formed formulas (wff) of $\mathcal{L}_{CRB}$,
- $cp_i^{=n}$ (which states that the value of agent i's communication counter is n) is a wff of $\mathcal{L}_{CRB}$ for all $n \in \{0, \ldots, n_C(i)\}$ and $i \in \mathcal{A}$,
- $B_i p$ (agent i believes p) and $B_i \rho$ (agent i believes ρ) are wffs of $\mathcal{L}_{CRB}$ for any $p \in P$, $\rho \in \Pi$ and $i \in \mathcal{A}$,
- If φ and ψ are wffs of $\mathcal{L}_{CRB}$, then so are $\neg\varphi$ and $\varphi \wedge \psi$,
- If φ and ψ are wffs of $\mathcal{L}_{CRB}$, then so are $X\varphi$ (in the next state φ), $\varphi U \psi$ (φ holds until ψ), $A\varphi$ (on all paths φ).

Other classical abbreviations for $\bot$, $\vee$, $\rightarrow$ and $\leftrightarrow$, and temporal operations: $F\varphi \equiv \top U \varphi$ (at some point in the future φ) and $G\varphi \equiv \neg F \neg \varphi$ (at all points in the future φ), and $E\varphi \equiv \neg A \neg \varphi$ (on some path φ) are defined as usual. For convenience, we also introduce the following abbreviations: $CP_i = \{cp_i^{=n} \mid n = \{0, \ldots, n_C(i)\}\}$ and $CP = \bigcup_{i \in \mathcal{A}} CP_i$.

The semantics of $\mathcal{L}_{CRB}$ is defined by $\mathcal{L}_{CRB}$ transition systems which are based on ω-tree structures. Let (T, R) be a pair where T is a set and R is a binary relation on T. (T, R) is a ω-tree frame iff the following conditions are satisfied.

1. T is a non-empty set.
2. R is total, i.e. for all $t \in T$, there exists $s \in T$ such that tRs.
3. Let $<$ be the strict transitive closure of R, namely $\{(s,t) \in T \times T \mid \exists n \geq 0, t_0 = s, .., t_n = t \in T$ such that $t_i R t_{i+1} \forall i = 0, \ldots, n-1\}$.
4. For all $t \in T$, the past $\{s \in T \mid s < t\}$ is linearly ordered by $<$.
5. There is a smallest element called the root, which is denoted by t_0.
6. Each maximal linearly $<$- ordered subset of T is order-isomorphic to the natural numbers.

A branch of (T, R) is an ω-sequence $(t_0, t_1, \ldots)$ such that t_0 is the root and $t_i R t_{i+1}$ for all $i \geq 0$. We denote $B(T, R)$ to be the set of all branches of (T, R). For a branch $\sigma \in B(T, R)$, σ_i denotes the element t_i of σ and $\sigma_{\leq i}$ is the prefix $(t_0, t_1, \ldots, t_i)$ of σ. A $\mathcal{L}_{CRB}$ transition system M is defined as a triple (T, R, V) where:

- (T, R) is a ω-tree frame,
- $V : T \times \mathcal{A} \to \wp(\Omega \cup CP)$ such that for all $s \in T$ and $i \in \mathcal{A}$: $V(s, i) = Q \cup \{cp_i^{=n}\}$ for some $Q \in \wp(\Omega)$ and $cp_i^{=n} \in CP_i$. We denote $V^*(s, i) = V(s, i) \setminus CP_i$.

The truth of a $\mathcal{L}_{CRB}$ formula at a point n of a path $\sigma \in B(T, R)$ is defined inductively as follows:

- $M, \sigma, n \models \top$,
- $M, \sigma, n \models start$ iff $n = 0$,
- $M, \sigma, n \models B_i \alpha$ iff $\alpha \in V(s, i)$,
- $M, \sigma, n \models cp_i^{=m}$ iff $cp_i^{=m} \in V(s, i)$,
- $M, \sigma, n \models \neg \varphi$ iff $M, \sigma, n \not\models \varphi$,
- $M, \sigma, n \models \varphi \wedge \psi$ iff $M, \sigma, n \models \varphi$ and $M, \sigma, n \models \psi$,
- $M, \sigma, n \models X\varphi$ iff $M, \sigma, n+1 \models \varphi$,
- $M, \sigma, n \models \varphi U \psi$ iff $\exists m \geq n$ such that $\forall k \in [n, m)$ $M, \sigma, k \models \varphi$ and $M, \sigma, m \models \psi$,
- $M, \sigma, n \models A\varphi$ iff $\forall \sigma' \in B(T, R)$ such that $\sigma'_{\leq n} = \sigma_{\leq n}$, $M, \sigma', n \models \varphi$.

The models of $\mathcal{L}_{CRB}$ satisfy a set of constraints on the accessibility relation. Intuitively, each R is composed of an n_A-tuple of agents' actions performed in parallel. We will next define precisely the set of actions that each agent can perform. They are $Rule_{i,\rho}$, $Copy_{i,\alpha}$ and $Idle_i$ where $i \in \mathcal{A}$, $\rho \in \Pi$ and $\alpha \in \Omega$. $Rule_{i,\rho}$ is the action of an agent i firing ρ; $Copy_{i,\alpha}$ the action of copying α from another agent and $Idle_i$ is when agent i does nothing and moves to the next state.

We set constraints on the set of models such that the two following conditions are satisfied: (i) any transition between two states of the model corresponds to the effect of actions done by all agents in $\mathcal{A}$ and (ii) for any action of an agent in $\mathcal{A}$ that is applicable at a state s of the model, then there exists another state s' and a transition from s to s' which corresponds to the effect of the action. To formalise those two conditions, we have the following definitions.

Definition 1. *Let (T, R, V) be a tree model. The set of effective transitions R_a for an action a is defined as a subset of R and satisfies the following conditions, for all $(s, t) \in R$*

1. $(s,t) \in R_{Rule_{i,\rho}}$ iff $\rho \in V(s,i)$, $V(s,i) \supseteq pre(\rho)$, $con(\rho) \notin V(s,i)$ and $V(t,i) = V(s,i) \cup \{con(\rho)\}$. This condition says that s and t are connected by agent i's *rule-fired* transition if the following is true: ρ is a rule of i, $V(s,i)$ contains all premises of ρ but not its conclusion and the conclusion of ρ is added to the next state t of i.

2. $(s,t) \in R_{Copy_{i,\alpha}}$ iff $\alpha \in V(s,j)$ where some $j \in \mathcal{A}$ and $j \neq i$, $cp_i^{=n} \in V(s,i)$ such that $n < n_C$, $\alpha \notin V(s,i)$ and $V(t,i) = V(s,i) \setminus \{cp_i^{=n}\} \cup \{cp_i^{=n+1}\} \cup \{\alpha\}$. In this condition, s and t are connected by a $Copy$ transition of agent i iff i has copied so far at most $n_C(i) - 1$ messages from other agents, at s, i does not have α in its working memory while another agent j does and at the next state t, α is added into the working memory of i and its message counter is increased by one.

3. $(s,t) \in R_{Idle_i}$ iff $V(t,i) = V(s,i)$. The $Idle$ transition does not change the state.

Below, we specify when an action is applicable. Note that we only enable deriving a formula if this formula is not already in the agent's working memory.

Definition 2. *Let* (T,R,V) *be a tree model. The set* $Act_{s,i}$ *of applicable actions that an agent i can perform at a state $s \in T$ is defined as follows:*

1. $Rule_{i,\rho} \in Act_{s,i}$ *iff* $\rho \in V(s,i)$, $pre(\rho) \subseteq V(s,i)$ *and* $con(\rho) \notin V(s,i)$.
2. $Copy_{i,\alpha} \in Act_{s,i}$ *iff* $n < n_C(i)$ *where n is from* $cp_i^{=n} \in V(s,i)$, $\alpha \notin V(s,i)$, $\alpha \in V(s,j)$ *for some* $j \in \mathcal{A}$.
3. *It is always the case that* $Idle_i \in Act_{s,i}$.

Finally, the definition of the set of models corresponding to a system of rule-based reasoners is given below:

Definition 3. $M(n_C)$ *is the set of models* (T,R,V) *which satisfies the following conditions:*

1. $cp_i^{=0} \in V(t_0,i)$ *where t_0 is the root of (T,R) for all* $i \in \mathcal{A}$.
2. $R = \bigcup_{\forall a} R_a$.
3. *For all* $s \in T$, $a_i \in Act_{s,i}$, *there exists* $t \in T$ *such that* $(s,t) \in R_{a_i}$ *for all* $i \in \mathcal{A}$.

Below are some abbreviations which will be used in the axiomatisation:

- $ByRule_i(p,n) = \neg B_i p \wedge cp_i^{=n} \wedge \bigvee_{\rho \in \Pi \wedge con(\rho) = p}(B_i\rho \wedge \bigwedge_{p \in pre(\rho)} B_i p)$.
  This formula describes the state before the agent comes to believe formula p by the $Rule$ transition. n is the value of i's communication counter.
- $ByCopy_i(\alpha,n) = \neg B_i\alpha \wedge B_j\alpha' \wedge cp_i^{=n-1}$.

Let us now introduce the axiomatisation systems.

A1. All axioms and inference rules of CTL^* [15].

A2. $B_i\rho \wedge \bigwedge_{p \in pre(\rho)} B_i p \wedge cp_i^{=n} \wedge \neg B_i con(\rho) \rightarrow EX(B_i con(\rho) \wedge cp_i^{=n})$ for all $\rho \in \Pi$ and $i \in \mathcal{A}$.

   Intuitively, this axiom says that it is always possible to make a transition to a state where agent i believes the conclusion of a rule ρ in its working memory. In addition, the communication counter of the agent does not increase.

   The next axiom **A3** similarly describes transitions made by copy with communication counter increased).

A3. $cp_i^{=n} \wedge \neg B_i\alpha \wedge B_j\alpha \rightarrow EX(B_i\alpha \wedge cp_i^{=n+1})$ for any $\alpha \in \Omega$, $j \in \mathcal{A}$, $j \neq i$, $n < n_C(i)$.

A4. $EX(B_i\alpha \wedge B_i\beta) \rightarrow B_i\alpha \vee B_i\beta$.

This axiom says that at most one new belief is added in the next state.

A5. $B_i\alpha \rightarrow AX B_i\alpha$ for any $\alpha \in \Omega$.

This axiom says that an agent always believes in what it already believed before.

A6. $EX(B_i\alpha \wedge cp_i^{=n}) \rightarrow B_i\alpha \vee ByRule_i(\alpha, n) \vee ByCopy_i(\alpha, n)$ for any $\alpha \in \cup\Omega$.

This axiom says that a new belief can only be added by one of the valid reasoning actions.

A7a. $start \rightarrow cp_i^{=0}$ for all $i \in \mathcal{A}$.

At the start state, the agent has not performed any $Copy$ actions.

A7b. $\neg EX\,start$

$start$ only holds at the root of the tree.

A8. $\bigvee_{n=0...n_C} cp_i^{=n}$ for all $i \in \mathcal{A}$.

There is always a number n between 0 and n_C corresponding to the number of $Copy$ actions agent i has performed.

A9. $cp_i^{=n} \rightarrow \neg cp_i^{=n'}$ for all $i \in \mathcal{A}$ and $n' \neq n$.

The number of previous $Copy$ actions by i in each state is unique.

A10. $\varphi \rightarrow EX\varphi$, where φ does not contain $start$.

This describes an $Idle$ transition by all agents.

A11. $\bigwedge_{i\in\mathcal{A}} EX(\bigwedge_{\alpha\in Q_i} B_i\alpha \wedge cp_i^{=n_i}) \rightarrow EX \bigwedge_{i\in\mathcal{A}}(\bigwedge_{\alpha\in Q_i} B_i\alpha \wedge cp_i^{=n_i})$ for any $Q_i \subseteq \Omega$.

If each agent i can separately reach a state where it believes formulas in Q_i, then all agents together can reach a state where for each i, agent i believes formulas in Q_i.

Let us now define the logic obtained from the above axiomatisation system.

Definition 4. $L(n_C)$ *is the logic defined by the axiomatisation* **A1** *-* **A11**.

We have the following result.

Theorem 1. $L(n_C)$ *is sound and complete with respect to* $M(n_C)$.

Proof Sketch. As usual, soundness is proved by showing that all axioms are valid and inference rules preserve validity. The proofs for axioms and rules included in **A1** are given in [15]. The validity of axioms **A2-A11** can be proved using the properties of models in $M(n_C)$. In the following, we provide the proof for **A2**. The proofs for other axioms are similar.

Let $M = (T, V, R) \in M(n_C)$, $\sigma \in B(T, R)$ and $n \geq 0$. Assume that $M, \sigma, n \models B_i\rho \wedge \bigwedge_{p\in pre(\rho)} B_i p \wedge cp_i^{=m} \wedge \neg B_i con(\rho)$ for some $\rho \in \Pi$. Then $p \in V(\sigma_n, i)$ for all $p \in pre(\rho)$ and $con(\rho) \notin V(\sigma_n, i)$. This means that $Rule_{i,\rho} \in Act_{\sigma_n, i}$. According to the definition of $M(n_C)$, there exists a $t' \in T$ such that $\sigma_n R t'$ and $V(t', i) = V(\sigma_n, i) \cup \{con(\rho)\}$. Let σ' be a branch in $B(T, R)$ such that $\sigma'_{\leq n} = \sigma_{\leq n}$ and $\sigma'_{n+1} = t'$. Then we have that $M, \sigma', n + 1 \models B_i con(\rho) \wedge cp_i^{=m}$. It is obvious, then, that $M, \sigma, n \models EX(B_i con(\rho) \wedge cp_i^{=m})$.

Completeness is shown by constructing a tree model for a consistent formula φ. The construction is the one introduced in [15]. Since the initial state of all agents does not restrict the set of formulas they may derive in the future, for simplicity we conjunctively add to φ a tautology that contains all the potentially necessary formulas and message counters, in order to have enough sub-formulas for the construction. We construct a model $M = (T, R, V)$ for

$$\varphi' = \varphi \wedge \bigwedge_{\alpha \in \Omega} (XB_i\alpha \vee \neg XB_i\alpha) \wedge \bigwedge_{n=0...n_C, i \in \mathcal{A}} (Xcp_i^{=n} \vee \neg Xcp_i^{=n})$$

We then prove that M is in $M(n_C)$ by showing that it satisfies all properties listed in Definition 3.

By axiom **A8**, it is straightforward that at a state t of M there exists $cp_i^{=n}$ for some $n \in \{0, \ldots, n_C\}$ and any $i \in \mathcal{A}$ such that $cp_i^{=n} \in V(t, i)$. Moreover, **A9** ensures that one and only one such n can be presented in $V(t, i)$.

At the root t_0 of (T, R), the construction of the model implies that there exists a MCS[2] Γ_0 such that $\Gamma_0 \supseteq V(t_0, i)$ and $start \in \Gamma_0$. By axiom **A7**, it is trivial that $cp_i^{=0} \in V(t_0, i)$.

We then need to prove that at a state t of M, if an action a_i of agent $i \in \mathcal{A}$ is applicable, then there exists $t' \in M$ such that tRt' and $V(t', i)$ is the result of $V(t, i)$ after i performs action a_i. The proof is done by induction on the cases of a_i. Let us consider the case when a_i is $Rule_{i,\rho}$ for some $\rho \in \Pi$. Since $Rule_{i,\rho}$ is applicable at t, $con(\rho) \notin V(t, i)$ and $p \in V(t, i)$ for all $p \in pre(\rho)$. Therefore there exists a MCS Γ such that $\Gamma \supseteq V(t, i)$. Then we obtain $\bigwedge_{p \in pre(\rho)} B_i p \wedge cp_i^{=n} \wedge \neg B_i con(\rho) \in \Gamma$ for some $n \in \{0, \ldots, n_C\}$. By axiom **A2** and **MP**[3], $EX(B_i con(\rho) \wedge cp_i^{=n}) \in \Gamma$. Therefore, according to the construction, there exists $t' \in T$ such that tRt' and $V(t', i) \subseteq \Gamma'$ for some Γ' such that $B_i con(\rho) \wedge cp_i^{=n} \in \Gamma'$. Therefore $V(t', i) = V(t, i) \cup \{con(\rho)\}$.

For other cases of a_i, the proofs are similar by using **MP** and axioms **A3** and axiom **A10**. Then, axiom **A11** enables us to show that, for any tuple of actions $(a_1, \ldots, a_{n_A})$ such that all a_i are applicable at a state t of M, there exists $t' \in T$ such that $V(t', i)$ is the result of performing a_i at t for all $i \in \mathcal{A}$. The proof is similar to that above, except that each case under consideration is a tuple of actions, and by using axiom **A11** and **MP**.

Finally, we prove that for any $t' \in T$ such that tRt', there exists a tuple of actions $(a_1, \ldots, a_{n_A})$ and $V(t', i)$ is the result of $V(t, i)$ when agent i performs a_i for all $i \in \mathcal{A}$. By axioms **A4** and **A5**, $V^*(t', i)$ is different from $V^*(t, i)$ by at most one formula added and no formula removed. If no formula is added (and no formula is removed), we set a_i to be $Idle_i$. Let us now consider the case where a formula α is added. By axiom **A6**, if $cp_i^{=n} \in V(t, i)$ for some $n \in \{0, \ldots, n_C\}$ then either cp_i^n or $cp_i^{n+1} \in V(t', i)$. If $cp_i^n \in V(t', i)$ then set a_i to be $Rule_{i,\rho}$ for some $\rho \in V(t, i)$ such that $\alpha = con(\rho)$ (this must happen according to **A6**). If $cp_i^{n+1} \in V(t', i)$ then set a_i to be $Copy_{i,\alpha}$ (this must happen according to **A6** that $\alpha \in V(t, j)$ for some $j \in \mathcal{A}$). Thereby, we have proved the existence of the tuple $(a_1, \ldots, a_{n_A})$ for tRt'. Then, we conclude that $M \in M(n_C)$. $\square$

---

[2] MCS stands for *maximally consistent set*.

[3] **MP** stands for Modus Ponens.

4   Mocha Encoding

It is straightforward to encode a $\mathcal{L}_{CRB}$ model for a standard model checker, and to verify resource bounds using existing model checking techniques. For the examples reported here, we used the Mocha model checker [1] due to the ease with which we can specify concurrently executing agents in *reactive modules*, the description language used by Mocha. Note that since belief operators in our logic are interpreted syntactically, we do not need to use a model-checker for temporal epistemic logic such as MCMAS [16].

The state of the system is described by a set of state variables and each system state corresponds to an assignment of values to the variables. The presence or absence of each fact in the working memory of an agent is represented by a boolean state variable $a_i A_j$ which represents the fact that agent i believes fact A_j. The initial values of these variables determines the initial distribution of facts between agents.[4] In the experiments reported below (which used the binary tree example, see Figure 2), all derived (non-leaf) variables were initialised to *false*, and only the allocation of leaves to each agent was varied.

The actions of firing a rule, copying a fact from another agent and idling were encoded as a Mocha *atom* which describe the initial condition and transition relation for a group of related state variables. Inference is implemented by marking the consequent of a rule as present in working memory at the next cycle if all of the antecedents of the rule are present in working memory at the current cycle. A rule is only enabled if its consequent is not already present in working memory at the current cycle. Communication is implemented by copying the value representing the presence of a fact in the working memory of another agent at the current cycle to the corresponding state variable in the agent performing the copy at the next cycle. Copying is only enabled if the fact to be copied is not already in the working memory of the agent performing the copy. In the experiments, we assumed that all rules are believed by all agents in the initial state, and did not implement copying rules. However, this can be done in a straightforward way by adding an extra boolean variable to the premises of each rule, and implementing copying a rule as copying this variable. To express the communication bound, we use a counter for each agent which is incremented each time a copy action is performed by the agent. To allow an agent to idle at any cycle, the atoms which update working memory in each agent are declared to be *lazy*.

The evolution of the system's state is described by an initial round followed by an infinite sequence of update rounds. The variables are initialised to their initial values in the initial round and new values are assigned to the variables in the subsequent update rounds. At each update round, Mocha non-deterministically chooses between the enabled rules and copy operations and idling.

Mocha supports hierarchical modelling through composition of *modules*. A module is a collection of atoms and a specification of which of the state variables updated

---

[4] We can also leave the initial allocation of facts undetermined, and allow the model checker to find an allocation which satisfies some property, e.g., that there is a proof which takes less than 7 steps. However for the experiments reported here, we specified the initial assignment of facts to agents.

by those atoms are visible from outside the module. In our encoding, each agent is represented by a module. A particular distributed reasoning system is then simply a parallel composition of the appropriate agent modules.

The specification language of Mocha is ATL, which includes CTL. We can express properties such as 'agent i may derive belief ϕ in n steps' as $EX^n\ tr(B_i\alpha)$, where EX^n is EX repeated n times, and $tr(B_i\alpha)$ is a state variable encoding of the fact that α is present in the agent's working memory (e.g. $tr(B_i\alpha) = a_iA_j$ if $\alpha = A_j$). To obtain the actual derivation, we can verify an invariant which states that $tr(B_i\alpha)$ is never true, and use the counterexample trace to show how the system reaches the state where α is proved. To bound the number of messages used, we can include a bound on the value of the message counter of one or more agents in the property to be verified. For example, $EX^n\ (tr(B_i\alpha) \wedge tr(cp_i^{=0} \vee cp_i^{=1}))$, where $tr(cp_i^{=0} \vee cp_i^{=1})$ is translated to the statement $a_i\_counter < 2$, bounds the number of messages used by agent i to be at most 1. The encoding of the models and translation of the properties from $\mathcal{L}_{CRB}$ into the Mocha specification language does not involve a significant overhead in comparison to other model-checking problems.

5   Experimental Results

In this section we describe the results of experiments for different sizes of the binary tree example (see Figure 2) and different distributions of leaves between the agents. The experiments were designed to investigate trade-offs between the number of steps and the number of messages exchanged (a shorter derivation with more messages or a longer derivation with fewer messages).

First, as a 'base case' and also to get an idea of the size of examples which can be model-checked in a reasonable time using our Mocha encoding, we ran experiments with just one agent, varying the size of the tree. The results are shown in Figure 3. As one would expect, the number of steps equals to the total number of rules in the example. While for our binary tree example the results are unsurprising, in a less uniform rule-based system such a result may be difficult to establish by a simple inspection of rules.

We then investigated different distributions of leaf facts between the agents. Figure 4 shows the number of derivation steps and the number of messages for each agent for varying distributions of 8 leaves. Note that there are several optimal (non-dominated) derivations for the same initial distribution of leaves between the agents. For example, when agent 1 has all the leaves apart from A_8, and agent 2 has A_8, the obvious solution is case 5, where agent 1 copies A_8 from agent 2, and then derives the goal in 7 steps, as

Case	# leaves	# steps
1.	8	7
2.	16	15
3.	32	31
4.	64	63
5.	128	127

Fig. 3. Resource requirements for one agent

Case	Agent 1	Agent 2	# steps	# messages agent 1	# messages agent 2
1.	$A_1 - A_8$		7	-	-
2.	$A_1 - A_7$	A_8	6	0	3
3.	$A_1 - A_7$	A_8	6	1	2
4.	$A_1 - A_7$	A_8	7	1	1
5.	$A_1 - A_7$	A_8	8	1	0
6.	$A_1 - A_6$	A_7, A_8	6	0	2
7.	$A_1 - A_6$	A_7, A_8	6	1	1
8.	$A_1 - A_6$	A_7, A_8	7	1	0
9.	$A_1 - A_4$	$A_5 - A_8$	5	1	0
10.	A_1, A_3, A_5, A_7	A_2, A_4, A_6, A_8	7	2	3
11.	A_1, A_3, A_5, A_7	A_2, A_4, A_6, A_8	11	0	4

Fig. 4. Resource requirements for optimal derivation in 8 leaf cases

in case 1. This derivation requires 8 time steps and one message. However, the agents can solve the problem in fewer steps by exchanging more messages. For example, case 2 describes the situation when agent 2 copies A_7 from agent 1, while agent 1 derives B_3 (step 1). Then agent 2 derives B_4 while agent 1 derives B_2 (step 2). Then agent 2 copies B_3 from agent 1, while agent 1 derives B_1 (step 3). At the next step agent 1 derives C_1 and agent 2 derives C_2 (step 4). Then agent 2 copies C_1 from agent 1 (step 5) and agent 1 idles; finally at step 6 agent 2 derives D_1. The effect of the bound on messages varies with the distribution, as can be seen in cases 10 and 11: if agent 1 has all the odd leaves and agent 2 all the even leaves, then to derive the goal either requires 7 steps and 5 messages, or 11 steps and 4 messages.

Similar trade-offs are apparent for a problem with 16 leaves, as shown in Figure 5. However in this case there are a larger number of possible distributions of leaves, and, in general, more trade-offs for each distribution. For example, when one of the agents has all the leaves but one, we again have the obvious solution where agent 1 copies the missing leaf and derives the goal on its own, which takes 16 steps and 1 message (case 7). In addition there are 15, 14, 13 and 12 step derivations, where the shorter the derivation the more messages the agents have to exchange (cases 2-7). We also see interesting trade-offs when agent 2 has two leaves (cases 8-13) or four leaves in the same subtree (cases 14-17). When agent 1 has 3 leaves in each subtree and agent 4 the fourth leaf in each subtree, there is again an obvious derivation in which agent 1 copies the 4 missing leaves and completes the derivation in 19 steps and 4 copy operations, and a more interesting one which takes 13 steps and the agents exchange more messages (agent 2 copies 3 leaves to complete a part of the proof, and then copies variables from higher up in the tree). The difference is also more marked in the 'odd and even' case (cases 20 and 21), where agent 1 has all the odd leaves and agent 2 all the even leaves, where increasing the message bound by 1 reduces the length of the proof by 10 steps.

Although these examples are very simple, they point to the possibility of complex trade-offs between time and communication bounds in systems of distributed reasoning agents. For more complex examples, we would anticipate that such trade-offs would be harder to predict *a priori*, and our framework would be of correspondingly greater utility.

Case	Agent 1	Agent 2	# steps	# m 1	# m 2
1.	$A_1 - A_{16}$		15	-	-
2.	$A_1 - A_{15}$	A_{16}	12	0	6
3.	$A_1 - A_{15}$	A_{16}	12	1	4
4.	$A_1 - A_{15}$	A_{16}	13	1	3
5.	$A_1 - A_{15}$	A_{16}	14	1	2
6.	$A_1 - A_{15}$	A_{16}	15	1	1
7.	$A_1 - A_{15}$	A_{16}	16	1	0
8.	$A_1 - A_{14}$	A_{15}, A_{16}	11	0	5
9.	$A_1 - A_{14}$	A_{15}, A_{16}	11	1	4
10.	$A_1 - A_{14}$	A_{15}, A_{16}	12	1	3
11.	$A_1 - A_{14}$	A_{15}, A_{16}	13	1	2
12.	$A_1 - A_{14}$	A_{15}, A_{16}	14	1	1
13.	$A_1 - A_{14}$	A_{15}, A_{16}	15	1	0
14.	$A_1 - A_{12}$	$A_{13}, A_{14}, A_{15}, A_{16}$	11	0	4
15.	$A_1 - A_{12}$	$A_{13}, A_{14}, A_{15}, A_{16}$	11	1	2
16.	$A_1 - A_{12}$	$A_{13}, A_{14}, A_{15}, A_{16}$	12	1	1
17.	$A_1 - A_{12}$	$A_{13}, A_{14}, A_{15}, A_{16}$	13	1	0
18.	A_1-A_3, A_5-A_7, A_9-A_{11}, A_{13}-A_{15}	A_4, A_8, A_{12}, A_{16}	13	2	6
19.	A_1-A_3, A_5-A_7, A_9-A_{11}, A_{13}-A_{15}	A_4, A_8, A_{12}, A_{16}	19	4	0
20.	$A_1, A_3, A_5, A_7, A_9, A_{11}, A_{13}, A_{15}$	$A_2, A_4, A_6, A_8, A_{12}, A_{14}, A_{16}$	13	4	5
21.	$A_1, A_3, A_5, A_7, A_9, A_{11}, A_{13}, A_{15}$	$A_2, A_4, A_6, A_8, A_{12}, A_{14}, A_{16}$	23	0	8

Fig. 5. Resource requirements for optimal derivation in 16 leaf cases

6 Conclusions

In this paper, we proposed an approach to modelling and verifying resource requirements of distributed rule-based reasoners. We showed how to reason about time and communication bounds in such systems, and defined a sound and complete logic, $\mathcal{L}_{CRB}$, in which such reasoning can be expressed. The models of the logic can be encoded as an input to a standard model-checker such as Mocha and properties of interest translated into CTL, without a significant overhead in comparison to other model-checking problems. We described results of some experiments on a synthetic example which show interesting trade-offs between time required by the agents to solve the problem and the number of messages they need to exchange.

References

1. Alur, R., Henzinger, T.A., Mang, F.Y.C., Qadeer, S., Rajamani, S.K., Tasiran, S.: MOCHA: Modularity in model checking. In: Y. Vardi, M. (ed.) CAV 1998. LNCS, vol. 1427, pp. 521–525. Springer, Heidelberg (1998)
2. Faltings, B., Yokoo, M.: Introduction: Special issue on distributed constraint satisfaction. Artificial Intelligence 161, 1–5 (2005)
3. Jung, H., Tambe, M.: On communication in solving distributed constraint satisfaction problems. In: Pěchouček, M., Petta, P., Varga, L.Z. (eds.) CEEMAS 2005. LNCS, vol. 3690, pp. 418–429. Springer, Heidelberg (2005)

4. Provan, G.M.: A model-based diagnosis framework for distributed embedded systems. In: Fensel, D., Giunchiglia, F., McGuinness, D.L., Williams, M.-A. (eds.) Proceedings of the 8th International Conference on Principles and Knowledge Representation and Reasoning (KR 2002), Toulouse, France, April 22-25, 2002, pp. 341–352. Morgan Kaufmann, San Francisco (2002)

5. Wooldridge, M., Dunne, P.E.: On the computational complexity of coalitional resource games. Artif. Intell. 170, 835–871 (2006)

6. Adjiman, P., Chatalic, P., Goasdoué, F., Rousset, M.-C., Simon, L.: Distributed reasoning in a peer-to-peer setting. In: de Mántaras, R.L., Saitta, L. (eds.) Proceedings of the 16th Eureopean Conference on Artificial Intelligence, ECAI 2004, including Prestigious Applicants of Intelligent Systems, PAIS 2004, August 22-27, 2004, pp. 945–946. IOS Press, Amsterdam (2004)

7. Amir, E., McIlraith, S.A.: Partition-based logical reasoning for first-order and propositional theories. Artificial Intelligence 162, 49–88 (2005)

8. Albore, A., Alechina, N., Bertoli, P., Ghidini, C., Logan, B., Serafini, L.: Model-checking memory requirements of resource-bounded reasoners. In: Proceedings of the Twenty-First National Conference on Artificial Intelligence (AAAI 2006), pp. 213–218. AAAI Press, Menlo Park (2006)

9. Alechina, N., Bertoli, P., Ghidini, C., Jago, M., Logan, B., Serafini, L.: Verifying space and time requirements for resource-bounded age nts. In: Stone, P., Weiss, G. (eds.) Proceedings of the Fifth International Joint Conference on Aut onomous Agents and Multi-Agent Systems (AAMAS 2006), Hakodate, Japan, pp. 217–219. IEEE Computer Society Press, Los Alamitos (2006)

10. Alechina, N., Bertoli, P., Ghidini, C., Jago, M., Logan, B., Serafini, L.: Verifying space and time requirements for resource-bounded agents. In: Edelkamp, S., Lomuscio, A. (eds.) Proceedings of the Fourth Workshop on Model Checking and Artificial Intelligence (MoChArt 2006), pp. 16–30 (2006)

11. Alechina, N., Jago, M., Logan, B.: Modal logics for communicating rule-based agents. In: Brewka, G., Coradeschi, S., Perini, A., Traverso, P. (eds.) Proceedings of the 17th European Conference on Artificial Intelligence (ECAI 2006), pp. 322–326. IOS Press, Amsterdam (2006)

12. Alechina, N., Logan, B., Nga, N.H., Rakib, A.: Verifying time, memory and communication bounds in systems of reasoning agents. In: Padgham, Parkes, Muller, Parsons (eds.) Proceedings of the Seventh International Conference on Autonomous Agents and Multiagent Systems (AAMAS 2008), Estoril, Portugal (May 2008)

13. Ågotnes, T., Alechina, N.: Knowing minimum/maximum n formulae. In: Brewka, G., Coradeschi, S., Perini, A., Traverso, P. (eds.) Proceedings of the 17th European Conference on Artificial Intelligence (ECAI 2006), Riva del Garda, Italy, pp. 317–321. IOS Press, Amsterdam (2006)

14. Ågotnes, T., Alechina, N.: The dynamics of syntactic knowledge. Journal of Logic and Computation 17, 83–116 (2007)

15. Reynolds, M.: An axiomatization of full computation tree logic. J. Symb. Log. 66, 1011–1057 (2001)

16. Lomuscio, A., Raimondi, F.: Mcmas: A model checker for multi-agent systems. In: Hermanns, H., Palsberg, J. (eds.) TACAS 2006. LNCS, vol. 3920, pp. 450–454. Springer, Heidelberg (2006)

Solving μ-Calculus Parity Games by Symbolic Planning

Marco Bakera, Stefan Edelkamp, Peter Kissmann, and Clemens D. Renner

Department of Computer Science
Dortmund University of Technology
{firstname.lastname}@cs.tu-dortmund.de

Abstract. This paper applies symbolic planning to solve parity games equivalent to μ-calculus model checking problems. Compared to explicit algorithms, state sets are compacted during the analysis. Given that $diam(G)$ is the diameter of the parity game graph G with node set V, for the alternation-free model checking problem with at most one fixpoint operator, the algorithm computes at most $O(diam(G))$ partitioned images. For d alternating fixpoint operators, $O(d \cdot diam(G) \cdot (\frac{|V|+(d-1)}{d-1})^{d-1})$ partitioned images are required in the worst case.

Practical models and properties stem from data-flow analysis, with problems transformed to parity game graphs, which are then compiled to a general game playing planner input.

1 Introduction

Symbolic μ-calculus model checking with BDDs [8] has been applied as a general framework for various verification problems like model checking of LTL and CTL formulas or testing for bi-simulation equivalence and language containment. One successful tool is μcke [3]. On the other hand, μ-calculus model checking problems have been converted to parity games [22]. Different tools like Omega [40] and MetaGame [43] have been developed.

Specialized game playing is one of the major successes in AI [29]. In general game playing [26], strategies are computed domain-independently without knowing which game is played. Best policies result in perfect play. The opponents can take actions alternately and independently and attempt to maximize the outcome. The game description language (GDL) is designed for use in defining complete information games. It is a subset of first order logic, using the syntax of the knowledge interchange format (KIF) [18].

This paper attempts to close the gap between general symbolic game playing and model checking, which is based on checking the satisfiability of formulas [25,4]. Here, we refer to symbolic exploration in the context of using binary decision diagrams (BDDs) [6].

For parity games, strategy improvement [39] and progress measure algorithms [23] are prominent. The latter one has been translated to a symbolic setting by providing an algorithm with $O(|V|^{d+3} \log(|V|))$ (ADD) images [7]. In this paper, we improve the results for the μ-calculus to $O(d \cdot diam(G) \cdot (\frac{|V|+(d-1)}{d-1})^{d-1})$ possibly partitioned (BDD) images, where $diam$ is the diameter of G and d is the fixpoint alternation depth of the formula. We also provide a theoretically faster algorithm for full alternation.

The paper is structured as follows. First, we review the symbolic classification algorithm for two-player zero-sum games that is included in our general game playing tool. Next, we introduce the basics of game-based model checking and the transformation of μ-calculus model checking problems to parity games. The transformation is illustrated with a simple example. We then show how the classification algorithm solves the problem of parity games that are generated by formulas in the alternation free μ-calculus. The extension to larger fragments of the μ-calculus is discussed together with a transformation of an existing explicit-state strategy synthesis algorithm. Independent proofs of correctness are given for both algorithms. In the empirical part, we analyze model checking problems from data-flow analysis and convert them to parity games and general game playing inputs, on which our planner is applied. Finally, we draw conclusions.

2   Symbolic Analysis of Two-Player Games

A two-player zero-sum game (with perfect information) is given by a set of states S, move-rules to modify states and two players, called player 0 and player 1. Since exactly one player is active at any given time, the entire state space of the game is $S \times \{0, 1\}$. A game has an initial state and some predicate *Goal* to determine whether the game has come to an end. For now, we assume that every path from the initial state is finite. Assuming optimal play and starting with all lost goal positions of one player, all previous lost positions have to be computed. A position is lost if all moves lead to an intermediate position in which the other player can force a move back to a lost position.

In symbolic search with BDDs, states are manipulated in form of sets by computing images. The image of a state set *States* wrt. the transition relation $Trans(x, x')$ is equal to computing $WeakImage(Trans, States) := \exists x. Trans(x, x') \wedge States(x)$, where x and x' are vectors of Boolean state variables. The result of this image operation is a representation of all states reachable from *States* in one step. In order to repeat the process, we substitute x with x'. In an interleaved representation this operation reduces to a textual replacement of node labels in the BDD. For computing the image, a monolithic transition relation is not required. Instead, a sub-relation $Trans_a$ is stored together with every move $a \in \{1, \ldots, k\}$. The image of a state set *States* is partitioned into $WeakImage(Trans, States) = \exists x. (Trans_1(x, x') \wedge States(x)) \vee \ldots \vee \exists x. (Trans_k(x, x') \wedge States(x))$.

In contrast to reachability analysis (which can be invoked to initialize the classification algorithm), the direction of the symbolic retrograde analysis is *backwards*. Fortunately, symbolic backward search causes no problem, as the representation of all moves is defined as a relation. With symbolic search, two-player games with perfect information can be classified iteratively using BDDs. For it we furthermore need to calculate strong preimages: $StrongPreImage(Trans, States) := \forall x'.$

Algorithm 1. Symbolic classification of two-player zero-sum games

---

Data: Transition Relation *Trans*, Initial State Set *Init*, Goal Sets *Goal*, Leaf
evaluation *Eval*.
Result: Four Classification Sets.

1 $(Reached, L(0), L(1)) \leftarrow Reachable(Init, Trans, Goal, Eval)$;
2 **foreach** $i \in \{0, 1\}$ **do**
3      $New \leftarrow Lose(i) \leftarrow L(i)$;
4      $Win(1 - i) \leftarrow \perp$;
5   **repeat**
6          $Weak \leftarrow Move(1 - i) \wedge WeakPreImage(Trans, New) \wedge Reached$;
7          $Win(1 - i) \leftarrow Win(1 - i) \vee Weak$;
8          $Strong \leftarrow Move(i) \wedge StrongPreImage(Trans, Win(1 - i)) \wedge Reached$;
9          $New \leftarrow Strong \wedge \neg Lose(i)$;
10         $Lose(i) \leftarrow Lose(i) \vee New$;
11   **until** $New = \perp$;
12 **return** $(Win(0), Lose(0), Win(1), Lose(1))$;

$Trans(x, x') \Rightarrow States(x')$. Fortunately, with it a partitioned computation also applies. Since $StrongPreImage(Trans, States) = \neg WeakPreImage(Trans, \neg States)$ with $WeakPreImage(Trans, States) := \exists x'. Trans(x, x') \wedge States(x')$, we can induce $StrongPreImage(Trans, States) = \forall x'.(Trans_1(x, x') \Rightarrow States(x')) \wedge \ldots \wedge \forall x'.(Trans_k(x, x') \Rightarrow States(x'))$.

Algorithm 1 shows the classification algorithm for computing strategies in turn-taking games as mentioned in [12]. The idea of attractors, however, goes back to [44]. First of all, we calculate all the reachable states through forward reachability analysis; a backward exploration can result in states that are unreachable from the initial state. Next, we construct four sets: The lost states $Lose(i)$ for each player and the won states $Win(i)$ for each player. The lost states for player i are initialized with the BDDs $L(i)$. From these we only take those goal states that are reachable. Won states are initialized with the BDD $\perp$ for the *false* function, representing the empty set. Now we construct the predecessors of the lost states. Here, the last move has to be made by player $(1 - i)$, the opponent of player i; this predicate is denoted by $Move(1 - i)$. These predecessors are then added to the won states of the opponent. Starting from those won states we calculate their predecessors. Here, the last move has to be made by the current player i. These new states are added to the lost states. If there are no new states at this point, the calculation terminates (for the current player).

Once the algorithm has ended for both players, we can simply check in which set the initial state resides. If it is in one of the sets of won states, the corresponding player can assure a victory; if it is in one of the lost states, the opponent can assure victory (independent of the other player's moves). If the initial state is in none of these four sets, a finite game surely ends in a draw – always assuming both players perform optimal play.

The number of images for determining all reachable states and the number of images for their classification is linear in the maximal BFS layer, known as the radius of the problem r. By introducing *no-ops*, one can transform any (non simultaneous) game into a turn-taking game by at most doubling the game graph. For games with loops and no draws, the classification algorithm (started for each player) still might leave a set of positions unclassified. These sets correspond to an infinite game play without further progress. Note that by applying retrograde analysis, some states may be classified despite the fact that they lie on a cycle.

Extensions of the algorithm to games with arbitrary costs are proposed in [14,15].

3   Preliminaries: Model Checking Based on Parity Games

Model checking is a procedure for the automated verification of software and hardware systems. The system model (e.g., in form of a Kripke transition system[1]) is checked for the validity of a formula in temporal logic.

3.1 μ-Calculus Model Checking

Modal μ-calculus formulas ϕ are built from propositions (basic properties of the system's states) $p \in AP$, standard Boolean operators, $\langle a \rangle \phi$ (*possibility*) and $[a]\phi$ (*necessity*) modal operators on actions $a \in A$, as well as minimal and maximal fixpoint operators $\mu X.\phi$ and $\nu X.\phi$. The μ and ν operators act as binders for fixpoint variables. The following (minimal) syntax denotes the modal μ-calculus with X being a fixpoint variable (the dual operators can be derived from this base set of operators):

$$\phi ::= true \mid p \mid \neg\phi \mid \phi_1 \vee \phi_2 \mid \langle a \rangle \phi \mid X \mid \mu X.\phi$$

For brevity, we write $\langle \cdot \rangle \phi := \bigvee_{a \in A} \langle a \rangle \phi$ and $[\cdot]\phi := \bigwedge_{a \in A} [a]\phi$.

3.2   Parity Games

A parity game graph $G = (V_\diamond, V_\square, E, p)$ is composed of two disjoint sets of vertices $V_\diamond$ and $V_\square$, an edge set $E \subseteq V \times V$, where $V = V_\diamond \cup V_\square$, and a priority function $p : V \to \{1, 2, \ldots, d\}$, for some integer d, defined on its vertices. The game is played by two players: *diamond* and *box*. The game starts at some vertex $v_0 \in V$. The players construct a possibly infinite path as follows: Let u be the last vertex added so far to the path. If $u \in V_\diamond$, then diamond chooses an edge $(u, v) \in E$. Otherwise, if $u \in V_\square$, then box chooses an edge $(u, v) \in E$. In either case, vertex v is added to the path, and a new edge is then chosen by either diamond or box. Let $v_0, v_1, \ldots$ be the path constructed by the two players, and $p(v_0), p(v_1), \ldots$ the sequence of the priorities of the vertices on the path. Diamond wins the game if the path ends in a leaf node in $V_\square$ or the smallest priority seen infinitely many times is even, while box wins otherwise.

---

[1] The model $M := (S, A, AP, \to, I)$ is composed of a set of states S, a set of actions A (from labeled transition systems), a set of atomic propositions AP (from Kripke structures), a transition relation $\to \subseteq S \times A \times S$, and an interpretation function $I : S \to 2^{AP}$ (assigning propositions to states).

4   Solving Parity Games for Alternation-Free Formulas

It has been shown that model checking systems with property specification in the μ-calculus is equivalent to solving a parity game, with the maximal priority roughly corresponding to the alternation depth of the μ-formula ϕ [9]. For each play there is a unique partitioning of the parity game in two winning sets, see for example [16].

Local model checking approaches like [9] generate a node for each state in the system and each sub-formula of ϕ. In the following we generally assume alternation-free μ-formulas. The transformation of ν-formulas is dual (changing the roles of box and diamond).

We transform the model and the μ-calculus formula into a parity game as implemented in the tool GEAR [1,2]. Figure 1 shows a simple model with respect to an alternation-free μ-calculus formula $\mu X.(good \vee [\cdot]X)$ and its translation to a parity game graph (nodes are of type either box or diamond, node priorities are all 1). The color shading will be explained below.

Marking a node won corresponds to a definite win for player diamond, marking it lost corresponds to a definite win for player box (assuming optimal play). For the recursive winning set computation we may apply the following rules (assuming player diamond's point of view).

– v is a $\diamond$ node
  • v is a leaf $\Rightarrow$ v is marked lost

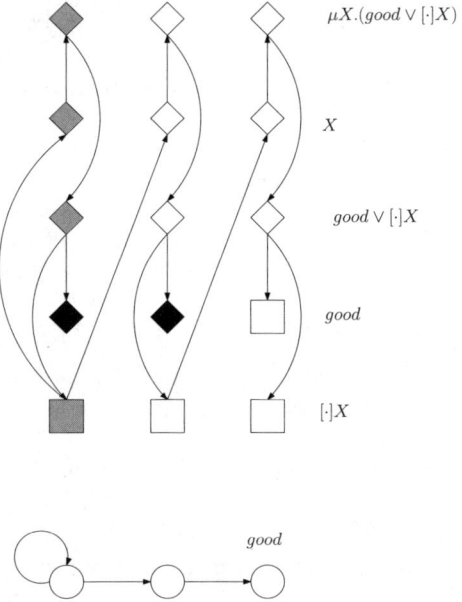

Fig. 1. A model (bottom) wrt. the alternation-free μ-calculus formula $\mu X.(good \vee [\cdot]X)$ and the classified parity game graph (top). Here, *good* is an atomic proposition.

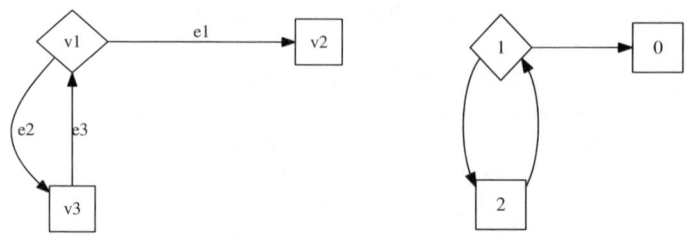

Fig. 2. Example game graph (left) and backward BFS layers (right)

- there is a successor u of v marked won $\Rightarrow$ mark v won
- all successors u of v are marked lost $\Rightarrow$ mark v lost
- v is a $\square$ node
  - v is a leaf $\Rightarrow$ v is marked won
  - there is a successor u of v marked lost $\Rightarrow$ mark v lost
  - all successors u of v are won $\Rightarrow$ mark v won

If there is a lasso in the graph, it is not immediate to determine a strategy defined as a subset of edges completely classifying optimal play of player diamond. Consider the parity game graph given in Fig. 2 (left). All states belong to the diamond player's winning set, but if he chooses to take the vertical edge leading to the state on the bottom of the graph, the box player will win, as the game results in an infinite cycle, which is won by the box player.

The idea to remedy this is to store the backward BFS layer each state was classified in. The player then has to take an edge that leads to a state that was detected earlier in the backward search and thus is stored in a smaller layer (smaller by 1). In the example game in Fig. 2 (right), the numbers in the nodes denote the backward layers. Following the strategy to take only actions to layers with smaller numbers, the diamond player easily wins – he just has to take the horizontal edge to the terminal state.

Theorem 1. *For the case of alternation-free parity games, given the backward layers of the classification from the calculation of the winning sets, it is possible to calculate the diamond player's strategy.*

Proof. Let L_i denote the set of states found in the ith layer of the backward search and $W_\diamond = \bigcup_{i>0} L_i$ the winning set of the diamond player as determined by the algorithm. We define the optimal strategy for player diamond as $E_\diamond := \{(u,v) \in W_\diamond \times W_\diamond \mid \exists i > 0. \ u \in L_i \wedge v \in L_{i-1}\}$.

We prove the correctness of this by induction on the BFS layer $i > 0$. For the states from the set L_1, it is clear that the diamond player will win by taking the edge to the terminal state (within L_0). For the states in L_i, the player can take an edge leading to a state in L_{i-1}. From there, we inductively already have a strategy.

Formulas in Hennessy-Milner logic [20] have no fixpoint operators. The corresponding game is finite and the classification algorithm will end up with a complete strategy for both players. The search for a strategy in a parity game matches the one in a two-player zero-sum game given that one player is box and the other player is diamond.

As only one reachability step and one call to the classification algorithm is executed, backward analysis is restricted to the reachable set in form of a DAG which is traversed bottom-up. Thus we obtain that the symbolic classification algorithm for parity games arising from model checking problems with temporal logic properties in Hennessy-Milner logic is correct and amounts to $O(radius(G, Init))$ possibly partitioned (BDD) images, where $radius(G, Init)$ is the maximum BFS-layer of the forward search of G starting from $Init$.

If one μ fixpoint operator is present in the according parity game, we have to search for strategies in which diamond must avoid a cycle. Otherwise, box can establish a cycle and wins the game. The translation to an ordinary game graph for cyclic solutions may become involved, as infinite games are played. In order to detect cycles, one might try adopting the state recording method for transforming safety into liveness [32]. However, an application is not immediate.

Next, we recognize that all states that remain unmarked lie on a cycle that player diamond cannot avoid; according to the winning condition, these states can be marked lost. Figure 1 displays the result of such a complete classification of the parity game graph. Black shading indicates that player box wins from there, white indicates nodes won by player diamond and gray denotes nodes won by player box due to an infinite cycle. The respective other player loses due to the zero-sum character of the game.

For alternation-free formulas, all priorities in the graph are the same. W.l.o.g. we consider μ formulas only, such that all priorities are 1 and player box wins the game (assuming optimal play) if he[2] can force player diamond to stay on a cycle. The remaining unclassified nodes all lie on a lasso[3]. Moreover, we need to show that player diamond cannot escape the cycle unless he navigates to some black node (where he loses). Let us assume that one of the remaining nodes is not on a lasso. This implies that the node would be on a path to a sink that can be marked won for one of the players. Therefore, the node itself could have been marked as well and would not be unclassified, contrary to our assumption.

Why can diamond not escape from this cycle (lasso)? Any diamond node v on the cycle must have at least one unclassified successor. It cannot have a white successor (marked 'won by diamond') because in that case v would have been marked 'won by diamond' as well. Diamond would not pick a black successor as this implies that he will lose eventually. The case for player box is analogous (no black successors, white successors are avoided). Therefore, only unclassified nodes are played. As an infinite path in a finite graph will eventually lead to a cycle, the unclassified nodes can be marked black. Therefore, all nodes are classified.

---

[2] For the sake of simplicity, we stay with *he* and *him* instead of *he / she* and *him / her*.

[3] A lasso is a cycle and a prefix of nodes (stem) leading to that cycle.

As only one reachability analysis and one call to the classification algorithm is executed, and given that backward analysis is restricted to the reachable set, the complexity of the algorithm in the number of images is linear in $diam(G)$ and $diam(G^{-1}) = diam(G)$, where G^{-1} is the inverse graph of G (all edges are reversed).

Therefore, we observe that the symbolic classification algorithm for parity games arising from model checking problems wrt. temporal logic properties in alternation-free μ-calculus formulas is correct and amounts to $O(diam(G))$ possibly partitioned (BDD) images, where $diam$ is the maximal shortest path length between every two states.

5   Extension to Full Alternation Depth

We now address an extension of our symbolic planning approach to cover parity games for μ-calculus model checking problems with alternation. No polynomial-time algorithm is to be expected, since according to [41] only the solution of games with so-called Büchi winning condition can currently be done in polynomial time. There are sub-exponential algorithms [5,24] with a complexity of $n^{O(\sqrt{n/\log n})}$, which are to be preferred only if the alternation depth is larger than $\Omega(\sqrt{n})$. Even specialized problems like finite-state controller synthesis for r request-response constraints [41] require an exponential time algorithm in r.

In adaptation of the notation used in the literature [42], we define the alternation depth d as the number of alternations between the fixpoint operators ν and μ plus 1 (resulting in the counter-intuitive result that alternation-free μ-calculus formulas have a value of $d = 1$).

In the following, we devise an efficient symbolic algorithm following the explicit-state strategy synthesis algorithm documented in [42], which re-assembles ideas from [9] and [28]. The strategy synthesis algorithm has a time complexity of $O(|E|(|V|/d)^{d-1})$ (assuming a uniform distribution of priorities). Compared to the algorithm of [23], the exponent $d - 1$ matches the value $\lceil d/2 \rceil$ as obtained in the small progress measure algorithm for $d = 2$ and $d = 3$. With further refinements, the results of [42] indicate that for these cases the strategy improvement algorithm will be faster for formulas with small alternation depth (which appear in practice).

Let V_i be the set of nodes for player i. The strategy synthesis algorithm relies on an iterative calculation of *forcing sets*. A forcing set for some subset $V' \subseteq V$ towards some fixed node set $A \subseteq V$ for player $i \in \{0, 1\}$ is defined by the condition that for each node u in V' player i can force player $(1 - i)$ to play towards the node set A. A maximal forcing set from V' to A for player i does not include an edge (v, w) with $v \in V' \cap V_{1-i}$ and $w \in V \setminus (V' \cup A)$.

On acyclic game graphs, the computation of winning sets reduces to the computation of forcing sets as mentioned above. Otherwise, cycles are handled in the synthesis algorithm 5.

First, the nodes are partitioned with respect to their priority (l. 5). There is no need for deeper recursion and refinement of the resulting winning sets when

---

Algorithm 2. Main

Result: Winning Sets W_0 and W_1.

1 $(R, W_0, W_1) \leftarrow Initialize()$;
2 $(W_0, W_1) \leftarrow Synthesize(R \wedge \neg(W_0 \vee W_1))$;
3 **return** (W_0, W_1);

Algorithm 3. Initialize

Result: Reachable set R, winning Sets W_0 and W_1.

1 $(R, W_1, W_0) \leftarrow Reachable(Init, Trans, Goal, Eval)$;
2 $W_0 \leftarrow Force(R, W_0, 0)$;
3 $W_1 \leftarrow Force(R, W_1, 1)$;
4 **return** (R, W_0, W_1);

---

all nodes share the same priority. In this case, winning sets are computed that respect the player that is currently predominating the game when considering priorities (ll. 5-5). Afterwards, an assumption of the winning set for the other player is made (ll. 5-5). The subsequent repeat loop tries to consolidate this assumption (ll. 5-5). The partitioning that emerges either breaks down into exactly two or more classes of nodes with the same priority. In the former case, the assumption is computed as in the cycle-free case (ll. 5-5). The latter case requires refining the assumption – by a new assumption based on the current one – in the recursive call (ll. 5-5). The remainder of the loop (ll. 5-5) collects the results and assigns them to the appropriate player until there is no more need for refinement (l. 5).

Following the presentation in [42], we show symbolic equivalents of the algorithms *Main* (Algorithm 2), *Initialize* (Algorithm 3), *Force*, (Algorithm 4), and *Synthesize* (Algorithm 5). For the ease of presentation, we assume that the parity game graph is *consistent*, such that priorities are consecutive (there is no gap). For game graphs that are translated from model checking tasks, this assumption is necessarily true. We further assume the transition relation *Trans*, the initial state set *Init*, the goal predicate *Goal*, the priority evaluation function *Priority*, and the leaf evaluation predicate *Eval* to be globally accessible.

After initialization, the synthesis algorithm refers to computing the forcing sets and a recursive call to itself. As shown before, all explicit state operations to determine the winning sets for both players can be performed symbolically. The initialization that computes the maximal forcing set for both players on the entire graph towards the terminal nodes matches the classification in Algorithm 1. For computing the forcing sets, the classification algorithm needs to be executed only for one player. Computing the subgraph can either be done in the game description language by specifying different graph and goal conditions (see Appendix B for an example) or via restricting the disjunctive representation of the transition relation to the part that corresponds to the remaining edges.

Algorithm 4. Force

Data: Set V', Target Set A, Player i.
Result: Forcing Set F.

1 $Trans' \leftarrow Trans \wedge (V' \times (V' \cup A))$;
2 $New \leftarrow Lose(1-i) \leftarrow (A \wedge Move(1-i))$;
3 $Win(i) \leftarrow (A \wedge Move(i))$;
4 **repeat**
5      $Weak \leftarrow Move(i) \wedge WeakPreImage(Trans', New) \wedge V'$;
6      $Win(i) \leftarrow Win(i) \vee Weak$;
7      $Strong \leftarrow Move(1-i) \wedge StrongPreImage(Trans', Win(i)) \wedge V'$;
8      $New \leftarrow Strong \wedge \neg Lose(1-i)$;
9      $Lose(1-i) \leftarrow Lose(1-i) \vee New$;
10 **until** $(New = \bot)$;
11 **return** $(Lose(1-i) \vee Win(i))$;

Lemma 1. *The worst-case number of partitioned images of the symbolic classification algorithm for parity games with d alternating fixpoint operators is bounded by $2 \cdot diam(G) \cdot d \cdot \prod_{k=1}^{d-1}(|Level_k| + 1)$.*

Proof. Let $T(G)$ denote the running time for the synthesis algorithms on the graph with $V = Support$, for the number of images we have $T(G) = 2 \cdot diam(G)$, if $d = 1$.

Given that $Upper \cup Lower \subseteq Layer$ and $W_1 \subseteq Layer$ we obtain a recursive equation for the asymptotic complexity of

$$T(G) = 1 + \sum_{j=0}^{r} 2 \cdot diam(G|_{Layer_j}) + T(G|_{Upper_j})$$

images, where r is the number of iterations of the repeat loop, $Layer_j$ is the set representing $Layer$ and $Upper_j$ is the set representing $Upper \wedge \neg W$ in the j-th iteration. Both calls to the $Force$ function induce at most $diam(G|_{Layer_j})$ many images and the plus 1 is due to the weak pre-image in line 5. $G|_{V'}$ is the subgraph restricted to $V' \subseteq V$, more precisely $G|_{V'} := (V', E \cap (V' \times V'))$.

The next step is to rewrite the equation to avoid recursion. Following the inductive argument in [42], see Appendix A, we have

$$T(G) \leq 2 \cdot \sum_{j=1}^{d-1} diam(G) \cdot \prod_{k=1}^{j}(|Level_k| + 1)$$

many images in the worst case, where $Level_k$ is the set of nodes in graph G with priority k.

$$T(G) \leq 2 \cdot \sum_{j=1}^{d-1} diam(G) \cdot \prod_{k=1}^{d-1}(|Level_k| + 1)$$

Algorithm 5. Synthesize

Data: Node Set *Support*.
Result: Winning Sets Z_0, Z_1.

1   **if** $(Support = \bot)$ **then**
2   **return** $(\bot, \bot)$;
3   $m \leftarrow MinPriority(Priority \wedge Support)$;
4   $m' \leftarrow m + 1$;
5   $i \leftarrow (m \bmod 2)$;
6   **if** $MaxPriority(Priority \wedge Support) = m$ **then**
7   **if** $(i = 0)$ **then**
8   **return** $(Support, \bot)$;
9   **else**
10   **return** $(\bot, Support)$;
11 $Layers \leftarrow Support$;
12 $Lower \leftarrow Priority_{<m'} \wedge Layers$;
13 $Upper \leftarrow Support \wedge \neg Lower$;
14 **repeat**
15   **if** $(Lower = \bot)$ **then**
16          $W \leftarrow Force(Upper, Lower, i)$;
17   **else**
18          $W \leftarrow \bot$;
19   **if** $(i = 0)$ **then**
20          $(W_0, W_1) \leftarrow Synthesize(Upper \wedge \neg W)$;
21   **else**
22          $(W_1, W_0) \leftarrow Synthesize(Upper \wedge \neg W)$;
23      $Upper \leftarrow Upper \wedge \neg W_1$;
24      $Layers \leftarrow Layers \wedge \neg W_1$;
25      $Z_1 \leftarrow Z_1 \vee W_1$;
26   **if** $(Lower \neq \bot \wedge W_1 \neq \bot)$ **then**
27          $W' \leftarrow Force(Layers, W_1, 1 - i)$;
28          $Lower \leftarrow Lower \wedge \neg W'$;
29          $Upper \leftarrow Upper \wedge \neg W'$;
30          $Layers \leftarrow Layers \wedge \neg W'$;
31   **else**
32          $W' \leftarrow \bot$;
33 **until** $(W' = \bot)$;
34 $Z_0 \leftarrow W \vee W_0 \vee (Lower \wedge Move(i) \wedge WeakPreImage(Trans, W \vee W_0 \vee Lower))$;
35 **if** $(i = 0)$ **then**
36   **return** (Z_0, Z_1);
37 **else**
38   **return** (Z_1, Z_0);

$$\leq 2 \cdot diam(G) \cdot d \cdot \prod_{k=1}^{d-1} (|Level_k| + 1).$$

Theorem 2. *The symbolic classification algorithm for parity games arising from model checking problems wrt. temporal logic properties in μ-calculus formulas with d alternating fixpoint operators is correct. For $d > 1$, the worst-case number of partitioned images is $O(d \cdot diam(G) \cdot (\frac{|V|+(d-1)}{d-1})^{d-1}))$.*

Proof. The correctness of the algorithm is inherited from the correctness of the explicit-state variant documented in [42].

The number of images for initialization is $O(radius(G, Init))$ for computing the reachable set and $O(diam(G))$ for computing the two forcing sets. Let $T(G)$ denote the running time for the synthesis algorithms on the graph with $V = Support$.

For $d > 1$, we have

$$T(G) \leq 2 \cdot diam(G) \cdot d \cdot \prod_{k=1}^{d-1}(|Level_k| + 1)$$

$$\leq 2 \cdot diam(G) \cdot d \cdot \left(\frac{\sum_{k=1}^{d-1}(|Level_k| + 1)}{d - 1} \right)^{d-1}$$

$$= 2 \cdot diam(G) \cdot d \cdot \left(\frac{|V| + (d - 1)}{d - 1} \right)^{d-1}$$

partitioned images in the worst case. For the penultimate step we used the inequality for the geometric wrt. the arithmetic mean.

The worst-case number of BDD images beats the value of $O(|V|^{d+3} \log(|V|))$ images obtained by [7]. For the important subclass $d = 2$, our algorithm reduces to only $O(diam(G) \cdot |V|)$ (BDD) images compared to $O(|V|^5 \log(|V|))$ (ADD) images [7].

6   Empirical Analysis

We draw experiments with our general game playing planning tool [14], which itself uses CUDD[4] by Fabio Somenzi as the underlying BDD library. The models and formulas were generated from data-flow analysis problems and translated into parity game graphs using GEAR. The export format of GEAR was adapted to suit the game-based planner. Moreover, we introduced no-operators to allow the game to be turn-taking. Parts of the specification of the GDDL encoding[5] for the example problem is provided in appendix B.

One important fact about our tool is the minimization of the state encoding by building groups of mutually exclusive propositions [13,19]. As a result, we can apply a binary state encoding. This is the key to a space-efficient representation of the states, since in a BDD many states share nodes and exponentially many nodes may be represented in a polynomially sized graph.

---

[4] http://vlsi.colorado.edu/~fabio/CUDD

[5] GDDL is a language introduced by [14]; a hybrid of GDL (Game Description Language) and PDDL (Planning Domain Definition Language).

6.1 Data-Flow Analysis as Model Checking

Data-flow analysis (DFA) is one step at the compile time of a program, prior to its optimization. Many DFA demands have been transformed into model checking problems [34]. The main idea is to interpret control flow graphs as Kripke transition systems with program steps labeling nodes and edges. Basic propositions at a node are $isDefined(x)$, denoting that variable x is written or changed, and $isUsed(x)$, denoting that variable x is read. A variable is *live* if it is used and was not redefined before – in terms of temporal logics this can be expressed as $\mu X.isUsed(x) \vee \neg isDefined(x) \wedge \langle \cdot \rangle X$.

Many such formulas are free of alternation as shown in [31]. This makes data-flow analysis via model checking a good testbed for our search algorithms.

6.2 Experiments

We have performed three experiments, obtaining matching results wrt. GEAR.

The first example is based on the Java byte code of an implementation of the *Fast Fourier Transformation*. The byte code has been transformed into a control-flow graph using Soot[6]. For its liveness analysis, 749 states are reachable in 366 steps. For these, 141 BDD nodes are needed. The classification algorithm can classify 517 states: 343 states are won for the diamond player, which are represented by 155 BDD nodes. These are found after 39 iterations through the loop. For the box player, 174 states are classified as won. Here, 11 iterations and 112 BDD nodes are needed. These states contain the initial state, i.e., it is surely won for the box player. The remaining 232 states are not classified by our algorithm, so they must lie on one or more lassos from which the diamond player cannot escape. Thus, they are also won for the box player. The total runtime of the forward and backward analysis was 0.8 seconds.

The second example consists of automatically generated code as described in [21], also used as an input to Soot. We expect that this leaves more room for data-flow analysis wrt. possible optimizations. We reached a total of 4,590 states after 3,086 steps and need 619 BDD nodes to represent them all. In this case, all states are also reachable in backward direction: The algorithm classifies 3,888 as won for the diamond player. For these, it needs 128 iterations and 770 BDD nodes. Within two steps it classifies the remaining 702 states as won for the box player using 350 BDD nodes. The initial state is contained within the set of states won for the box player. The total runtime for the forward and backward analysis was 24 seconds.

Instead of source code, the third example for the DFA-MC paradigm considers process graphs edited by the jABC tool[7], where a model is converted to a characteristic formula, which is checked together with a failure specification. The explicit model had 49,141 nodes in the parity graph. The reachability analysis converts the graph into a turn-taking game with 96,616 states and 13,110 BDD nodes, generated in 63 steps. The number of states (BDD nodes) that are won

---

[6] http://www.sable.mcgill.ca/soot
[7] http://jabc.cs.uni-dortmund.de

for diamond are 22,682 (12,198); the number of states directly won by player box are 26,510 (12,736). The remaining 43,421 non-classified states correspond to the situation that box can enforce player diamond to stay on a cycle. The entire classification took 123 seconds.

7   Conclusion and Discussion

We have seen a fruitful approach for the symbolic analysis of parity games that arise when transforming μ-calculus model checking problems. The algorithms for the Hennessy-Milner and alternation-free μ-calculus are efficient and have been implemented. Testbeds arose during data-flow analysis. Moreover, an implementation for formulas with large alternation depth has been presented.

The historical roots of the work are as follows. As a winning condition for games, the parity condition was already considered by Emerson and Jutla [16]. It was shown that parity games always result in memoryless winning strategies – determinicity of parity games follows directly from the determinicity of Borel games. The algorithmic presentation of McNaughton [28] and the early analyses of Zielonka [44] lay the basis for algorithms based on recursive reachability. No implementation was provided. Thomas [37] realized the importance of parity games. One of the first implementations is the (explicit-state) fixpoint analysis machine [35], which provides a tool based on [9], which was in turn the basis for (explicit-state) strategy synthesis algorithm by [42]. For uniform priorities, [42] shows an advantage wrt. FAM, and $d \leq 3$ (the practical cases) an advantage to Jurdzinski [42]. There are two recent improvements for enumeration we are aware of: the $O(|E| \cdot |V|^{d/3})$ algorithm by [30], and an acceleration for the 3-priorities [11]. A distributed implementation for parity games shows a rather direct adaption of Jurdzinski's small progress measurement algorithm for multi-core architectures based on different state-space partitioning functions [38].

Applying symbolic game playing has different advantages. First, the representation of the winning sets (e.g., in a binary encoding of the nodes) is implicit and can be much smaller than the explicit one. Wrt. space consumption for progress measures, no vectors have to be stored together with each state. Moreover, the analysis can be extended to implicit parity game graphs. Last but not least, BDDs show advantages to SAT and QBF solvers in combinatorial games [27].

Given a symbolic parity game graph representation in a BDD, the above algorithm is capable of solving much larger problems. In other words, we cover a more powerful input language, which allows the succinct specification of nontrivial game graphs using Boolean formulas. So far we have extracted explicit-state models from the GEAR model checker [1,2]. In the future we will likely integrate our implementation to the global model checker in the jABC framework to access the model checking problem, prior to the explicit graph construction.

References

1. Bakera, M., Margaria, T., Renner, C.D., Steffen, B.: Game-based model checking for reliable autonomy in space. Journal of the American Institute of Aeronautics and Astronautics (AIAA) (to appear)
2. Bakera, M., Margaria, T., Renner, C.D., Steffen, B.: Verification, diagnosis and adaptation: Tool supported enhancement of the model-driven verification process. In: Revue des Nouvelles Technologies de Information (RNTI-SM-1), pp. 85–98 (to appear) ISBN 2854288148
3. Biere, A.: μcke – efficient μ-calculus model checking. In: Grumberg, O. (ed.) CAV 1997. LNCS, vol. 1254, pp. 468–471. Springer, Heidelberg (1997)
4. Biere, A., Cimatti, A., Clarke, E.M., Zhu, Y.: Symbolic model checking without BDDs. In: Proc. Tools and Algorithms for the Construction and Analysis of Systems (1999)
5. Björklund, H., Sandberg, S., Vorobyov, S.G.: A discrete subexponential algorithm for parity games. In: Alt, H., Habib, M. (eds.) STACS 2003. LNCS, vol. 2607, pp. 663–674. Springer, Heidelberg (2003)
6. Bryant, R.E.: Symbolic manipulation of Boolean functions using a graphical representation. In: ACM/IEEE Design Automation Conference, pp. 688–694 (1985)
7. Bustan, D., Kupferman, O., Vardi, M.Y.: A measured collapse of the modal μ-calculus alternation hierarchy. In: Diekert, V., Habib, M. (eds.) STACS 2004. LNCS, vol. 2996, pp. 522–533. Springer, Heidelberg (2004)
8. Clarke, E.M., Grumberg, O., Peled, D.: Model Checking. MIT Press, Cambridge (2000)
9. Cleaveland, R., Klein, M., Steffen, B.: Faster model checking for the modal μ-calculus. Theoretical Computer Science 663, 410–422 (1992)
10. Cleaveland, R., Steffen, B.: A linear-time model-checking algorithm for the alternation-free modal mu-calculus. Formal Methods in System Design 2(2), 121–147 (1993)
11. de Alfaro, L., Faella, M.: An accelerated algorithm for 3-color parity games with an application to timed games. In: Damm, W., Hermanns, H. (eds.) CAV 2007. LNCS, vol. 4590, pp. 108–120. Springer, Heidelberg (2007)
12. Edelkamp, S.: Symbolic exploration in two-player games: Preliminary results. In: AIPS-Workshop on Model Checking, pp. 40–48 (2002)
13. Edelkamp, S., Helmert, M.: Exhibiting knowledge in planning problems to minimize state encoding length. In: Biundo, S., Fox, M. (eds.) ECP 1999. LNCS, vol. 1809, pp. 135–147. Springer, Heidelberg (2000)
14. Edelkamp, S., Kissmann, P.: Symbolic exploration for general game playing in PDDL. In: ICAPS-Workshop on Planning in Games (2007)
15. Edelkamp, S., Kissmann, P.: Symbolic classification of general two-player games. In: Dengel, A.R., Berns, K., Breuel, T.M., Bomarius, F., Roth-Berghofer, T.R. (eds.) KI 2008. LNCS, vol. 5243, pp. 185–192. Springer, Heidelberg (2008)
16. Emerson, E.A., Jutla, C.S.: Tree automata μ-calculus and determinacy. In: Foundations of Computer Science, pp. 368–377 (1991)
17. Emerson, E.A., Lei, C.-L.: Efficient model checking in fragments of the propositional mu-calculus. In: Symposium on Logic in Computer Science, pp. 267–278 (1986)
18. Genesereth, M.R.: Knowledge interchange format. In: Second International Conference on Principles of Knowledge Representation and Reasoning, pp. 238–249 (1991)

19. Helmert, M.: A planning heuristic based on causal graph analysis. In: International Conference on Automated Planning and Scheduling, pp. 161–170 (2004)
20. Hennessy, M., Milner, R.: On observing nondeterminism and concurrency. In: de Bakker, J.W., van Leeuwen, J. (eds.) ICALP 1980. LNCS, vol. 85, pp. 299–309. Springer, Heidelberg (1980)
21. Jørges, S., Kubczak, C., Pageau, F., Margaria, T.: Model driven design of reliable robot control programs using the jabc. In: 4th IEEE International Workshop on Engineering of Autonomic and Autonomous Systems (EASe), March 2007, pp. 137–148 (2007)
22. Jurdzinski, M.: Deciding the winner in parity games is UP∩co-UP. Information Processing Letters 68(3), 119–124 (1998)
23. Jurdzinski, M.: Small progress measures for solving parity games. In: Reichel, H., Tison, S. (eds.) STACS 2000. LNCS, vol. 1770, pp. 290–301. Springer, Heidelberg (2000)
24. Jurdzinski, M., Paterson, M., Zwick, U.: A deterministic subexponential algorithm for solving parity games. In: SODA, pp. 117–123 (2006)
25. Kautz, H., Selman, B.: Pushing the envelope: Planning propositional logic, and stochastic search. In: European Conference on Artificial Intelligence, pp. 1194–1201 (1996)
26. Love, N.C., Hinrichs, T.L., Genesereth, M.R.: General game playing: Game description language specification. Technical Report LG-2006-01, Stanford Logic Group (April 2006)
27. Madhusudan, P., Nam, W., Alur, R.: Symbolic computational techniques for solving games. Electronic Notes in Theoretical Computer Science 89(4) (2004)
28. McNaughton, R.: Infinite games played on finite graphs. Annals of Pure and Applied Logic 65, 129–284 (1993)
29. Schaeffer, J., Björnsson, Y., Burch, N., Kishimoto, A., Müller, M., Lake, R., Lu, P., Sutphen, S.: Solving checkers. In: International Joint Conference on Artificial Intelligence, pp. 292–297 (2005)
30. Schewe, S.: Solving parity games in big steps. In: CAV, pp. 449–460 (2007)
31. Schmidt, D.A.: Data flow analysis is model checking of abstract interpretations. In: Conference Record of POPL 1998: The 25th ACM SIGPLAN-SIGACT Symposium on Principles of Programming Languages, San Diego, California, Janary 19–21, 1998, pp. 38–48 (1998)
32. Schuppan, V., Biere, A.: Efficient reduction of finite state model checking to reachability analysis. STTT 5(2-3), 185–204 (2004)
33. Seidl, H.: Fast and simple nested fixpoints. Information Processing Letters 59(6), 119–124 (1996)
34. Steffen, B.: Data flow analysis as model checking. In: Ito, T., Meyer, A.R. (eds.) TACS 1991. LNCS, vol. 526, pp. 346–365. Springer, Heidelberg (1991)
35. Steffen, B., Classen, A., Klein, M., Knoop, J., Margaria, T.: The fixpoint-analysis machine. In: Lee, I., Smolka, S.A. (eds.) CONCUR 1995. LNCS, vol. 962, pp. 72–87. Springer, Heidelberg (1995)
36. Stirling, C.: Local model checking games. In: Lee, I., Smolka, S.A. (eds.) CONCUR 1995. LNCS, vol. 962, pp. 1–11. Springer, Heidelberg (1995)
37. Thomas, W.: On the synthesis of strategies in infinite games. In: Mayr, E.W., Puech, C. (eds.) STACS 1995. LNCS, vol. 900, pp. 1–13. Springer, Heidelberg (1995)
38. van de Pol, J., Weber, M.: A multi-core solver for parity games. In: PDMC 2008 (to appear, 2008)

39. Vöge, J., Jurdzinski, M.: A discrete strategy improvement algorithm for solving parity games. In: Emerson, E.A., Sistla, A.P. (eds.) CAV 2000. LNCS, vol. 1855, pp. 202–215. Springer, Heidelberg (2000)
40. Vöge, J., Ulbrand, S., Matz, O., Buhrke, N.: The automata theory package omega. In: Wood, D., Yu, S. (eds.) WIA 1997. LNCS, vol. 1436, pp. 228–231. Springer, Heidelberg (1998)
41. Wallmeier, N., Hütten, P., Thomas, W.: Symbolic synthesis of finite-state controllers for request-response specifications. In: H. Ibarra, O., Dang, Z. (eds.) CIAA 2003. LNCS, vol. 2759, pp. 11–22. Springer, Heidelberg (2003)
42. Yoo, H.: Fehlerdiagnose beim Model-Checking durch animierte Strategiesynthese. PhD thesis, Universität Dortmund (2007)
43. Yoo, H., Müller-Olm, M.: MetaGame: An animation tool for model-checking games. In: Jensen, K., Podelski, A. (eds.) TACAS 2004. LNCS, vol. 2988, pp. 163–167. Springer, Heidelberg (2004)
44. Zielonka, W.: Infinite games on finite coloured graphs with applications to automata on infinite trees. Theoretical Computer Science 200, 135–183 (1998)

A   Compiling Away the Recursion

We have to show that

$$T(G) = 1 + \sum_{j=0}^{r} 2 \cdot diam(G|_{Layer_j}) + T(G|_{Upper_j}).$$

induces

$$T(G) \le 2 \cdot \sum_{j=1}^{d-1} diam(G) \prod_{k=1}^{j} (|Level_k| + 1)$$

Proof. For the induction we observe that $r \le |Lower_0|$ (at least a one-element set is processed in each iteration) and $G|_{Layer_{|Lower_0|}} = \emptyset$ (no forcing sets in the last iteration) we induce

$$T(G) \le 1 + \sum_{j=0}^{|Lower_0|} 2 \cdot diam(G|_{Layer_j}) + \sum_{j=0}^{|Lower_0|} T(G|_{Upper_j})$$

$$\le 1 + \sum_{j=0}^{|Lower_0|-1} 2 \cdot diam(G) + \sum_{j=0}^{|Lower_0|} T(G|_{Upper_j})$$

$$\le 1 + |Lower_0| \cdot 2 \cdot diam(G) + \sum_{j=0}^{|Lower_0|} T(G|_{Upper_j})$$

We additionally observe that $Level_1 = Lower_0$ and that $\sum_{j=0}^{|Lower_0|} T(G|_{Upper_j})$ is bounded by $(|Lower_0| + 1) \cdot T(G|_{Upper_s})$ for some $0 \le s \le |Lower_0|$. Hence, by inserting the induction hypothesis (Ind.) we have

$$
\begin{aligned}
T(G) \ &\le\ 1 + |Level_1| \cdot 2 \cdot diam(G) + \sum_{j=0}^{|Level_1|} T(G|_{Upper_s}) \\
&\le\ 1 + |Level_1| \cdot 2 \cdot diam(G) + (|Level_1| + 1) \cdot T(G|_{Upper_s}) \\
&\overset{\text{Ind.}}{\le}\ (1 + |Level_1|) \cdot 2 \cdot diam(G) + (|Level_1| + 1) \cdot 2 \cdot \sum_{j=2}^{d-1} diam(G) \prod_{k=2}^{j} (|Level_k| + 1) \\
&\le\ (1 + |Level_1|) \cdot 2 \cdot diam(G) + 2 \cdot \sum_{j=2}^{d-1} diam(G) \prod_{k=1}^{j} (|Level_k| + 1) \\
&\le\ 2 \cdot \sum_{j=1}^{d-1} diam(G) \prod_{k=1}^{j} (|Level_k| + 1)
\end{aligned}
$$

B   GDDL Encoding

The parity games have been translated to GDDL. The domain model for the problem looks as follows.

```
(define (domain alternation-free)
 (:types state role)
 (:predicates (at ?s - state) (connect ?s1 ?s2 - state)
        (box ?s - state) (diamond ?s - state) (control ?player - role))
(:action move-box
  :parameters (?player - role ?s1 ?s2 - state ?nextplayer - role)
  :precondition (and (at ?s1)(connect ?s1 ?s2)(control ?player) (box ?s1)
                (= ?player box_player)(not (= ?player ?nextplayer)))
  :effect (and (not (at ?s1)) (at ?s2)
               (not (control ?player))(control ?nextplayer)))
(:action noop-box
  :parameters (?player - role ?s - state ?nextplayer - role)
  :precondition (and (at ?s) (box ?s) (control ?player)
                 (= ?player diamond_player)(not (= ?player ?nextplayer)))
  :effect (and (not (control ?player)) (control ?nextplayer)))
(:action move-diamond ...)
(:action noop-diamond ...)
(:lost (?player - role)
  (exists (?s - state) (and (at ?s) (= ?player diamond_player)
  (not (control ?player)))))
(:won (?player - role)
  (exists (?s - state) (and (at ?s) (= ?player diamond_player)
  (not (control ?player)))))
(:lost ...)
(:won ...)
```

The example problem from Fig. 1 is encoded as follows.

```
(define (problem check)
  (:domain modelcheck)
  (:objects box_player diamond_player - role
    s1 s2 s3 s4 s5 s6 s7 s8 s9 s10 s11 s12 s13 s14 s15 - state)
  (:init
    (diamond s1) (diamond s6) (diamond s11) (diamond s2) (diamond s7)
    (diamond s12) (diamond s3) (diamond s8) (diamond s13) (diamond s4)
    (diamond s9) (box s14) (box s5) (box s10) (box s15)
    (connect s2 s1) (connect s1 s3) (connect s3 s5) (connect s3 s4)
    (connect s5 s7) (connect s5 s2) (connect s6 s8) (connect s7 s6)
    (connect s8 s10) (connect s8 s9) (connect s10 s12) (connect s11 s13)
    (connect s12 s11) (connect s13 s15) (connect s13 s14)
    (at s1) (control box_player))
  (:goal (exists (?s1 - state)
    (and (at ?s1)
      (or (and (control box_player) (box ?s1))
          (and (control diamond_player) (diamond ?s1)))
      (forall (?s2 - state) (not (connect ?s1 ?s2)))))))
```

Verifying Robocup Teams*

Clara Benac Earle[2], Lars-Åke Fredlund[1], José Antonio Iglesias[2],
and Agapito Ledezma[2]

[1] LSIIS, Facultad de Informática, Universidad Politécnica de Madrid
fred@babel.ls.fi.upm.es
[2] grupo CAOS, Universidad Carlos III de Madrid
{cbenac,jiglesia,ledezma}@inf.uc3m.es

Abstract. Verification of multi-agent systems is a challenging task due
to their dynamic nature, and the complex interactions between agents.
An example of such a system is the RoboCup Soccer Simulator, where
two teams of eleven independent agents play a game of football against
each other. In the present article we attempt to verify a number of properties of RoboCup football teams, using a methodology involving testing.
To accomplish such testing in an efficient manner we use the McErlang
model checker, as it affords precise control of the scheduling of the agents,
and provides convenient access to the internal states and actions of the
agents of the football teams.

1 Introduction

The analysis and verification of multi-agent systems is not an easy task due to
their dynamic nature, and the complex interactions between agents. One method
that is often advocated to verify such systems is model-checking. However, in
performing model-checking on multi-agent systems two main issues arise: i) a
model needs to be constructed, and ii) the state space is bound to grow too
large. In this paper we propose an alternative approach to the verification of
properties in multi-agent systems by means of testing, in particular we use a
model checker to simulate RoboCup teams and verify properties during such
simulation runs. The tool we use, McErlang [6], permits precise control of concurrency and communication, and detailed access to the internal states of agents
and communication channels.

The RoboCup Soccer Simulator, the soccer server [4], is a research and ed-
ucational tool for multi-agent systems and artificial intelligence. It enables two
teams of eleven simulated autonomous players to play a game of football. A
match is carried out in client/server style: the server provides a virtual field
and simulates all movements of a ball and the players, and each client controls

* This work has been partially supported by the FP7-ICT-2007-1 project ProTest
(215868), a Ramón y Cajal grant from the Spanish Ministerio de Educación y Cien-
cia, and the Spanish national projects TRA2007-67374-C02-02, TIN2006-15660-C02-
02 (DESAFIOS) and S-0505/TIC/0407 (PROMESAS).

D. Peled and M. Wooldridge (Eds.): MOCHART 2008, LNAI 5348, pp. 34–48, 2009.
© Springer-Verlag Berlin Heidelberg 2009

the movements of one player. Communication is done via UDP/IP sockets, enabling players to be written in any programming language that supports UDP communication.

Erlang [1] is a programming language developed at Ericsson for implementing telecommunication systems. The principal characteristics of Erlang, i.e., a clear separation between data and processes and a high level of abstraction thanks to its functional style, together with excellent support for developing distributed applications, makes writing code for RoboCup teams in Erlang an easy task. Indeed, undergraduate students at the IT university of Gothenburg have been developing such teams to compete in their local RoboCup simulation tournament. Given the rather complex nature of the application, and the availability of capable verification tools for Erlang such as e.g. McErlang[6] , it seemed natural to try to use these verification tools in the task of analyzing some interesting properties of multi-agent RoboCup teams.

The use of tool support in the task of verifying multi-agent systems is recently attracting significant interest from the agent community. In [2], for example, a variant of the abstract agent-oriented programming language AgentSpeak, AgentSpeak(F), is proposed. By translating AgentSpeak(F) programs into Promela or Java, properties written in LTL can be model-checked with SPIN or the Java Path Finder [11], a general purpose model checker for Java. A difference between their approach and ours is that AgentSpeak is based on the BDI agent architecture while we do not consider any specific agent architecture. In [7] a combination of UML statecharts and hybrid automata was proposed for modeling multi-agent systems, and the method was applied to the task of model checking agents of the RoboCup rescue simulation league. In [3] a trace based approach is used to study a complex agent scenario.

This paper is organized as follows. In the next section we introduce the Erlang programming language, and in Sect. 3 a description of the McErlang tool is given. In Sect. 4 the implementation of a RoboCup soccer team in Erlang is explained. Our approach to checking properties on the football players is explained in Sect. 5, together with a discussion of the type of experiments we have carried out. We conclude in Sect. 6 with a discussion on the present results, and directions for future work.

2   The Programming Language Erlang

Erlang [1] is a programming language developed at Ericsson for implementing concurrent, distributed, fault-tolerant systems. Erlang software is typically organized into modules, which at runtime execute as a dynamically varying number of lightweight processes communicating through asynchronous message passing.

3   The McErlang Tool

The internal construction of the model checker is parametric, enabling a user to easily change its configuration for different verification runs. The input to the model checker is the name of an Erlang function which starts the execution of the program to verify, together with a special call-back module also written in Erlang which specifies the behavioral property to be checked (called the *monitor*). The output of a verification can be either a positive answer saying that the property holds, or a negative one together with a counterexample.

Moreover, a tool user can also specify:

– the name of a *language* module providing an operational semantics[1],
– the particular *verification algorithm* to use, (e.g., a safety property checker, a liveness property checker, or simulation of the program in conjunction with a correctness property),
– the name of a *state table* implementation, that records encountered program states (typically a hash table),
– the name of an *abstraction module* that abstracts program states, and
– the name of a *stack module* that implements the stack of program states (storing all or some of the states occurring on the path from the initial program state to the current one)

3.1   Programming Language Semantics for Erlang

The main idea behind McErlang is to re-use as much of a normal Erlang programming language implementation as possible, but adding a model checking capability. To achieve this, the tool replaces the part of the Erlang runtime system which implements concurrency and message passing, while still using the runtime system for the evaluation of the sequential part of the input programs.

The model checker has a complex internal state in which the current state of the runtime system is represented. The structure that is maintained by the model checker records the state of all alive processes (their process identifiers, mailboxes, computation state, etc). Moreover the global state kept by the model checker runtime system includes a structure to record process links, information about registered process identifiers, etc.

McErlang has built-in support for some Erlang/OTP component behaviours that are used in almost all serious Erlang programs such as the supervisor component (for fault-tolerant applications) and the generic server component (implementing a client–server component), and a module for programming finite-state machines. The presence of such high-level components in the model checker significantly reduces the gap between original program and the verifiable model, compared to other model checkers.

3.2   Correctness Properties

The model checker implements full linear-temporal logic (LTL) checking. Correctness properties are represented as Büchi automatons (*monitors* coded in Erlang) which are checked using a standard on–the–fly dept–first model

---

[1] Apart from Erlang, we have also for instance implemented a semantics for the web service specification language WS-CDL, thus providing a WS-CDL model checker[5].

checking algorithm [8]. For efficiency, there is a dedicated safety property only checker available. A *monitor* checks whether the correctness property holds for the combination of the new program state and the monitor state. If successful, the monitor returns an updated monitor state (for safety checking). A *Büchi monitor* (automaton) is a monitor that additionally may mark certain states as accepting states. As is well known [10], linear temporal logic formulas can be automatically translated to Büchi automata. Correctness properties can be implemented, therefore, as finite state machines where depending on the monitor state, actions leading to new states. The Erlang/OTP programming environment is a comparatively rich programming environment for programming systems composed of (possibly) distributed processes that communicate by message passing. Fault tolerance is implemented by means of failure detectors, a standard mechanism in the distributed algorithms community. Moreover there is a process fairness notion, something which often makes it unnecessary to explicitly specify fairness in correctness properties. The language provides explicit control of distribution, and a clean model of distribution semantics. For distributed processes (processes executing on separate nodes) the communication guarantees are far weaker than for processes co-existing on the same processor node. are accepted or not. Such correctness properties have full access to the internal state of the program run (including message queues, state of processes, and so on).

The memory aspect of monitors is implemented by sending along the old monitor state as an argument to the Erlang function implementing the monitor. Concretely a monitor defines two callback functions: init (*parameters*) and stateChange(*programState,monitorState,runStack*). The init function returns {ok,*monState*} where *monState* is the initial state of the monitor.

The stateChange function is called when the model checker encounters a new program state *programState*, and the current monitor state is monitorState, and the execution history (a subset of the program states, and actions, between the initial program state and the current one) is provided by the *runStack* parameter. If a safety monitor finds that the combination of program and current monitor state is acceptable, it should return a tuple {ok,*newMonState*} containing the new monitor state. If future states along this branch are uninteresting the monitor can return skip (e.g., to implement a search path depth limit), any other value signals a violation of the correctness property implemented by the monitor. A Büchi automatons should return a set of states, each state either accepting {accepting, *state*} or not {nonaccepting,*state*}.

As an example, the code fragment below implements a simple safety monitor that guards against program deadlocks: (a process is considered deadlocked if its execution state as recorded by the process data structure in the run-time system is blocked).

```
stateChange(State, MonState, RunStack) ->
    case lists:any(fun (P) -> P#process.status =/= blocked end,
                State#state.processes) of
        true -> {ok, MonState};
        false -> {deadlock, MonState}
    end.
```

The syntax *variable#recordName.field* is used to access the field *field* of the record variable *variable*, of type *recordName*.

The Erlang language standard requires that process schedulers must be fair. The McErlang tool accordingly implements (weak) process fairness directly in its (liveness) model checking algorithm by omitting non-fair loops (i.e., ones that constantly bypass some enabled process) from the accepting runs.

3.3   Using the Model Checker for Simulation

Recently we have added a simulation facility to the model checker, whereby instead of exploring the whole state space of an application only a single execution branch is followed. Which execution to branch to follow is by default a random choice, however finer control can be exercised by the monitor module above, which in addition to checking safety properties can mark certain states an "uninteresting", preventing the model checker to examine them and instead choosing an alternative state in simulation mode.

The checking of the RoboCup agents has necessitated implementation of "real-time support" for the McErlang model checker as well. The player agents are time dependent, and have to respond in a timely fashion to information sent from the soccer server by means of actuation commands.

Moreover the model checker had to be "opened up to the outside world". Agents send commands to the soccer server using UDP sockets, and the soccer server regularly broadcasts sensory information to all agents. To support sending UDP commands was trivial (we modified the Erlang API function that supports UDP sending), whereas receiving messages was a bit more tricky. The solution was to program a new Erlang process, constantly listening for incoming UDP messages. This (real) Erlang process keeps a map of virtual (simulated) Erlang processes to which incoming messages should be resent (using the virtual message communication mechanism). Thus virtual processes wanting to receive UDP messages on a certain UDP port communicates this to the UDP Erlang process, which in turn starts receiving and forwarding incoming messages on behalf of the virtual process.

4   RoboCup Teams in Erlang

The IT-university of Gothenburg has been organizing local RoboCup competitions for their students[2]. Students were asked to developed in groups a RoboCup soccer simulation team in Erlang to play against teams developed by other groups. We have taken two such teams as a starting point for a case-study in verifying properties of complex multi-agent systems.

In the case of the first team we have considered, each of the football players is composed of four Erlang processes as shown in Fig. 1: a communicator process, a planner process, an executor process and a timer process. All communication

---

[2] See http://www.ituniv.se/~jalm/ecc06/

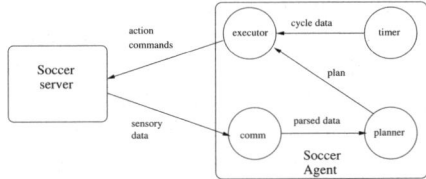

Fig. 1. The soccer server and one player

between the processes uses Erlang's built-in asynchronous message passing communication facility. Thus the total Erlang application comprises around $11 * 4$ processes.

In each cycle, the player receives messages from the soccer server through an UDP connection containing sensor information, for example, a message "`(see Time ObjectInfo)`" reports the objects currently seen by the player in a simulation cycle of the soccer server. The messages are parsed and sent to a process which updates and stores the contextual knowledge of the agent, and also to the planner process which elaborates a plan (a list of actions) and sends it to the executor process. During each cycle of the game, each player can send a limited number of action commands. The executor process sends the action commands to the server, for example, the command "`(kick Power Direction)`" to accelerate the ball with the given power in the given direction. The soccer server executes the commands at the end of the cycle and simulates the next cycle using the received commands and data from the previous cycles.

In total the number of lines of codes for this RoboCup team comprises around 3500 lines of Erlang code (including parsing), whereas the more complex (and better playing) team comprises around 8400 lines of Erlang code.

5   Checking Robocup Agents

Seen as a verification task, checking properties of a RoboCup team is very challenging. A team consists of eleven to a large extent independently acting agents with complex internal states, that cooperate to solve a common task in real-time. Unfortunately the hostile environment, i.e., the opponent team, strives to greatly complicate the task of the "home" team. Moreover, the setting is not static, the opponents will vary, and in addition the soccer simulation server contains random features[3] that will alter the outcome of various actions of the agents.

To apply model checking techniques to such a verification problem one would have to construct, with substantial effort, a simplified model of the soccer server and the agents (of both teams). Even so the real state space would be huge, and a model checking run would be unlikely to cover more than a very tiny fragment of that state space. For this reason we decided upon a different "verification" strategy: to use the McErlang model checker for executing the agents, and to formulate correctness properties to check as monitors, but instead of model checking

---

[3] E.g. reporting all positional information to an agent with a possible slight error.

a team we used the model checker as a testing/simulation environment. What we lose by not performing a complete verification, which could anyway never be complete due to the abstractions needed to obtain a verifiable model, we hope to gain by checking the actual source code of the agents.

Concretely to check a football team we ran a number of simulated football matches against a number of opposition teams. Each match consisted of two halves of 300 seconds each, with time ticks (events during which the soccer server calculates game changes, and transmits positional information to every player) every 100 milliseconds. These are configurable parameters in the soccer server; McErlang was sufficiently quick to keep up at the default settings. If time deadlines are not met, then football agents would not act timely on sensory information resulting in bad playing; a symptom of such a problem is increasing message queues of processes, a property we did check during games. To accomplish such real-time execution, with over 50 simulated Erlang processes and checking safety monitors in every global system state, proves that the simulated runtime implementation is not overly slow.

To check a team in varying situations the opposition teams were chosen with care. To evaluate defensive play we matched the team to check against good teams from previous international Robocup competitions[4]. Concretely such teams include `fcportugal2004` and `tokyotech2004`, both from the 2004 international Robocup competition[5]. For evaluating offensive play a particularly bad student team was selected as an opponent. Finally, to evaluate the team in a more fluctuating situation we played the team against itself. All games were repeated multiple times, to increase the coverage of the verification experiment.

By using McErlang compared to using traditional testing frameworks we obtain a number of advantages:

- correctness properties can be elegantly expressed as automatons rather than sets of tests,
- compared to running a team under the normal Erlang runtime system, the McErlang tool provides detailed control of the scheduling of processes, and delivery of messages (which control a traditional runtime system does not provide at all). Testing a multi-agent system under different scheduling assumptions can often reveal errors that are difficult to reproduce using normal testing procedures,
- no or very little source code modification is necessary to interpret testing outcome (i.e., as all the team state – including all its agents, and all the processes implementing an agent – can be inspected, there is generally little need to export extra information from an agent).
- since we are using an untyped functional programming language (Erlang) we can treat programs (e.g., pending function calls, sent messages, etc) as data, and analyse such data using powerful data abstraction functions. Moreover we can often reuse functions and data structures used in the program itself, when formulating correctness properties.

---

[4] As the level of play of the student teams is generally not very good, this was easy.
[5] http://www.robocup2004.pt/

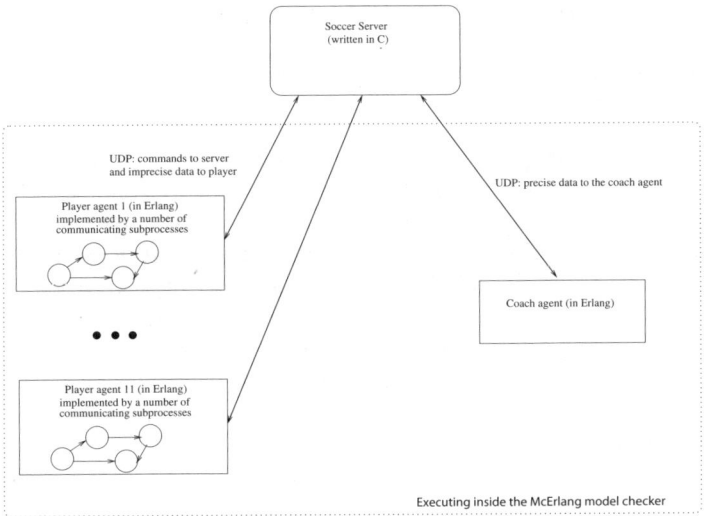

Fig. 2. RoboCup verification setup

We use the monitor concept of McErlang to check properties of a RoboCup team programmed in Erlang during games with opponents. Monitors to check correctness properties of the team are written in Erlang as well, and have full access to the state of all agents (players), messages in communication channels, and so on.

However, the states of player agents may of course not reflect reality, as they may have incorrect or simply insufficient knowledge of the state of the game. Clearly to determine whether a property holds, in general we need access to the state of the soccer server as well. As the server is not written in Erlang, McErlang does not have direct access to its internal state. However, by programming a "Coach agent" in Erlang[6], that repeatedly gets truthful and complete situational information from the soccer server (e.g., ball position, and the position and movement of all players), we gain access, using the McErlang tool, to the complete simulation state.

In case a property violation is detected by a monitor, the complete trace of the simulation up to that point, including the states and actions of all agents and the coach, are available for further analysis in the McErlang debugger.

The experimental setup is depicted in Fig. 2; note that there is no direct communication between agents comprising a team.

5.1 Correctness Property Classification

Roughly we can separate desirable properties of RoboCup teams into three kinds:

- **observable properties** can be evaluated by observing only the actions (or inactions) of an agent and its external stimuli, without considering the internal state of an agent

---

[6] The coach interface is provided by the soccer simulation server.

- **discrepancy properties** concern the difference between an agents's beliefs and the objective reality
- **internal properties** concern the general consistency of an agent, and the efficacy of its internal logic decisions

Externally observable properties can be decided solely by examining the data the soccer server sends to the coach process, and the actions (UDP data) sent from an agent to the soccer server. There are countless such properties that can be formulated and checked. For example: "players stay inside the playing field" (*op1*), "the goalie doesn't leave the goal area" (*op2*), "a pass cannot be intercepted by a player from the opponent team" (*op3*), and so on. An obvious externally observable property is that an agent may never crash (*nocrash*).

If we find that such an observable property is violated, the cause can either be that the internal logic of the agent is faulty, or that the agent is acting correctly but on faulty data.

An example of a discrepancy property is: "the difference between the believed position of a player and its real position must not exceed some safety margin" (*dp1*). Discrepancy properties requires us to examine both the objective state of the RoboCup simulation (the information sent to the coach process) as well as the internal beliefs (internal data structures) of the processes comprising a player agent.

Internal properties range from quite general properties such that: "the size of a message queue is never greater than some limit l" (*mq*) to very specific properties. As an example, we can reformulate the property about safe passes (*op3*) above into a property about the internal state of agents: "the agent never attempts a pass when it knows that an opponent player may intercept the ball" (*ip3*). Note that it is perfectly possible for an agent to fail the property *ip3* while not failing *op3* (or vice verse) if the knowledge of the position of the players of the opposition team is particularly poor (a discrepancy property).

While it is easy to formulate such high-level properties in English, with much ambiguity, the challenge is to formulate these properties precisely, and to provide a framework for determining whether they are satisfied by Robocup teams or not. Below we exemplify how this is achieved for two such teams.

5.2   Verification of the First RoboCup Team

The first RoboCup team analysed by us was rather simplistic in nature, generally being reactive (every new sensor information causes a complete new plan to be formed) rather than proactive (players have long term plans that they attempt to realise).

We exemplify the specification of properties by formulating a simple observable property, i.e., that no player strays far outside the playing area (*op1*). As explained earlier, such a property can be checked by examining the accurate information sent to the coaching process, without considering the internal states of agents.

```
stateChange(State, MonState, Stack) ->
  try
    {ok, CoachState} = coach:getCoachState(State),
    AllPlayers = coach:getOwnPlayers(CoachState),

    %% Verify that all players are in the allowed area
    {LowerX, LowerY, UpperX, UpperY} = MonState,
    case lists:any
        (fun (P) ->
            {PosX, PosY} = P#player.position,
            (PosX < LowerX) orelse (PosX > UpperX) orelse
            (PosY < LowerY) orelse (PosY > UpperY)
          end, AllPlayers) of
        true -> error
        false -> {ok, MonState}
      end
  catch _ -> {ok, MonState} end.
```

The function stateChange is called by the model checker every time a new state is generated. Its arguments are the new state State, the previous monitor state MonState (for this property the coordinates for the allowable area for a player), and the entire stack of program states leading to the current state[7].

The implemented monitor begins by extracting the state of the "coach" process using the function coach:getCoachState. This function attempts to retrieve the process datastructure of the coach process using its name "coach", and from that structure the internal datastructure that records the data sent from the soccer server. This is achieved by accessing the expr field of a process datastructure, that records the current state of the process (always waiting for a new UDP message to arrive from the soccer server) together with the state data (a part of which is the internal datastructure that records data sent by the soccer server).

```
getCoachState(State) ->
  %% Retrieve process named "coach"
  P = findProcessByRegisteredName("coach", State),
  case P#process.expr of
    {recv, {_,_,{_, CoachState}}, _} -> CoachState
  end.
```

If this fails (e.g., probably because the coach process has not been created yet) the **try** ... **catch** statement ensures that the simulation continues. Given the coach state, the coach:getOwnPlayers function returns the information sent by the soccer server regarding the team players (e.g., position and so on). It is then easy to compute whether any player strays outside the allowable area, and if so the monitor returns error which indicates to the model checker that an error has been encountered. As a result the simulator will offer the possibility to examine in detail the trace leading to the erroneous state detected by the monitor. During testing, the checker quickly produced a run leading to a violation of this property.

---

[7] The stack implementation is also parametric and we frequently use a bounded stack which forgets old states when runs become too large.

As another example, we formulated the *op2* property, i.e., that the goalie doesn't leave the goal area, and attempted to verify that property. This property is also easily checked using the knowledge from the coach process. Unfortunately the first team fails even this simple property: the goalkeeper was very far from his penalty area. However, from visual inspection (using the soccer monitor to view a game progress) the goalie did not appear to have left his penalty area. Program inspection found the source of the error: the team had assumed a fixed assignment of player numbers to their processes, whereas the soccer server could randomly assign player numbers. In other words, the player which resided in the penalty area was in fact not the goal keeper, thus the player did not have permission to handle the ball with his hands.

In conclusion, the first team analysed possessed grave problems indeed, and we didn't think it interesting to consider the analysis further at that point but continued with the second team.

5.3   Verification of the Second RoboCup Team

The second RoboCup team analysed is far more complex, comprising more lines of code, and having a much more complex internal state. Although generally playing much better than the first team, we were able to discover a number of bugs that had gone undetected using normal testing techniques. We illustrate the kinds of properties checked, and the bugs found, using a number of small examples below.

Observable properties. When trying to execute the second RoboCup team under the McErlang model checker, and playing a game, the program sometimes crashed with an error message. This had never been experienced when running the team outside the model checker. The reason for the crash turned out to be typical of a class of hard–to–reproduce errors which occur only for some very intricate sequences of concurrent actions. Players of the second team are composed of different processes; one such process responsible for executing plans have two states: idle when it awaits a new plan, and execute when it executes a received plan. The execution of each step of a plan is performed by a subordinate process, which reports the success or failure of the step back to the executor process. The executor process and its subordinates communicate using asynchronous message passing. The error occurs when a second plan reaches the executor process before it has finished executing a prior plan. In such a situation the process (correctly) terminates the subordinate process, resends the second plan to itself, and enters the idle state (awaiting the second plan sent to itself). However, it turns out that the subordinate process may have sent a message to the executor process that arrived after it was itself terminated, but arriving before the second plan (when the executor process was in the idle state). Moreover the executor process was not able to handle incoming messages from a subordinate process in its idle state, leading it to crash.

A graphical depiction of the error is shown in Fig. 3, where the idle state (of the executor process) is in white, and the executor state is in gray.

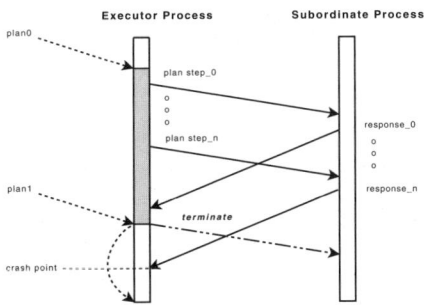

Fig. 3. RoboCup Agent Bug

During extensive testing of the team this error had never been seen, however using McErlang (which has a much less deterministic agent scheduler compared to the normal Erlang runtime system) the error was immediately discovered.

We also coded up the property of safe passes (*op3*); however, it turned out that agents could attempt quite unsafe passes. A possible reason for such unsafe behaviour is analysed below, in the formalisation of a logic property (*lp3*).

A discrepancy property. A central correctness property is whether the agent's beliefs of the position of the ball in the field are accurate or not.

To formulate the property we have to compare the belief about the ball position, as retrieved from the internal store of an agent, compared to the real position of the ball as given by the coach agent. Clearly these values can be substantially different, for instance if the ball is kicked away behind the back of a player. However, we want to require the agent to eventually correct his ball estimate.

The formulation of the property should thus be parametric on two parameters: i) what is a bad estimate, and ii) for how long time must an estimate be continuously bad until an error is signalled.

The implementation of the property as a state monitor is as follows:

```
stateChange(State,_,Mst={Time,Params={BadEstim,Intval}}) ->
try
    %% Fetch coach info; check if game is halted, get pos info
    {ok, CoachState} = coach:getCoachState(State),
    play_on == CoachState#coachInfo.play_mode,
    CurrentTime = CoachState#coachInfo.time,
    CoachPlayer = coach:getOwnPlayer(Number,CoachState),
    CoachPlayerPos = coach:playerPos(CoachPlayer),
    CoachBall = coach:getGall(CoachState),
    CoachBallPos = coach:ballPos(CoachBall),

    %% Fetch Agent internal data, with ball & player position
    Player = kb:ask({player,myself}),
    Ball = kb:ask(ball),
```

```
%% Calculate Players distance approximation and error
DistPlayer = dist(Player#player.position, Ball#ball.position),
DistCoach = dist(CoachPlayerPos, CoachBallPos),
Error = abs(DistCoach-DistPlayer)/DistCoach,

if Error >= BadEstim ->
  case Time of
    %% First time bad estimate seen, set timer
    ok -> {ok,{{until, CurrentTime+Intval}, Params}};

    %% Estim bad during interval, report error
    {until, EndTime} when EndTime =< CurrentTime -> badEstim;

    %% Estim continously bad, not end of interval
    {until, EndTime} when EndTime > CurrentTime -> {ok, Mst}
  end;

  %% Estim is good
  true -> {ok, {ok, Params}}
end
catch ... end
```

The function dist calculates the distance between two points, and the function kb:ask (present in the agent source code) returns the belief of the agent regarding its parameter. Note that the kb:ask function is called without a parameter specifying the player; this is because the monitor is executed in the context of the agent that caused the last program step.

The error is calculated as the absolute difference between the believed distance to the ball and the real distance to the ball, divided by the real distance.

There are indeed dubious beliefs in the second agent. The model checker found, for instance, a sequence of states where a player thought the distance to be around 7.6 meters, for over a second, while the real distance hovered around 17 meters (with an error of 0.5 meters and interval of 10 time units – a second).

A logic property. To illustrate the coding of a logic property we considered first the property (*ip3*): "the agent never attempts a pass when it knows that an opponent player may intercept the ball".

We can illustrate the idea of the property using Fig. 4; there may be no opponent player in the gray zone around the (believed) path of the ball from its originating player to the destination.

In each state the formalisation of the property has to determine whether a pass attempt has been made. This turned out to be rather difficult, as the difference between what is a pass, shooting or just clearing the ball in a dangerous situation is hidden quite deep in the code (and all three operations are executed by sending a "kick" command to the soccer server). In the end it turned out to be easier to modify one line of the player program, by introducing a new (artificial) state

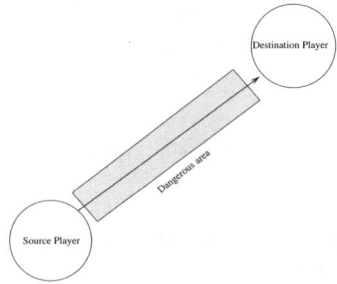

Fig. 4. Property *ip3*

labelled by a tuple encoding the operation of passing the ball, and the destination position of the corresponding kick:

{ do_pass , TargetPosition }

After the introduction of this "probe state", the property is easily specified. Essentially whenever a kick is made, it is necessary to retrieve from the player agent its beliefs about the opponent players and calculate whether any of these players are too close to the path of the ball between source and target.

Running an example quickly reveals that the second agent exhibits dubious behaviour. We found a situation when, using as the unsafe distance 0.5 meters, an agent could attempt a pass in the following situation: source player at $\{-23.9, -24.27\}$, destination player at $\{-13.57, -8.4\}$, and an opposition player at $\{-17.56, -14.59\}$ which could quite easily intercept the pass.

6   Conclusions

In this paper we have used the McErlang model checking tool to perform runtime verification on a set of agents comprising a RoboCup soccer simulation team written in the Erlang programming language. Correctness properties were specified as monitors (automatons) observing the detailed behavior and states of all the players in the team, and the opponent team. The agents checked were not modified nor abstracted for the purpose of the study, rather the standard source code of the agents was used essentially unchanged. One of the key functionalities of the McErlang tool is the capability to observe the inner state of agents, and of coping with temporal agent behaviors.

The properties checked include a number of obvious correctness criteria for football play (respecting playing field boundaries etc), including also a number of properties that concern the inner logic of the agents. We aim to continue this experiment in order to formulate further more detailed properties regarding the internal state of agents (beliefs, plans, etc) of more RoboCup teams and agents, to further illustrate the practicality of the approach.

References

1. Armstrong, J., Virding, R., Wikström, C., Williams, M.: Concurrent Programming in Erlang. Prentice-Hall, Englewood Cliffs (1996)
2. Bordini, R.H., Fisher, M., Visser, W., Wooldridge, M.: Verifying multi-agent programs by model checking. Autonomous Agents and Multi-Agent Systems 12(2), 239–256 (2006)
3. Bosse, T., Lam, D.N., Barber, K.S.: Automated analysis and verification of agent behavior. In: AAMAS 2006: Proceedings of the fifth international joint conference on Autonomous agents and multiagent systems, pp. 1317–1319. ACM Press, New York (2006)
4. Chen, M., Dorer, K., Foroughi, E., Heintz, F., Huang, Z., Kapetanakis, S., Kostiadis, K., Kummeneje, J., Murray, J., Noda, I., Obst, O., Riley, P., Steffens, T., Wang, Y., Yin, X.: RoboCup Soccer Server (2003); Manual for Soccer Server Version 7.07 and later (obtainable from sserver.sf.net)
5. Fredlund, L.: Implementing WS-CDL. In: Proceedings of the second Spanish workshop on Web Technologies (JSWEB 2006). Universidade de Santiago de Compostela (November 2006)
6. Fredlund, L., Svensson, H.: McErlang: a model checker for a distributed programming language. In: Proceedings of the 2007 ACM SIGPLAN International Conference on Functional Programming (2007)
7. Furbach, U., Murray, J., Schmidsberger, F., Stolzenburg, F.: Model checking hybrid multiagent systems for the roboCup. In: Visser, U., Ribeiro, F., Ohashi, T., Dellaert, F. (eds.) RoboCup 2007: Robot Soccer World Cup XI. LNCS, vol. 5001, pp. 262–269. Springer, Heidelberg (2008)
8. Holzmann, G.: Design and Validation of Computer Protocols. Prentice-Hall, Englewood Cliffs (1991)
9. Torstendahl, S.: Open telecom platform. Ericsson Review 1 (1997)
10. Vardi, M., Wolper, P.: An automata-theoretic approach to automatic program verification, pp. 332–344 (1986)
11. Visser, W., Havelund, K., Brat, G., Park, S.: Java pathfinder - second generation of a java model checker (2000)

Scaling Search with Pattern Databases*

Stefan Edelkamp, Shahid Jabbar, and Peter Kissmann

Technische Universität Dortmund

Abstract. In this paper, we illustrate efforts to perform memory efficient large-scale search. We first generate sets of disjoint symbolic pattern databases on disk. These pattern databases are then used for heuristic guidance, while applying explicit-state external-memory heuristic search. Different options for parallelization to save time and memory are presented. The general techniques are mapped to the $(n^2 - 1)$-puzzle as a large-scale case study.

1 Introduction

Abstraction-directed search [35] joins abstraction-based search [4, 5, 30] and heuristic search [13, 34]. An abstract state space model is obtained from a concrete one by grouping together concrete states that share some common properties into abstract states. The distances in the abstract model serve as heuristic estimates for the search in the original one. A pattern database [6, 14, 25, 27, 36, 38] for an abstract state space model is a lookup table that maps each abstract state to its shortest path distance to the closest abstract goal state. For undirected and unweighted graphs, it is easiest to create a pattern database by conducting a breadth-first search in backward direction. For a better time-space trade-off, it is possible to fully traverse the abstract state space symbolically with binary decision diagrams (BDDs), yielding symbolic pattern databases [2, 7]. These pattern databases can then be used to obtain admissible and consistent heuristic estimates in order to guide the search for errors in the concrete model.

Unfortunately, even with improved guidance, the space requirements for search in concrete models are the major bottleneck while dealing with large real-world systems. External-memory devices such as hard disks, on the other hand, provide bulk but cheaper storage capacities. External-memory heuristic search has shown significant success in dealing with large AI and model checking problems [10, 19]. In this paper, we extend the scope of external-memory directed search by incorporating large symbolic pattern databases for a more effective guidance. Besides this mixture of technologies, we study a number of refinements to push the limits of pattern databases in practice, including automated construction of super-database for control rule pruning, shared databases, partitioned construction, and distributed usage. Furthermore, we propose the integration of iterative-deepening with external-memory A* search, the delayed generation of successors, and an external-memory relay version of A* for computing approximate solutions.

---

* This research was supported by the German Research Council (DFG) in the projects *heuristic search*, *directed model checking* and *algorithm engineering*.

D. Peled and M. Wooldridge (Eds.): MOCHART 2008, LNAI 5348, pp. 49–64, 2009.

	1	2	3
4	5	6	7
8	9	10	11
12	13	14	15

	1	2	3	4
5	6	7	8	9
10	11	12	13	14
15	16	17	18	19
20	21	23	23	24

	1	2	3	4	5
6	7	8	9	10	11
12	13	14	15	16	17
18	19	20	21	22	23
24	25	26	27	28	29
30	31	32	33	34	35

Fig. 1. The end position of the $(n^2 - 1)$-puzzle for $n = 4$, $n = 5$ and $n = 6$

As a large-scale case study, we have chosen sliding tiles puzzles, a standard sample in AI search[1]. Some instances of this puzzle are shown in Fig. 1. This puzzle, commonly referred to as $(n^2 - 1)$-puzzle, has been used as a testbed for model checkers[2] that successfully solve 8- but tend to fail on 15-puzzle instances. The game consists of $(n^2 - 1)$ numbered tiles, squarely arranged, that can be slid into a single empty location, called the *blank*. The goal is to re-arrange the tiles such that a specific layout (like in Fig. 1) is reached. For modeling the puzzle, every state is represented as a state vector. Each component of this vector corresponds to one location, indicating the tile (including the blank) occupying it. The state spaces consist of $16!/2 \approx 1.05 \cdot 10^{13}$ for the 15-Puzzle, and $25!/2 \approx 7.75 \cdot 10^{24}$ for the 24-Puzzle, while the set of reachable states for the 35-Puzzle consists of $36!/2 \approx 1.86 \cdot 10^{41}$ states. Optimally solving the puzzle is infeasible for current technology [37], so that it serves as a valid testbet for pushing the envelope of state space search techniques. Due to its fast depth-first node generation and linear space requirements, IDA* [24] is probably the best choice for solving this puzzle. However, IDA* comes with no duplicate detection, which hinders its application to other model checking problems.

The paper is structured as follows. First, we discuss external-memory explicit-state A* search for solving problems that are larger than main memory. We then explain pattern databases and give a brief overview of disjoint databases. We introduce symbolic pattern databases based on BDDs and show how to improve their quality. Due to better tie-breaking, the integration of IDA* to external-memory A* search exhibits another time-space trade-off. We briefly discuss and analyze the impact of a delayed generation of successors in terms of disk accesses. We then address the distributed, space-efficient lookup, which on each client selectively loads only the pattern databases that are needed to incrementally compute the heuristic estimate. This allows to load larger pattern databases on individual processors. Last but not least, we propose an incremental version of A* to generate approximate solutions.

2 External-Memory Heuristic Search

The limitation of main memory is the major bottleneck for practical model checking applications. Relying on traditional virtual memory can drastically slow down the performance. External-memory search algorithms explicitly manage the transfer of data between fast RAM and slow hard disk, while minimizing the number of *seek* operations

---

[1] See [29] for related large-scale search study in Rubik's Cube.
[2] http://anna.fi.muni.cz/models/cgi/model_info.cgi?name=loyd

on the disk. These algorithms are more informed about the future data accesses than the virtual memory offered by the operating system. The complexity of these algorithms is measured in terms of the asymptotic number of I/Os they incur. For simplicity, instead of single I/Os, the complexity is often expressed in terms of number of external scanning or sorting operations.

Search algorithms, such as breadth-first search (BFS), rely on a duplicate removal mechanism, typically realized by a hash table, to avoid re-expansions of states. Naïvely running internal-memory BFS in the same way on external memory may result in many file accesses for removing duplicate nodes. The external-memory BFS algorithm [33] operates on undirected explicit graphs (provided before-hand in the form of adjacency lists). For implicit problem graphs (generated from a set of initial states and a set of transformation rules), this technique has been termed as delayed duplicate detection [26]. For directed implicit graphs, a constant bound on the number of BFS levels required to remove all the duplicates made the basis for internal sparse-memory algorithms, such as breadth-first heuristic search [39].

A* is a famous best-first search algorithm that exploits heuristic guidance to arrive at a goal state faster. It requires a priority queue to always select the state with the minimum $f = g + h$ value, where g is the depth, and h is the heuristic estimate of the state to the goal. External-memory A* [10] combines delayed duplicate detection, frontier and best-first search into one algorithm. It shares similarities with SetA* [21]. External-memory A* (Algorithm 1) maintains the search space on disk in the form of a (g, h) matrix, where each cell represents a *bucket* of states. The initial state (resp. set of target states) is represented by $\mathcal{I}$ (resp. $\mathcal{T}$). In the course of the algorithm, a bucket $Open(i, j)$ contains all states s with path length $g(s) = i$ and heuristic estimate $h(s) = j$. It simulates a priority queue by always selecting the buckets with the minimum f-value; ties are broken by selecting the one with the minimum g-value.

Duplicate detection wrt. previous layers can be restricted to the buckets of the same h-value. Each bucket, when active, is represented in RAM as a small buffer. If the buffer becomes full, it is sorted and flushed to the disk; if it becomes empty while reading, it is refreshed with new states from the disk. Duplicates are removed by first performing external sorting, followed by a operation to remove the states from a bucket in a mere scan. Next, the previous two buckets are subtracted to guarantee a duplicate-free bucket file. The state sets addressed by A in the pseudo-code are temporary files used to collect all the successor states generated by applying expansion rules *Succ* on a state set.

Using the Manhattan distance estimate, external-memory A* can optimally solve all 15-puzzle instances proposed in [24]. We furthermore exploited the property that due to the undirected nature of the $(n^2 - 1)$-puzzle and the parity condition, duplicates for bucket $Open(i, j)$ can only exist in the buckets $Open(i, j)$ and $Open(i - 2, j)$ and not in $Open(i - 1, j)$. For the hardest instance it expanded 999,442,568 nodes in less than an hour using a single processor[3] and 17,769 megabytes of disk space. In the subsequent discussion, for the sake of brevity, we avoid prefix *Open* for accessing a bucket.

---

[3] Experiments were carried out on a Linux cluster, equipped with Opteron 2.2-2.6GHz processor nodes (2.6GHz 4-processor nodes with 16 GB RAM, 2.2GHz 2-processor nodes with 4 GB RAM) and 3 terabytes hard disk connected via NFS. The time limit varied from 48h–480h.

Algorithm 1: External A* for Consistent and Integral Heuristics

---

$Open(0, h(\mathcal{I})) \leftarrow \{\mathcal{I}\}$
$f_{\min} \leftarrow \min\{i \mid Open(0, i) \neq \emptyset\}$ // Select the minimum $f_{\min}$ diagonal to expand
while $(f_{\min} \neq \infty)$ **do**
    $g_{\min} \leftarrow \min\{i \mid Open(i, f_{\min} - i) \neq \emptyset\}$ // Select the first non-empty bucket
    while $(g_{\min} \leq f_{\min})$ **do**
        // Loop for the whole $f_{\min}$ diagonal $h_{\max} \leftarrow f_{\min} - g_{\min}$;
        if $h_{\max} = 0$ **and** $\exists u \in Open(g_{\min}, h_{\max})$ s.t. $u \in \mathcal{T}$ **then**
            return $Path(u)$ // Return the path found from $\mathcal{I}$ to u
        $Open(g_{\min}, h_{\max}) \leftarrow external\text{-}sort(Open(g_{\min}, h_{\max}))$ // External sorting
        $Open(g_{\min}, h_{\max}) \leftarrow remove\text{-}duplicates(Open(g_{\min}, h_{\max}))$;
        // Subtract the previous two buckets
        $Open(g_{\min}, h_{\max}) \leftarrow$
        $Open(g_{\min}, h_{\max}) \setminus (Open(g_{\min} - 1, h_{\max}) \cup Open(g_{\min} - 2, h_{\max}))$;
        // Generate and distribute the successors based on their f-values
        $A(f_{\min}), A(f_{\min} + 1), A(f_{\min} + 2) \leftarrow Succ(Open(g_{\min}, h_{\max}))$;
        $Open(g_{\min} + 1, h_{\max} - 1) \leftarrow A(f_{\min}) \cup Open(g_{\min} + 1, h_{\max} - 1)$;
        $Open(g_{\min} + 1, h_{\max}) \leftarrow A(f_{\min} + 1) \cup Open(g_{\min} + 1, h_{\max})$;
        $Open(g_{\min} + 1, h_{\max} + 1) \leftarrow A(f_{\min} + 2)$;
        $g_{\min} \leftarrow g_{\min} + 1$;
    $f_{\min} \leftarrow \min\{i + j > f_{\min} \mid Open(i, j) \neq \emptyset\} \cup \{\infty\}$ // New f diagonal
return $\emptyset$

---

3 Pattern Databases

Better search heuristics are the keys for solving large problems. A pattern database is a lookup table containing the distance from any abstract state to the abstract error (the abstract goal state). It serves as an admissible search heuristic for the concrete state space. The size of a pattern database is the number of states it contains. The simplest abstractions are state vector projections, the so-called patterns. For the $(n^2 - 1)$-puzzle domain, a pattern is a particular selection of tiles, while replacing the other tiles with *don't-cares*. The selection of tiles has been provided manually, but pattern selection can be automated [9, 17].

Disjoint pattern databases [27] allow combining multiple abstraction databases, while still preserving the consistency of the estimate. If the selected patterns (in our case, the tiles) in each database are disjoint, the entries in each database can be added to get a better estimate. As only one tile moves at a time, for the $(n^2 - 1)$-puzzle, the move action acts locally in one group only.[4] Together with IDA* search, disjoint explicit-state pattern databases suffice to solve fully random 24-puzzle instances [27]. Each of the 6-tile pattern databases consists of 127,512,000 abstract states; due to structural regularities, only 2 of 4 pattern databases need constructed. In symmetric pattern databases, automorphisms in the state vector are exploited to allow multiple lookups. For the $(n^2 - 1)$-puzzle, the reflection along the main diagonal leads to a pattern database that is addressed twice for each state by additionally posing symmetric state queries.

---

[4] If an action modifies more than one group, one has to distribute its costs [12, 22, 23].

Symbolic pattern databases [7] are compact representations of pattern databases. The functional representation of state sets is maintained as a Binary Decision Diagram (BDD) [3]. For a given state vector, the BDD evaluates to 1, if the corresponding state is contained in the encoded set. The additional compaction refers to the two BDD reduction rule, which lead to a unique diagram representation.

A symbolic pattern database is a sequence of BDDs $H_0, \ldots, H_k$ with H_i covering all abstract state vectors that have a heuristic h-value of i, $i \in \{0, \ldots, k\}$. The symbolic pattern databases are generated by traversing the abstract state space with BDDs. The abstract operators are utilized to compute all successor sets of a state set in partitioned form in an operation called image [31]. The other option would have been to generate explicit-state pattern databases and then compact them into BDDs.

We observed that the symbolic construction 6-tile pattern databases for the 24-puzzle (in about half an hour each) led to only about 30% savings wrt. the explicit-state storage. One possible cause for this moderate reduction is that half of all possible permutations over $\{0, \ldots, n^2 - 1\}$ refer to reachable layouts in the $(n^2 - 1)$-puzzle. Moreover, the characteristic function f_N of all permutations on $0, \ldots, N - 1$ has has more than $2^{N/2}$ BDD nodes for every variable ordering [11, 18].

4   Refined Database Construction

The quality of symbolic pattern databases can be improved. Consider a pattern database for the sliding-tile puzzle with a set of tiles that surround the blank in the top-left corner. We know that the last action necessarily has to move a tile that is adjacent to the blank. The last but one action may also have restrictions.

Algorithm 2: Refinement for the construction of the pattern databases.

// Construction of the super-database
$H_{-1} \leftarrow \bot; H_0 \leftarrow \mathcal{T}; step \leftarrow 1;$
while $step < maxStep$ **and** $H_{step-1} \neq \bot$ **do**

$\quad H_{step} \leftarrow pre\text{-}image\left(H_{step-1}\right) \wedge \neg H_{step-2}$; // Remove duplicates from predecessors
$\quad step \leftarrow step + 1;$
$max \leftarrow step - 1;$

foreach *abstraction* i **do**
$\quad$ // Construction of the database for the i-th abstraction
$\quad H^i_{-1} \leftarrow \bot; H^i_0 \leftarrow \mathcal{T}^i; step \leftarrow 1; super \leftarrow \top;$
$\quad$ **while** $H^i_{step-1} \neq \bot$ **do**

$\quad\quad H \leftarrow pre\text{-}image\left(H^i_{step-1}\right) \wedge \neg H^i_{step-2}$; // Remove duplicates from predecessors
$\quad\quad$ **if** *super* **and** $step \leq max$ **then**
$\quad\quad\quad H^i_{step} \leftarrow H \wedge \exists v \in \left(V \setminus V^i\right) . H_{step}$; // Retain only states also in super-database
$\quad\quad\quad$ **if** $H^i_{step} \neq H_{step}$ **then**
$\quad\quad\quad\quad super \leftarrow \bot$; // Stop using the super-database
$\quad\quad\quad\quad H^i_{step} \leftarrow H$; // Store all predecessors
$\quad\quad$ **else** $H^i_{step} \leftarrow H;$
$\quad\quad step \leftarrow step + 1;$

These restrictions can be calculated automatically (cf. Algorithm 2). To do this, we construct a part of the super-database H, i.e., the database for the original space. This is done by creating the set of predecessors (called pre-image in symbolic search), starting at the target states T. As we do not need the complete database, *maxStep* backward steps suffice; in case of the $(n^2 - 1)$-puzzle, we need no more than three.

When constructing the pattern databases H^i we start at the abstract space's target states T^i. During each backward step, we retain only those states that are also in the super-database (in the same step), projected into the current abstraction. This projection is done by existential-quantification over the variables not in the abstract space ($V \setminus V^i$). This may only be done until the result does not equal the projection of the super-database's step. From then onwards, we forget about the super-database and construct the pattern database as before.

For a 5-tile (the 5 tiles nearest the top-left corner) pattern database of the 15-puzzle, the use of the super-database leads to an increase of the radius (i.e., the number of backward steps needed to construct the complete database) from 23 to 25. Similarly, for a 6-tile pattern database of the 24-puzzle, the radius increases from 32 to 35. Thus, the resulting databases are more accurate.

5   Incremental External Search

One disadvantage of external-memory A* is its unfortunate tie-breaking strategy.[5] As it processes the f-diagonal the with increasing depth, external-memory A* expands almost all the states with optimal f-value. In contrast, the depth-first order in iterative-deepening A* search (IDA*) often results in fewer states to be explored. Moreover, IDA* does not perform duplicate detection and thus trades time for space.

Therefore, we also tried to combine the advantages of IDA* and external-memory A*. This is done by initiating IDA* runs from the states generated in external-memory A*. For a fixed threshold on the f-value, external-memory A* is stopped. All states in still unexpanded buckets are are processed by calling IDA*.[6]

Table 1. Combining IDA* with external-memory A* in a some 24-puzzle instance

Threshold	Length	Nodes Generated	Time
68 (Pure IDA*)	82	9.47694×10^7	3m:06s
70 (Hybrid)	82	1.33633×10^8	4m:23s
72 (Hybrid)	82	1.27777×10^8	4m:03s
74 (Hybrid)	82	6.95716×10^7	2m:24s
76 (Hybrid)	82	6.37333×10^7	2m:22s
78 (Hybrid)	82	1.08334×10^8	3m:35s
80 (Hybrid)	82	9.66122×10^7	3m:36s
82 (Hybrid)	82	2.29965×10^8	8m:25s
84 (External-Memory A*)	82	1.71814×10^8	8m:48s

---

[5] A similar problem can be observed in breadth-first heuristic search [39].

[6] These runs are independent and can be distributed.

In Table 1, we show results of solving one simpler instance of the 24-puzzle (number 40 in [27]), according to different threshold values. The first entry shows that our implementation of IDA* generates more nodes than [27] (65,099,578) – likely due to different tie-breaking and further fine-tuning. Pure IDA* generated 94 million nodes, while external-memory A* generated 171 million. With increasing threshold value, we see a potential for a better algorithm in between the two.

Optimally solving another 24-puzzle instance (49 in [27]) with 100 moves and a split value of 84 and 367,243,074,706 generated nodes in 217 hours, shows that even with only one disjoint pattern database in use, hard instances are tractable. Therefore, we concentrate on solving the 35-puzzle.

During the implementation we observed that IDA*'s pruning strategies such as not re-generating predecessors save time for delayed duplicate detection.

6   External-Memory Symbolic Pattern Databases

External-memory pattern databases [8] are constructed in layers and maintained on the hard disk. Each BFS level is flushed in form of a BDD to disk, so that the memory for representing this level can be re-used. As the BDD representation of a state set is unique, no effort for eliminating duplicates in one BFS-level is required. Before expanding a state set in BFS-level i, however, we apply delayed duplicate detection, eliminating states that have appeared in BFS-level $i - 2$. As the external construction of large-scale pattern databases takes time, the process can be paused and resumed at any time.

For the 35-puzzle either seven 5-tile, five 6-tile + one 5-tile, or five 7-tile databases complete a disjoint set. The cumulated space consumption for explicit-state disjoint sets of pattern databases (without exploiting structural regularities) is 302 megabytes (for seven 5-tile pattern databases), 6.9 gigabytes (for five 6-tile + one 5-tile pattern databases), and 195 gigabytes (for five 7-tile pattern databases). For the disjoint 6-tile pattern database in the 35-puzzle the results are shown in Fig. 2. In total, the additive set consumes 2.6 gigabytes; a gain of factor 2.65 wrt. the explicit construction. We generated four more additive 6-tile pattern databases with sizes 4.0, 2.3, 2.3, and 3.2 gigabytes. The construction of all five disjoint 6-tile pattern databases took about 50h. Fig. 2 also depicts the memory profile for generating one 7-tile pattern database[7]. The total size of the database is 6.6 gigabytes, which compares well with the space needed for explicit construction. When RAM became sparse, for constructing larger BFS levels, partitioned images were calculated and unified.

Together with the space of about one gigabyte for the search buckets ($5 \cdot 10^6$ entries), one would expect a main memory requirement of more than 15 gigabytes when loading all 5 disjoint pattern databases. However, about 13 gigabytes RAM were actually needed. This additional memory gain is due to loading the different layers stored on disk into a shared BDD [32]. There are also cross-pattern database savings, obtained by BDD sharing. These savings are due to shifting the set of BDD variable indices for every pattern database to the same range, i.e., all BDDs are rooted at index 0.

---

[7] The full disjoint set of 7-tile databases has not been completed due to time limitation of more than 48h for generating one BFS layer.

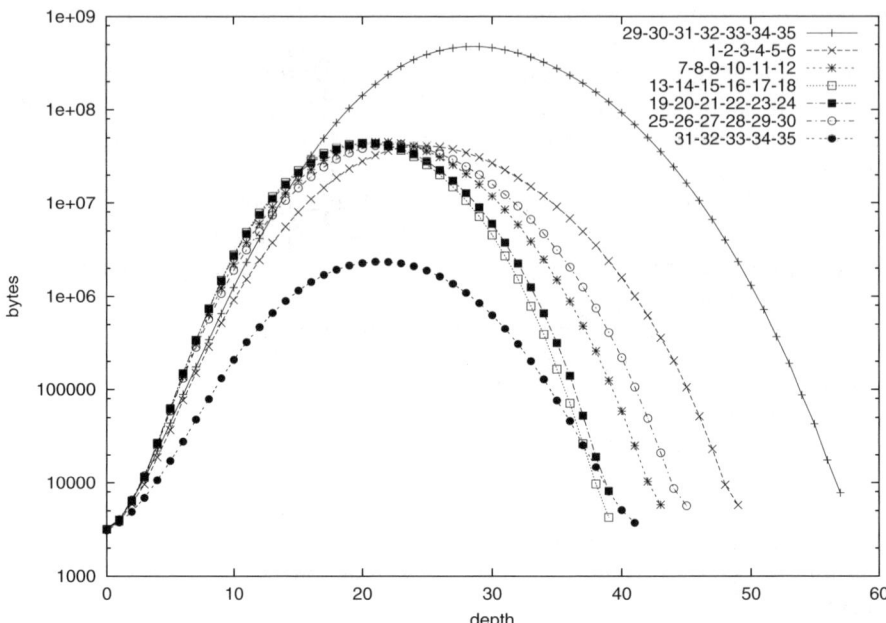

Fig. 2. Memory profile for 5-, 6- and 7-tile symbolic pattern databases (logscale)

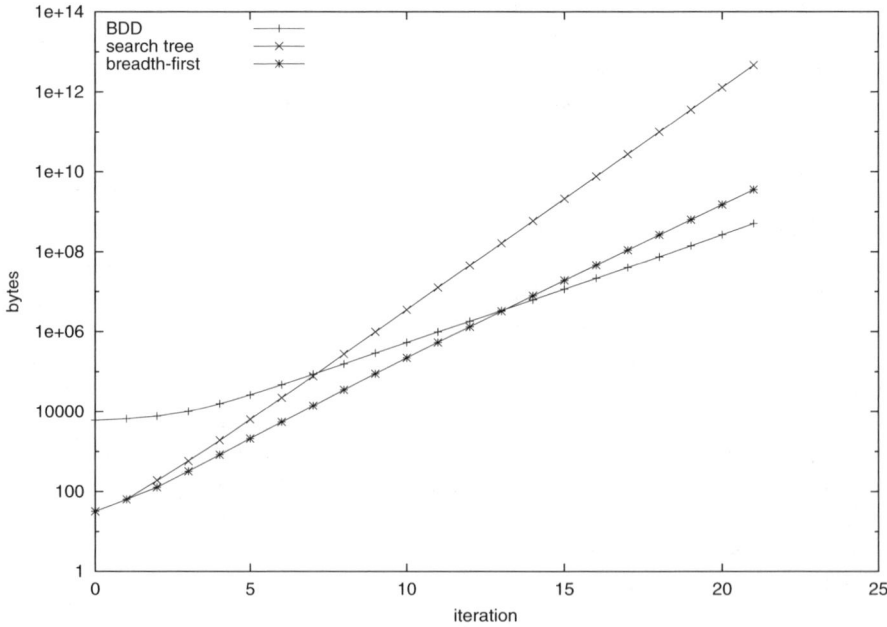

Fig. 3. Memory profile for backward search (logscale)

For the construction of large pattern databases, we found that the intermediate result for the image became too large to be completed in main memory. As a solution, we computed all sub-images (one for each individual move), flushed them, and unified them in the form of a binary tree using a separate program.

The question arises [28], whether or not symbolic pattern databases cooperate with symbolic perimeter search, an issue that has recently been denoted as partial or perimeter database [1, 12, 16]. For this we drew a small experiment constructing a limited-depth pattern database for the full problem. The memory needs for explicit-state search tree, breadth-first exploration, and symbolic exploration (residing on disk) are compared in Fig. 3.

7 Delayed Successor Generation

First, we emphasize that for a search with large internal buffers, as in our case, a multi-level merge-sort is not needed, such that external sorting is reduced to external scanning. This is due to the fact that in most operating systems, the number of file pointers is larger than the ratio between disk and main memory. Given that a single merging pass suffices, the I/O complexity is bounded by $O(|E|/B)$, with $E = \{(s, s') \mid s'$ is successor of $s \wedge f(s) \leq f^*\}$ and B being the block size.

To save space and work on the last diagonal, we have extended external-memory A* by expanding each f-diagonal twice. In the first pass, only the successors on the active

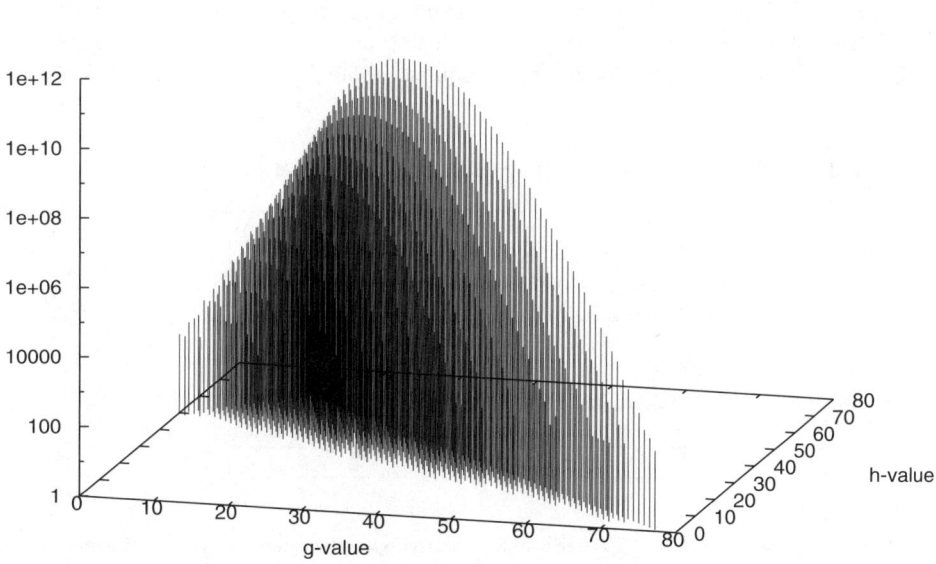

Fig. 4. Memory profile external-memory A* (logscale) for solving a partially random instance of the 35-puzzle with symbolic pattern databases

9	10	8	2		7
3	1	12	4	14	13
5	11	6	15	16	17
18	19	20	21	22	23
24	25	26	27	28	29
30	31	32	33	34	35

27	20	35	30	33	26
32	12	4	15	6	23
3	5	8	34	14	29
22		21	7	31	28
25	2	10	1	24	16
18	17	13	9	11	19

7	1	12		3	2
6	4	9	8	10	14
13	15	16	5	17	11
33	21	26	24	22	25
18	20	34	32	35	28
19	30	23	31	27	29

Fig. 5. Sample instances to the 35-puzzle, with rising level of difficulty

diagonal are generated, leaving out the generation of the successors on the $(f + 2)$-diagonal. In the second pass, the remaining successors on the $(f + 2)$-diagonal are generated. We can avoid computing the estimate twice, since all successor states that do not belong to the bucket $(g + 1, h - 1)$, belong to $(g + 1, h + 1)$. In the second pass we can, therefore, generate all successors and subtract bucket $(g + 1, h - 1)$ from the result. The I/O complexity of this strategy decreases to $O(|E'|/B)$, with $E' = \{(s, s') \mid s'$ is successor of $s \wedge f(s') \leq f^*\}$.

Fig. 4 shows the memory profile of external-memory A* for the partially random instance in Fig.5 (left). The exploration starts in bucket $(50, 0)$ and ends, while expanding bucket $(77, 1)$. For this experiment three disjoint 3-tile and three disjoint 5-tile pattern databases were loaded, which, together with the buckets for reading and flushing consumed about 4.9 gigabytes RAM. The total disk space taken was 1,298,389,180,652 bytes, or 1.2 terabytes, with a state vector of 188 bytes[8]. The exploration took about 2 weeks (cf. Table 2). As the maximum time for one process is 2 days, we had to resume the algorithm six times – a facility offered by the external-memory A* algorithm.

As we explore on every f-diagonal twice, we avoid the generation of nodes for diagonal $f^* + 2$. For the 35-puzzle, such delayed successor generation saved disk traffic by a factor of about 2.22. As a consequence, external-memory A* without support for delayed successor generation would have required about 3.9 terabytes disk space.

Table 2. External-memory A* for three disjoint 3- and three disjoint 5-tile databases

CPU Time	Total Time	RAM
12h:32m:20s	48h:00m:10s	4,960,976 kilobytes
9h:55m:59s	48h:00m:25s	4,960,980 kilobytes
8h:35m:43s	45h:33m:02s	4,960,976 kilobytes
8h:45m:53s	39h:36m:22s	4,960,988 kilobytes
10h:25m:31s	46h:31m:35s	4,960,976 kilobytes
11h:38m:36s	48h:00m:40s	4,960,988 kilobytes
8h:04m:14s	26h:37m:30s	4,960,984 kilobytes
66h:58m:16s	302h:19m:44s	

---

[8] $32 + 2 \times (6 \times 12 + 6 \times 1) = 188$ bytes: 32 bytes for the state vector + information for incremental heuristic evaluation: 1 byte for each value stored, multiplied by 6 sets of at most 12 pattern databases + 1 value each for their sum. Factor 2 is due to symmetry lookups.

Table 3. External-memory A* for three disjoint 5- and five disjoint 6-tile databases

CPU Time	Total Time	RAM
20h:57m:43s	48h:00m:35s	13,164,060 kilobytes
2h:18m:47s	5h:08m:44s	13,164,068 kilobytes
18h:28m:38s	42h:23m:08s	13,164,064 kilobytes
22h:55m:48s	45h:33m:47s	13,164,068 kilobytes
12h:38m:31s	24h:16m:32s	13,164,068 kilobytes
77h:19m:27s	165h:22m:46s	

In Table 3, we solved the instance again, now with the same three disjoint 5-tile pattern databases and additionally with the five disjoint 6-tile databases. The total exploration time reduces to about a week. The hard-disk consumption accumulated to 505 gigabytes with a state of 160 bytes.

8   Distributed Pattern Database Evaluation

Concerning several large pattern databases our solver faced the problem of high memory consumption exceeding RAM resources on one machine. Lazy loading of pattern databases on demand, however, significantly slowed down the performance[9]. Hence, we decided to distribute the heuristic evaluation to multiple machines across the network. We exploit the fact that the order of processing within a bucket does not matter. Different to distributed expansion in [20], pattern database evaluation is distributed.

For solving the 35-Puzzle we chose one master to expand and distribute the states in a bucket, and parallelized the heuristic evaluation for them to 35 client processes p_i, each one responsible for one tile i for $i \in \{1, \ldots, 35\}$. All client processes operate individually and communicate with the master via shared files.

During the expansion of a bucket (see Fig. 6), the master writes a file T_i for each client process p_i. The file T_i contains all the successors generated by moving the i-th tile. Once it has finished the expansion of a bucket, the master p_m announces that each p_i should start evaluating its file T_i. Additionally, the client is informed on the current g- and h-value. After that, the master p_m is suspended, and waits for all p_i to complete their task. To prevent the master from load, no sorting takes place in this phase.

Next, the client processes start evaluating the file T_i and distribute their results into the files $E_i(h-1)$ and $E_i(h+1)$, depending on the observed difference in the h-values. All files E_i are additionally sorted to eliminate duplicates; internally (when a buffer is flushed) and externally (for each generated buffer). As only 3 buffers are needed (one for reading and two for writing) internal buffers can be large.

After its evaluation, each process p_i is suspended. When all clients are done, the master p_m is resumed to merge the individual $E_i(h-1)$ and $E_i(h+1)$ files into $E_m(h-1)$ and $E_m(h+1)$. The merging preserves the order in the files $E_i(h-1)$ and $E_i(h+1)$, so that the files $E_m(h-1)$ and $E_m(h+1)$ are sorted with all bucket duplicates eliminated.

---

[9] Reading the largest disjoint pattern database set from disk took about half an hour.

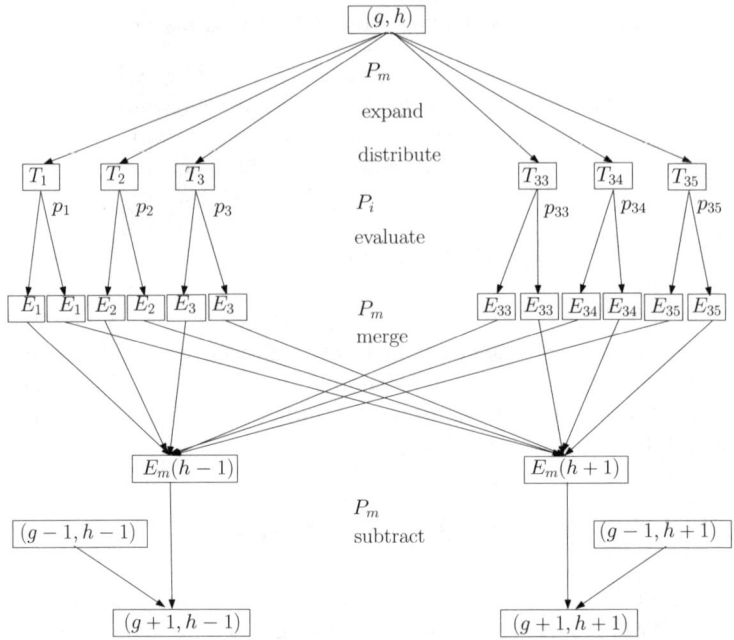

Fig. 6. Distributed expansion/evaluation of one bucket

The subtraction of the bucket $(g-1, h-1)$ from $E_m(h-1)$ and $(g-1, h+1)$ from $E_m(h+1)$ now eliminates duplicates using a parallel scan of both files[10].

Besides the potential for speeding up the evaluation, the chosen distribution mainly saves space. On the one hand, the master process does not need any additional memory for loading pattern databases. It can invest all its available memory for internal buffers required for the distribution, merging and subtraction of nodes. On the other hand, during the entire lifetime of client process p_i, it has to maintain only the pattern database D_j that includes tile i in its pattern (see Fig. 7). This saves RAM by a factor of about 5.

We started two parallel external-memory A* explorations for solving the half instances using 35 clients and one master process. The individual RAM requirements for the clients reduced to 1.3 gigabytes so that 2 processes could be run on one node. This proves that a considerable amount of RAM can be saved on a node using parallel execution - the most critical resource for the exploration with pattern databases. The first exploration (first 17 tiles permuted) took 3h:34m and 4.3 gigabytes to complete, while the second exploration (last 18 tiles permuted) took 4h:29m and 19 gigabytes.

As the above instance is moderately hard (the mean Manhattan distance in the puzzle is about 135 [15]) we compared the single-process version with the distributed one in the fully random instance in Fig.5 (right). The single-process version used the disjoint 5- and 6 tile pattern databases, while the parallel version took the 3- and 5-tile pattern

---

[10] A refined implementation concatenates the E-files using the system command `cat`. As the concatenated files are partially sorted, the merging and subtraction process used for the duplicate elimination of the entire bucket then catches all duplicates.

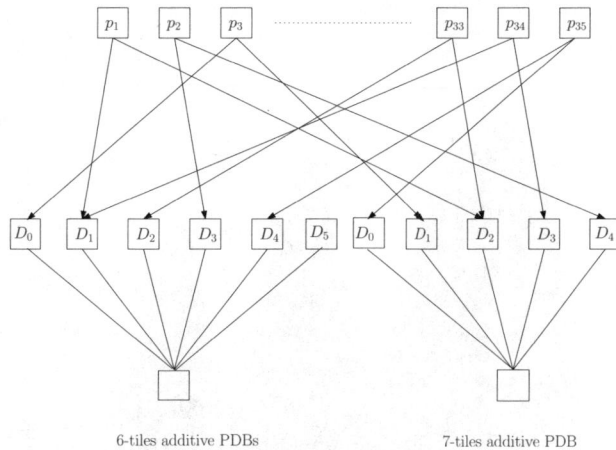

6-tiles additive PDBs   7-tiles additive PDB

Fig. 7. Selection of pattern databases for evaluation

databases. In two days, the distributed version found its best solution at $(87, 75)$ with 338, while the single version found $(85, 77)$ with 270 gigabytes, so that node generation in the distributed version was slightly faster even though it generated many intermediate files. The masters' CPU time accumulated to less than 1/6 of its total time (using 2.2 gigabytes RAM). For large buckets the partition based on the tile that gives an almost uniform distribution of the state sets so that no additional load balancing between the clients is needed. For the very small savings in time we blame the NFS file system for being slow. The clients' CPU time almost matches their total time, showing that they mostly wait for the master, without wasting time for writing and reading data.

9   External-Memory Relay A*

We have also solved an instance consisting of a random permutation of the upper and lower part with the mentioned three disjoint 3-tile and three disjoint 5-tile pattern databases (Fig. 5, middle). We found optimal solutions for the first half using 55 steps in about 10 minutes, as well as for the second half of the puzzle using 66 steps in about 40 minutes. As the other half remains untouched, this establishes a relay 2-approximation of 121 steps. Additionally, we terminated external-memory A* with the disjoint 5- and 6-tile pattern databases in solving the full instance at $f = 121$ after generating 1.3 terabytes disk space (in about 8 days). The best two states in diagonal $f = 99$ had a h-value of 22. When solving these remaining problems from scratch, we established a minimum of 42 moves giving rise to a relay solution of $77 + 42 = 119$ steps, such that the optimal solution length is an odd number in $[101, 119]$.

   Last, but not least, we solved the fully random problem in a relay fashion, restarting external A* on a selection of buckets. When we terminate based on limited disk space, we choose the ones with large g-value on the last completed f-diagonal. Successors of the previous buckets with small g-values are discarded. Assuming an undirected search graph, the problem remains solvable. Of course the solution quality degrades with each

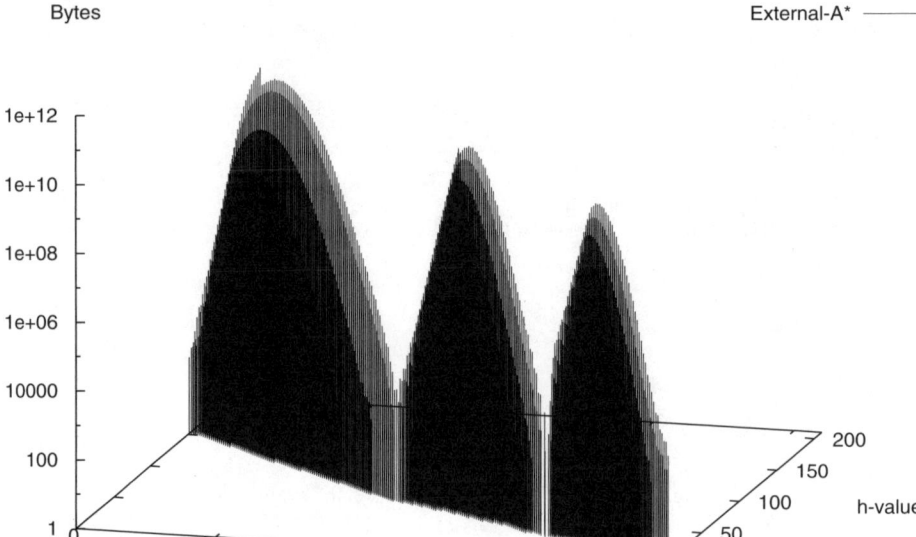

Fig. 8. Memory profile of external-memory relay A* for solving a fully random instance of the 35-puzzle with symbolic pattern databases (on a log-scale)

restart. We call the resulting procedure relay A*. As we have not implemented a resume support for the distributed version yet, we invoked the single-process version three times to finally find a valid solution.

Fig. 8 illustrates the memory profile for external-memory relay A* in the example. We see three exploration peaks. When the search has consumed too much disk space or time, it was restarted with the bucket having the lowest h-value. The initial h-value is 152 and the remaining interval for the optimal solution length imposed by the first iteration and established solution is $[166, 214]$. This large-scale exploration consumed $2,566,708,604,768 + 535,388,038,560 + 58,618,421,920$ bytes ≈ 2.9 terabytes in about 3 weeks.

10   Conclusion

Driven by a challenging case study, this paper opens a series of new research avenues to improve the time-space trade-off in searching with pattern databases. External-memory, iterative-deepening and distributed versions of A* have been engineered to solve instances of the $(n^2 - 1)$-puzzle with large symbolic pattern databases.

Although twisted to the $(n^2 - 1)$-puzzle, some techniques likely generalize. For example, the theory of the restricted number of layers for undirected search spaces has been extended to directed graphs [38]. In retrospective, the choice of the $(n^2 - 1)$-puzzle was not always favorable. Only moderate memory savings have been achieved by using BDDs. The succinctness of the state encoding of the $(n^2 - 1)$-puzzle limits the structural advantage of BDDs – much larger savings have been observed for other domains [11].

References

1. Anderson, K., Holte, R., Schaeffer, J.: Partial pattern databases. In: Miguel, I., Ruml, W. (eds.) SARA 2007. LNCS, vol. 4612, pp. 20–34. Springer, Heidelberg (2007)
2. Ball, M., Holte, R.: The compression power of symbolic pattern databases. In: International Conference on Automated Planning and Scheduling (ICAPS), pp. 2–11 (2008)
3. Bryant, R.E.: Symbolic boolean manipulation with ordered binary-decision diagrams. ACM Computing Surveys 24(3), 142–170 (1992)
4. Clarke, E., Grumberg, O., Long, D.: Model checking and abstraction. ACM Transactions on Programming Language Systems 16(5), 1512–1542 (1994)
5. Cousot, P., Cousot, R.: Abstract interpretation: A unified lattice model for static analysis of programs by construction or approximation of fixpoints. In: Principles of Programming Languages (POPL), pp. 238–252 (1977)
6. Culberson, J.C., Schaeffer, J.: Pattern databases. Computational Intelligence 14(4), 318–334 (1998)
7. Edelkamp, S.: Symbolic pattern databases in heuristic search planning. In: Artificial Intelligence Planning and Scheduling (AIPS), pp. 274–293 (2002)
8. Edelkamp, S.: External symbolic heuristic search with pattern databases. In: International Conference on Automated Planning and Scheduling (ICAPS), pp. 51–60 (2005)
9. Edelkamp, S.: Optimizing admissible planning pattern database heuristics with genetic programming. In: Workshop on Model Checking and Artificial Intelligence (MoChArt), pp. 35–50 (2007)
10. Edelkamp, S., Jabbar, S., Schrödl, S.: External A*. In: Biundo, S., Frühwirth, T., Palm, G. (eds.) KI 2004. LNCS (LNAI), vol. 3238, pp. 233–250. Springer, Heidelberg (2004)
11. Edelkamp, S., Kissmann, P.: Limits and possibilities of BDDs for state space search. In: National Conference on Artificial Intelligence (AAAI), pp. 1452–1453 (2008)
12. Edelkamp, S., Kissmann, P.: Partial symbolic pattern databases for optimal sequential planning. In: Dengel, A.R., Berns, K., Breuel, T.M., Bomarius, F., Roth-Berghofer, T.R. (eds.) KI 2008. LNCS, vol. 5243, pp. 193–200. Springer, Heidelberg (2008)
13. Edelkamp, S., Leue, S., Lluch-Lafuente, A.: Directed explicit-state model checking in the validation of communication protocols. International Journal on Software Tools for Technology Transfer 5, 247–267 (2004)
14. Edelkamp, S., Lluch-Lafuente, A.: Abstraction in directed model checking. In: ICAPS-Workshop on Connecting Planning Theory with Practice (2004)
15. Felner, A., Korf, R., Hanan, S.: Additive pattern databases. Journal of Artificial Intelligence Research 22, 279–318 (2004)
16. Felner, A., Ofek, N.: Combining perimeter search and pattern database abstractions. In: Miguel, I., Ruml, W. (eds.) SARA 2007. LNCS, vol. 4612, pp. 155–168. Springer, Heidelberg (2007)
17. Haslum, P.: Domain-independent construction of pattern database heuristics for cost-optimal planning (2007); Personal communications
18. Hung, N.N.W.: Exploiting symmetry for formal verification. Master's thesis, Faculty of the Graduate School, University of Texas at Austin (1997)
19. Jabbar, S., Edelkamp, S.: I/O efficient directed model checking. In: Cousot, R. (ed.) VMCAI 2005. LNCS, vol. 3385, pp. 313–329. Springer, Heidelberg (2005)
20. Jabbar, S., Edelkamp, S.: Parallel external directed model checking with linear I/O. In: Emerson, E.A., Namjoshi, K.S. (eds.) VMCAI 2006. LNCS, vol. 3855, pp. 237–251. Springer, Heidelberg (2005)
21. Jensen, R.M., Bryant, R.E., Veloso, M.M.: SetA*: An efficient BDD-based heuristic search algorithm. In: National Conference on Artificial Intelligence (AAAI), pp. 668–673 (2002)

22. Katz, M., Domshlak, C.: Optimal additive composition of abstraction-based admissible heuristics. In: International Conference on Automated Planning and Scheduling (ICAPS), pp. 174–181 (2008)
23. Katz, M., Domshlak, C.: Structural pattern heuristics via fork decomposition. In: International Conference on Automated Planning and Scheduling (ICAPS), pp. 182–189 (2008)
24. Korf, R.E.: Depth-first iterative-deepening: An optimal admissible tree search. Artificial Intelligence Journal 27(1), 97–109 (1985)
25. Korf, R.E.: Finding optimal solutions to Rubik's Cube using pattern databases. In: National Conference on Artificial Intelligence (AAAI), pp. 700–705 (1997)
26. Korf, R.E.: Breadth-first frontier search with delayed duplicate detection. In: Workshop on Model Checking and Artificial Intelligence (MoChArt), pp. 87–92 (2003)
27. Korf, R.E., Felner, A.: Disjoint Pattern Database Heuristics. In: Chips Challenging Champions: Games, Computers and Artificial Intelligence, pp. 13–26. Elsevier, Amsterdam (2002)
28. Korf, R.E., Felner, A.: Recent progress in heuristic search: A case study of the four-peg towers of hanoi problem. In: International Joint Conference on Artificial Intelligence (IJCAI), pp. 2324–2329 (2007)
29. Kunkle, D., Cooperman, G.: Solving Rubik's Cube: disk is the new RAM. Communications of the ACM 51(4), 31–33 (2008)
30. Kurshan, R.: Computer-Aided Verification of Coordinating Processes: The Automata-Theoretic Approach. Princeton University Press, Princeton (1994)
31. McMillan, K.: Symbolic Model Checking. Kluwer Academic Publishers, Dordrecht (1993)
32. Minato, S., Ishiura, N., Yajima, S.: Shared binary decision diagram with attributed edges for efficient boolean function manipulation. In: Design Automation Conference (DAC), pp. 52–57. IEEE Computer Society Press, Los Alamitos (1990)
33. Munagala, K., Ranade, A.: I/O-complexity of graph algorithms. In: ACM-SIAM Symposium on Discrete Algorithms (SODA), pp. 687–694 (1999)
34. Pearl, J.: Heuristics: Intelligent Search Strategies for Computer Problem Solving. Addison-Wesley, Reading (1984)
35. Qian, K.: Formal Verification Using Heuristic Search and Abstraction Techniques. PhD thesis, Computer Science & Engineering, The University of New South Wales (2006)
36. Qian, K., Nymeyer, A.: Guided invariant model checking based on abstraction and symbolic pattern databases. In: Jensen, K., Podelski, A. (eds.) TACAS 2004. LNCS, vol. 2988, pp. 497–511. Springer, Heidelberg (2004)
37. Ratner, D., Warmuth, M.K.: The $(n^2 - 1)$-puzzle and related relocation problems. Journal of Symbolic Computation 10(2), 111–137 (1990)
38. Zhou, R., Hansen, E.: External-memory pattern databases using structured duplicate detection. In: National Conference on Artificial Intelligence (AAAI), pp. 1398–1405 (2005)
39. Zhou, R., Hansen, E.A.: Breadth-first heuristic search. Artificial Intelligence Journal 170(4–5), 385–408 (2006)

Survey on Directed Model Checking

Stefan Edelkamp, Viktor Schuppan, Dragan Bošnački, Anton Wijs,
Ansgar Fehnker, and Husain Aljazzar*

Dortmund University of Technology, Germany
FBK-IRST, Trento, Italy
Eindhoven University of Technology, Netherlands
INRIA/VASY, Montbonnot St Martin, France
National ICT, Sydney, Australia
University of Konstanz, Germany

Abstract. This article surveys and gives historical accounts to the algorithmic essentials of *directed model checking*, a promising bug-hunting technique to mitigate the state explosion problem. In the enumeration process, successor selection is prioritized. We discuss existing guidance and methods to automatically generate them by exploiting system abstractions. We extend the algorithms to feature partial-order reduction and show how liveness problems can be adapted by lifting the search space. For deterministic, finite domains we instantiate the algorithms to directed symbolic, external and distributed search. For real-time domains we discuss the adaption of the algorithms to timed automata and for probabilistic domains we show the application to counterexample generation. Last but not least, we explain how directed model checking helps to accelerate finding solutions to scheduling problems.

1 Introduction

The presence of a vast number of computing devices in our environment imposes a challenge for designers to produce reliable software and hardware. Testing if a system works as intended becomes increasingly difficult. Formal verification aims to overcome this problem. The process of fully-automatic verification is referred to as *model checking* [27, 63]. Given a formal model of a system and a property specification in some form of temporal logic [45], the task is to validate, whether the specification is satisfied. If not, a model checker returns a counterexample for the system's flawed behavior, helping the designer to debug the model.

The major disadvantage of model checking is that it scales poorly. For a complete verification every state has to be looked at. Among the techniques to overcome the *state-explosion* problem, *directed model checking* has been established as one of the key technologies. It lessens the burden to find short counterexamples for design bugs quickly. Driven by the success of directed state-space

---

* The course of writing the article was initiated by forming a working group at the Dagstuhl seminar on *Directed Model Checking* that took place in April 2006.

D. Peled and M. Wooldridge (Eds.): MOCHART 2008, LNAI 5348, pp. 65–89, 2009.

exploration in artificial intelligence, model checking algorithms exploit the property specifications to orient the search towards their falsification.

In this paper we provide an overview of directed model checking with a focus on algorithmic aspects. Section 2 presents the development of directed model checking. In Sect. 3 we introduce notation and basic concepts. Section 4 covers directed model checking algorithms for safety and Sect. 5 extends the discussion to ω-regular properties. The implications of directed model checking on partial-order reduction are explained in Sect. 6. Section 7 shows application of directed model checking in external (disk-based) settings, for real-time systems, for generation of probabilistic counterexamples, and for scheduling problems.

2   History of Directed Model Checking

Elements of Directed Search in Jan Hajek's Approver. Some basic ideas of directed model checking have been present since the very first days of the automated verification of concurrent systems. For instance, *Approver*, which was probably the first tool for the automated verification of communication protocols, used a directed search of the state space. Approver, from Algorithmic and Proven PROtocol VERifier, was written in the second half of the 70's [54, 55, 56] by Jan Hajek from the Eindhoven University of Technology (at that time Technische Hogeschool Eindhoven). In fact the tool was capable of dealing with a broader class of concurrent systems than the classical communication protocols, like, for instance, mutual exclusion algorithms.

One of the most elaborate parts of Approver were the techniques for fast bug finding. Instead of a depth- or breadth-first search of the state space, that have been usually applied in model checkers, Approver used a general search algorithm based on priority queue. For efficiency this queue was implemented as a heap. Each element of the queue contained a pointer to the state vector in the hash table and a priority field. The records were ordered and selected based on this priority field. The value of the priority field was computed according to the priority function that corresponded to the global invariant that was verified. Directed search was used for the verification of safety properties.

Validation with Guided Search. Yang and Dill [113] wrote a seminal paper on the validation with guided search of the state space. The *SpotLight* system already applied the basic AI search algorithm A* [79] to combat the state explosion problem. A general search strategy, called the *target enlargement analysis*, computed nodes around the goal by applying some pre-images starting from the target description before starting the forward search, similar to *perimeter search* [35].

Symbolic Directed Model Checking. A first study of symbolic directed model checking algorithm simulating the A* exploration in the symbolic μ-calculus model checker μcke [17] has been given by Reffel and Edelkamp [88]. As an input, the proposed BDDA* algorithm assumes a heuristic estimate function in form of a BDD and operates on uniform cost graphs with integer-valued heuristic relations H. This relation partitions the state space in regions of the same heuristic estimates and exploits the succinctness of BDDs to store large state sets. The algorithm simulates the working of a bucket-based priority queue [32]. Instead of selecting only one element with best $f = g + h$ value (where g is a measure of the cost to reach that element from the initial states and h is an estimation of the cost to reach the target), the BDDA* algorithms selects all elements with minimal f-value and expands them in common. The successors are computed in form of a symbolic image operation and evaluated using BDD arithmetics. The resulting f-ordered state sets are put back into the queue. Later on, different authors have extended the framework of symbolic heuristic search, for example SetA* [66] introduces partitioned heuristics, ADDA* [59] employed ADDs instead of BDDs, and in SA*, [82] studied the strength of symbolic estimates.

While they can represent some sets compactly, BDDs still often grow too large for reachability analysis to complete. Getting an element of DFS into the default BFS exploration mode can help to alleviate that problem. When the BDD holding the current search frontier becomes too large, *high-density reachability analysis* [85] prunes away states that require relatively more BDD nodes to represent than the other states, i.e., to increase the ratio of states per BDD node. When the search frontier becomes empty the whole set of states reached so far is used in the next image computation [85] to bring the states back in that have been pruned away. As this step frequently exhausts the available resources, [86] suggests some alternatives, e.g., storing the pruned states in a separate BDD.

In [87] user-supplied *hints* are used to restrict the transition relation such that parts of the state space are avoided at first that are presumed to lead to a blow-up and only added towards the end of the traversal. This limits the effect that in a sequence of BDD operations such as computing the reachable set of states the intermediate BDDs are often much bigger than the end result. Experimental results show improved performance for both false and true properties.

Fraer et al. present an algorithm for reachability that employs frontier splitting to keep BDDs small and selects the part of the frontier to be expanded next based on BDD size [50].

Explicit-State Directed Model Checking. Edelkamp, Leue, and Lluch-Lafuente [39] coined the term *directed model checking* and implemented a guided variant of the explicit-state model checker SPIN [63]. In *HSF-SPIN*, safety violation checking is handled by replacing standard search by A*. Besides some *deadlock*-specific estimates, two generic estimates are supported. For liveness properties an improved nested-DFS algorithm based on the classification of the automata representation of the property in strongly-connected components has been proposed. Later on, partial-order reduction was added [40]. Directed model checking has also been applied to guide the search process to obtain a better counterexample for the same error. This is particularly useful if, e.g. due to memory constraints, suboptimal search algorithms were used to obtain a first counterexample [76].

3   Concepts and Notation

State-Space Model. We assume a state-space model $\mathcal{M}$ to include $\mathcal{S}$ as the set of states, $\mathcal{T}$ as the set of transitions, and $\mathcal{I} \subseteq \mathcal{S}$ as the set of initial states. The set $\mathcal{S}$ is often not known a priory, but generated *on-the-fly*. States are mapped to a set of atomic propositions AP true in that state by a labeling function $\mathcal{L} : \mathcal{S} \to 2^{AP}$. The set of transitions $\mathcal{T}$ induces a transition relation T on triples (s, t, s') where t leads from s to s'. We use the shorthand notation $s \xrightarrow{t} s'$. When analyzing safety properties we additionally assume a set of bad states $\mathcal{B} \subseteq \mathcal{S}$.

Cost algebras. Cost algebras [38] generalize edge weights to more general cost structures. A cost algebra is defined as $\langle A, \times, \preceq, \mathbf{0}, \mathbf{1} \rangle$, such that $\langle A, \times, \mathbf{1} \rangle$, is a monoid, $\preceq$ is a total order, $\mathbf{0} = \sqcap A$ and $\mathbf{1} = \sqcup A$, and A is isotone[1]. Intuitively, A is the domain set of cost values, $\times$ is the operation used to cumulate values and $\sqcup$ is the operation used to select the best (the least) amongst values. Consider for example, the following instances of cost algebras: $\langle I\!R^+ \cup \{+\infty\}, +, \leq, +\infty, 0 \rangle$ (optimization), $\langle I\!R^+ \cup \{+\infty\}, min, \geq, 0, +\infty \rangle$ (max/min), $\langle [0,1], \cdot, \geq, 0, 1 \rangle$ (probabilistic), or $\langle [0,1], min, \geq, 0, 1 \rangle$ (fuzzy). Not all algebras are isotone, e.g. take $A \subseteq I\!R \times I\!R$ with $(a,c) \times (b,d) = (\min\{a,b\}, c+d)$ and $(a,c) \preceq (b,d)$ if $a > b$ or $c < d$ if $a = b$. We have $(4,2) \times (3,1) = (3,3) \succ (3,2) = (3,1) \times (3,1)$ but $(4,2) \prec (3,1)$. However, the reader may easily verify that the related cost structure implied by $(a,c) \times (b,d) = (a+b, \min\{c,d\})$ is isotone. For a path $p = (s_0 \xrightarrow{t_0} s_1 \xrightarrow{t_1} \ldots \xrightarrow{t_{k-2}} s_{k-1} \xrightarrow{t_{k-1}} s_k)$ we define the *cumulated cost* $c(p)$ as $c(t_0) \times c(t_1) \times \ldots \times c(t_{k-1})$. As there can be many paths between two states s and s', with $\delta(s, s')$ we refer to the cost of an optimal one. We will also use the shorthand notation $\delta(s, X)$ for the optimum of $\delta(s, s')$ for any s' in X.

Heuristics. Cost-algebraic heuristics h map $\mathcal{S}$ to A. We assume that $h(e) = \mathbf{1}$ for each bad state $e \in \mathcal{B}$ saying that there is no cost estimated for reaching an error when having encountered it. A heuristic function $h : \mathcal{S} \to A$ is *admissible*, if for all $s \in \mathcal{S}$ we have $h(s) \preceq \delta(s, \mathcal{B})$, and *consistent*, if for each $s, s' \in \mathcal{S}$ and $t \in T$ s.t. $s \xrightarrow{t} s'$, we have $h(s) \preceq c(t) \times h(s')$. If h is consistent, then it is admissible.

The *formula-based heuristic* H_f used is recursively defined on the (safety) property specification. Let v be a Boolean variable, a some constant value in A, and g and h logical predicates. The recursive definition of H_f is as follows.

f	$H_f(s)$	$\overline{H}_f(s)$	f	$H_f(s)$	$\overline{H}_f(s)$
true	$\mathbf{1}$	$\mathbf{0}$	$\neg g$	$\overline{H}_g(s)$	$H_g(s)$
false	$\mathbf{0}$	$\mathbf{1}$	$g \vee h$	$\sqcup\{H_g(s), H_h(s)\}$	$\overline{H}_f(s) \times \overline{H}_g(s)$
v	if v then $\mathbf{1}$ else a	if v then a else $\mathbf{1}$	$g \wedge h$	$H_g(s) \times H_h(s)$	$\sqcup\{\overline{H}_g(s), \overline{H}_h(s)\}$

---

[1] Isotonicity is the key property of the algebra. It states that the order relation between the costs of any two paths is preserved if both of them are either prefixed or appended by a common, third, path. It has been shown that isotonicity is both necessary and sufficient for a generalized Dijkstra's algorithm to yield optimal paths [101].

In the definition of $H_{g \wedge h}$ and $\overline{H}_{g \vee h}$, the use of $\times$ suggests that g and h are independent, which may not be true. When choosing $\sqcap\{H(g), H(f)\}$ instead, (under some additional conditions on the value of a), the formula-based heuristic is consistent. The main reason is that the greatest of two consistent estimates is consistent, while the cumulation might not even be admissible.

The *finite state machine (FSM) distance heuristic* is based on projecting the system state to the program counter. The abstract state spaces are analyzed prior to the search to capture the shortest path distances of all local states to the set of *dangerous* states. The distances are cumulated for each running process. More formally, we assume that the global state space is generated based on the asynchronous compositions of processes p_i, $i \in \{1, \ldots, n\}$. In other words, each global system state is partitioned into n local states. The state of a local process p_i is called its *program counter*, $i \in \{1, \ldots, n\}$, pc_i for short. The FSM distance heuristic is defined as $H_m(s, s') = \times_{i=1}^{n} \delta_i(pc_i(s), pc_i(s'))$, where $\delta_i(pc_i(s), pc_i(s'))$ denotes the least-cost path from $pc_i(s)$ to $pc_i(s')$ in the automaton representation of p_i. The values for δ_i are computed prior to the search. The FSM distance heuristic assumes that both states s and s' are known to the exploration module. It has mainly been used in trail-directed search. As the product of different processes is asynchronous, it is not difficult to see [40] that the FSM distance is *consistent*.

One option to derive a heuristic automatically is to take the optimal cost from the current state to the error in an abstract space derived by any *homomorphic abstraction* as an admissible estimate, where a homomorphic abstraction is an over-approximation, for which each path in the concrete space induces a corresponding path in the abstract [26, 74]. Abstractions may contract states into one and merge edges accordingly. More precisely, if we contract states s_1 and s_2 and there are transitions $s_1 \xrightarrow{t_1} s_3$, $s_2 \xrightarrow{t_2} s_3$ or transitions $s_3 \xrightarrow{t_1} s_1$, $s_3 \xrightarrow{t_2} s_2$, we merge t_1 and t_2 to t_3 with $c(t_3) = c(t_1) \sqcup c(t_2)$. Self-loops usually do not contribute to an optimal solution and can be omitted. It is not difficult to see that such abstraction heuristics are consistent. Unfortunately, re-computing the heuristic estimate from scratch cannot speed-up the search [105]. A solution is to completely evaluate the abstract space prior to the search in the concrete space.

For a model $\mathcal{M}$ with abstraction $\hat{\mathcal{M}}$, an *abstraction database* [41, 83] is a lookup table indexed by $\hat{s} \in \hat{\mathcal{S}}$ containing the shortest distance from $\hat{s}$ to $\hat{\mathcal{B}}$. The size of an abstraction database is the number of states in $\hat{\mathcal{S}}$. For undirected graphs with uniform edge weights (usually equal to 1) it is easiest to create an abstraction database by conducting a breadth-first search in backward direction, starting at $\hat{\mathcal{B}}$. This assumes that for each (abstract) transition t we can devise an inverse (abstract) transition t^{-1} such that $\hat{s} \xrightarrow{t} \hat{s}'$ iff $\hat{s}' \xrightarrow{t^{-1}} \hat{s}$. To construct an abstraction database for weighted and directed graphs, the shortest path exploration in abstract space uses inverse transitions and Dijkstra's algorithm. If inverse operators are not available, we reverse the state space graph as generated in a forward chaining search. With each state $\hat{s}'$ we attach the list of all predecessor states $\hat{s}$. In case a bad state is encountered, the traversal is not terminated but the abstract bad states are collected in a (priority) queue. Next, backward

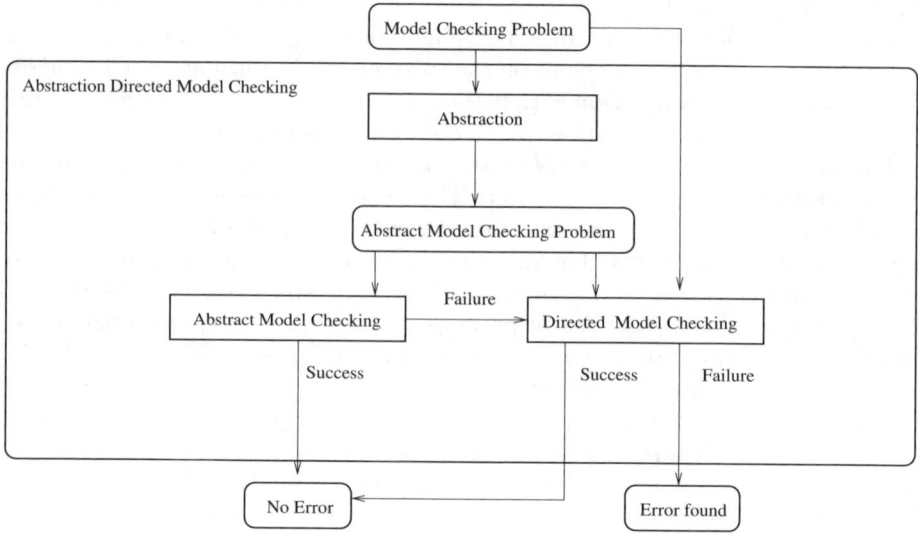

Fig. 1. Abstraction Directed Model Checking

traversal is invoked on the inverse of the state space graph, starting with the queued set of abstract bad states. The shortest path distances to the abstract bad states are stored with each state in a hash table. For a better time-space trade-off it is possible to fully traverse the abstract state space symbolically, yielding *symbolic abstraction databases* [36].

Abstraction directed model checking [81] combines model checking based on abstraction [26, 29, 74] and directed model checking as follows. An initial model checking run is performed on the abstract model. If the property holds, then the model checker returns true. If not, in a *directed model checking* attempt, the *same* abstraction is used to guide the search in the concrete state space to falsify the property. If the property does not hold there, a counterexample is returned; if it does, the property has been verified (see Fig. 1). If the abstraction (heuristic) turns out to be too coarse, it is possible to iterate the process with a refined abstraction.

4   Directed Model Checking Algorithms

Standard Forward Reachability A pseudo-code implementation of a forward reachability model checking algorithm (for safety properties) based on sets is provided in Fig. 2. In Line 1 the structures are initialized while Lines 2–7 perform the search for an error in a loop. If terminated without finding an error, Line 8 returns that the property is verified due to a complete exploration. Line 3 is a generic selection mechanism that determines the search traversal policy. Line 4 moves the selected set from *Open* to *Closed*, while Line 5 detects and

Procedure ModelCheck
Input: Model $\mathcal{M} = (\mathcal{S}, \mathcal{T}, \mathcal{I}, \mathcal{L})$, set of bad states $\mathcal{B}$, cost algebra $\mathcal{A}$
Output: *true* if property is satisfied or counterexample if not

```
1    Closed ← ∅; Open ← I
2    while (Open ≠ ∅)
3        S ← SelectA(Open)
4        Open ← Open \ S; Closed ← Closed ∪ S
5        if (S ∩ B ≠ ∅) return GeneratePath(S ∩ B)
6        Succ ← {s' | s ∈ S, (s, t, s') ∈ T}
7        Succ ← Succ \ Closed; Open ← Open ∪ Succ
8    return true
```

Fig. 2. General Model Checking Algorithm

handles bad states. Line 6 generates the successor set from which Line 7 eliminates duplicates. It also inserts the remaining elements into the search frontier.

In $Select_\mathcal{A}$ we can incorporate any specialized selection strategy. For BFS, we select the states with smallest depth, while for DFS we select the one(s) with the largest depth. For Dijkstra-like search we select one element with the least cost. Let $\mathcal{C}$ be the cost relation that relates a state to a cost-algebraic value. In such case, $Select_\mathcal{A}(Open)$ returns *some* s' in $Open$ with $(s', a) \in \mathcal{C}$ and for all s in $Open$ with $(s, b) \in \mathcal{C}$ we have $a \preceq b$. In the explicit-state version one candidate is selected, while in the set-based version all states are selected.

Forward Reachability with Costs. The algorithm in Fig. 2 does not say anything about updating the cost relation $\mathcal{C}$, which is modified during the execution of the algorithms. At invocation time, we have $(s, \mathbf{1}) \in \mathcal{C}$ for all $s \in \mathcal{I}$, and $(s, \mathbf{0}) \in \mathcal{C}$ for all $s \notin \mathcal{I}$. Whenever we reach a new state s' from s via transition t we perform *cost relaxation*, i.e., if $a \times c(t) \prec b$ with $(s, a) \in \mathcal{C}$ and $(s', b) \in \mathcal{C}$ we update $\mathcal{C} \leftarrow \mathcal{C} \setminus \{(s', b)\} \cup \{(s', a \times c(t))\}$. Strictly speaking, full initialization of the cost relation is not possible for the on-the-fly analysis of the system. Therefore, cost values are stored together with the states in the list $Open$ and $Closed$.

The update of relation $\mathcal{C}$ depends on the search algorithm. We call a state *settled*, if $(s, a) \in \mathcal{C}$ and $a = \delta(\mathcal{I}, s)$. Moreover, a cost relation is called *monotone*, if for $(s, a) \in \mathcal{C}$ and $(s', b) \in \mathcal{C}$ and $(s, t, s') \in T$, we have $a \preceq b$.

The selection strategy in Dijkstra's algorithm only considers settled states and monotone cost relations [34]. If it is not monotone, different approaches have been suggested. The main observation is that a cost update has to be executed more than once for a transition. It can be shown that BFS settles at least one unsettled state on an optimal path π^* in the $Open$ list, such that after $|\pi^*|$ iterations of *ModelCheck* without re-initializing $\mathcal{C}$ the bad state on π^* is settled [15]. In *k-best first search* [49] we select the k least-cost elements from $Open$ and compute their set of successors in common. The algorithm is complete but the counterexample might not be optimal. *k-beam search* [19] additionally prunes away all states from $Open$ that are not among the k best ones. In this case, completeness is sacrificed to search for errors in larger models. By iteratively performing k-beam search with larger k we get *iterative-broadening* [51], by which we gain back completeness.

Guided Forward Reachability. All exploration variants of the general model checking algorithm that we have seen so far are *blind* in the sense, that they do not incorporate any guidance towards a quicker falsification of the property. Directed model checking algorithms *reorder* the states to be expanded in order to accelerate error-detection in the case of choosing a different selection strategy.

The estimated cost of a counterexample at a given state s is the accumulation of the costs of reaching s and the heuristic estimate for reaching a bad state starting from s. For the latter we assume a static estimate relation $\mathcal{H}(s,b)$ that associates a state s with its estimate $b \in \mathcal{A}$. A* selects elements with least estimated counterexample costs. In other words, $Select_A(Open)$ returns *some* s in $Open$ with $(s,a) \in \mathcal{C}$ and $(s,b) \in \mathcal{H}$ such that for all s' in $Open$ with $(s',a') \in \mathcal{C}$ and $(s',b') \in \mathcal{H}$ we have $a \times b \preceq a' \times b'$. The initialization and the cost updates to the cost relation $\mathcal{C}$ remain unchanged. For consistent heuristics the selection strategy of A* only considers settled states. More precisely, at each extraction of a state s with $(s,a) \in \mathcal{C}$ and $(s,b) \in \mathcal{H}$ from the *Open*-List we have $a = \delta(\mathcal{I},s) \times b$. At a bad state $e \in \mathcal{B}$ b is trivial, as $\mathcal{H}(e,\mathbf{1})$. This implies $a = \delta(\mathcal{I},e)$. Therefore, A* with $\mathcal{H}(\mathcal{B},\mathbf{1})$ returns the cost-optimal counterexample. Optimality is only granted, if the goal check is performed at the expanded state. BFS is an exception, which terminates at a generated goal.

For inconsistent heuristics, it can happen that a better path to an already expanded state is encountered during the search process. For such case a *re-opening* strategy has been proposed [79]. It moves states from the set of already expanded states *Closed* back to the search frontier *Open*. Although in theory an exponential increase in the number of expanded nodes may happen, re-opening produces optimal counterexamples for admissible heuristics and works well in practice. The underlying problem of searching with non-consistent heuristics is equivalent to the search with non-monotone paths in a problem graph.

Bounded Forward Reachability. In Fig. 3 we display a cost-bounded variant of the general model checking algorithm. It extends the algorithm in Fig. 2 by an additional pruning condition in Line 8. The algorithm includes cost threshold U as an additional parameter. In the guided form shown here, it is based on the relations $\mathcal{C}$ and $\mathcal{H}$, as introduced above. There are various reasons for introducing parameter U. An upper bound prevents the algorithm from searching too deep e.g. when using depth-first selection strategies. Any generated counterexample has a quality not worse than U. If $U = \delta(\mathcal{I},\mathcal{B})$ then up to tie-breaking and the choice of $\mathcal{H}$ the optimal number of states are expanded [30]. The reason is that any optimal exploration strategy has to explore all states with costs smaller than $\delta(\mathcal{I},\mathcal{B})$. In some cases $U = \delta(\mathcal{I},\mathcal{B})$ is already known, the only task is to generate a counterexample matching it. If U is not known, one may adjust U interactively. Automated strategies are *iterative-deepening* [67] (increasing U by the smallest amount possible), *branch-and-bound* [69] (decreasing U to the

Procedure CostBoundedDirectedModelCheck
Input: Model $\mathcal{M} = (\mathcal{S}, \mathcal{T}, \mathcal{I}, \mathcal{L})$, set of bad states $\mathcal{B}$, cost algebra $\mathcal{A} = \langle A, \times, \preceq, \mathbf{0}, \mathbf{1} \rangle$,
        bound on cost U, cost relation $\mathcal{C}$, estimate relation $\mathcal{H}$
Output: *true* if property satisfied on U cost-bounded paths or counterexample

```
1    Closed ← ∅; Open ← 𝓘
2    while (Open ≠ ∅)
3        S ← Select_A(Open)
4        Open ← Open \ S; Closed ← Closed ∪ S
5        if (S ∩ B ≠ ∅) then return GeneratePath(S ∩ B)
7        Succ ← {s' | s ∈ S, (s,t,s') ∈ T}; Succ ← Succ \ Closed
8        Succ ← Succ \ {s ∈ Succ | ∃a,b ∈ A.C(s,a) ∧ H(s,b)∧ U ≺ a × b}
9        Open ← Open ∪ Succ
10   return true
```

Fig. 3. Cost-Bounded Model Checking Algorithm

largest value smaller than the latest cost value obtained), or *refined threshold determination* [107] (an exponential or binary search compromise between the two). In memory-limited A* search [91], full duplicate elimination in the *Closed*-list is sacrificed in order to gain space. U can control the memory needs. If the cost-updates do not preserve monotonicity, the cost values of some states in *Closed* are not optimal on the first visit and some nodes may remain unsettled.

According to the selection mechanism in *Select$_A$* we arrive at different branch-and-bound strategies. *Depth-bounded depth-first search* imposes an upper bound on the solution depth, to prevent the algorithms from searching too deep. As our algorithm, it takes U as an additional input parameter. *Admissible depth-first search* guarantees to find an error of cost smaller than the given threshold.

For cost-optimal depth-bounded search with duplicate detection there is a potential pitfall [40]. It is apparent in depth-first depth-bounded search but applies to many cost-bounded variants. The problem is that a cached duplicate may not be reached with optimal cost on the first visit such that on the second visit it is stored with suboptimal cost. Even worse, if the successor of a such cached duplicate has a bad state outside the cost threshold as a successor then this error might not be detected even if its cost are below the cost threshold. A possible solution is to re-open a state if reached with better costs.

Sparse Memory Forward Reachability. In model checking practice, the limitation of (main) memory is likely to be the most challenging problem. Set *Closed* is mainly kept to prevent exploring states twice and it tends to take up most space. In Fig. 4 we show a pseudo-code implementation of frontier search that has shown significant improvements in solving action planning and sequence alignment problems [68]. The assumption here is that not the entire set of states needs to be stored completely for detecting an error. How many layers are sufficient for full duplicate detection in general is dependent on a property of the search graph called *locality*. For uniform weighted problem graphs, it is defined

Procedure CostBoundedDirectedFrontierModelCheck
Input: Model $\mathcal{M} = (\mathcal{S}, \mathcal{T}, \mathcal{I}, \mathcal{L})$, set of bad states $\mathcal{B}$, cost algebra $\mathcal{A} = \langle A, \times, \preceq, \mathbf{0}, \mathbf{1} \rangle$,
      bound on cost U, locality L, cost relation $\mathcal{C}$, estimate relation $\mathcal{H}$
Output: *true* if property satisfied on U cost-bounded paths or counterexample

```
1     Succ ← I; for each k = 1, . . . , L Closed(k) ← ∅
2     while (Succ ≠ ∅)
3         Closed(0) ← Open ← Succ; Succ ← ∅
4         while (Open ≠ ∅)
5             S ← Select_A(Open)
6             Open ← Open \ S
7             if (S ∩ B ≠ ∅) then return GeneratePath(S ∩ B)
8             Succ ← Succ ∪ {s' | s ∈ S, (s, t, s') ∈ T}
9             Succ ← Succ \ ⋃_{k=0}^{L} Closed(k)
10            Succ ← Succ \ {s ∈ Succ | ∃a, b ∈ A.C(s, a) ∧ H(s, b) ∧ U ≺ a × b}
11        for each k = L, . . . , 1 Closed(k) ← Closed(k − 1)
12    return true
```

Fig. 4. Directed Frontier Search Model Checking Algorithm

as the maximum $\max\{\delta(\mathcal{I}, s) - \delta(\mathcal{I}, s')\} + 1$ of all states s, s', with s' being a successor of s. It determines the *thickness* of the boundary slice of the graph needed to prevent duplicates to occur in the search.

One observation for state selection is that breadth-first branch-and-bound frontier search often results in a smaller search frontier than best-first branch-and-bound frontier search. In AI literature, the according search strategy is called *breadth-first heuristic search* [114]. In *beam-stack-search* this strategy has been extended to feature partial state selection [115]. For such memory-limited frontier search, (divide-and-conquer) solution reconstruction is needed, for which certain relay layers are additionally stored in main memory.

5 ω-Regular Properties

The exposition has so far been restricted to checking *reachability* of a set of states. We now show how the machinery can be used to check ω-regular properties, which properly include propositional LTL [45].

We assume that the reader is familiar with the automaton-based approach to model checking of ω-regular properties [106]. We extend our state space model with a Büchi fairness constraint $\mathcal{F} \subseteq \mathcal{S}$ to $\mathcal{M} = (\mathcal{S}, \mathcal{T}, \mathcal{I}, \mathcal{L}, \mathcal{F})$ and restrict the discussion below to the search of a fair lasso-shaped path in $\mathcal{M}$. See also [27, 63].

Nested Depth-First Search. The most popular algorithm to search for fair lasso-shaped paths in explicit-state model checking is probably *nested depth-first search* [28, 65]. A first DFS finds all reachable states. When backtracking from a fair state it starts a second DFS that tries to close a fair cycle by hitting a state on the stack of the first DFS. When that happens, a counterexample can be reconstructed easily from both search stacks. States are marked as visited by either DFS, hence, each state is visited at most twice. Marking can be done with just two bits per state, which is the main reason for the frequent use of this algorithm in explicit-state model checking. On the downside, starting the second DFS in post order tends to produce long counterexamples.

In the inner search it's obvious that the search should be directed to some state in the stack of the outer search. Potential heuristics for this case include the Hamming and the FSM distance heuristic [40]. In the outer search it's less clear what a promising direction should look like. Clearly, the likelihood of finding a fair cycle should be high. If the state space of $\mathcal{M}$ is the synchronous product of smaller state spaces $\mathcal{M}_1, \mathcal{M}_2, \ldots$, some $\mathcal{M}_i$ can be analyzed beforehand to obtain approximate information on whether a state $s = (s_1, s_2, \ldots)$ in $\mathcal{M}$ can be part of a strongly connected component with a fair cycle at all. Only if all s_i are part of an SCC that includes a fair path in $\mathcal{M}_i$ then s can be part of an SCC with a fair path itself. Hence, if any s_i is known not to be in such SCC then the search should be directed to the edge of the current SCC [39].

Liveness Checking as Safety Checking. Transforming a liveness checking problem into a safety checking problem immediately makes the algorithms in Sect. 4 available for all ω-regular properties. Here, we consider the *state-recording translation* that reformulates the problem of finding a fair lasso as a reachability problem [18, 95, 96, 97]. The translation extends the original model with a copy for each state variable and a number of flags. It splits the search for a fair lasso into 3 steps: (1) non-deterministically guess and record a loop start in a copy of the set of state variables, (2) search a fair state and record its occurrence in a flag, and (3) return to the guessed and recorded loop start. Shortest fair lassos can be found when breadth-first search or A* [79] are used.[2] Although the reformulation roughly squares the size of the state space, performance of BDD-based symbolic model checking is improved for some examples [95, 96]. The method has been applied to SAT-based interpolation [78], to external distributed explicit-state directed model checking [37], and, independently, to regular model checking [22].

The heuristics should distinguish whether a loop start has been guessed or not. If not (step 1), we are effectively in the outer part of a nested search and should seek for promising loop starts. Once a state has been saved, a fair state (step 2) and, after that (step 3), the loop start are preferred targets. Applicable heuristics in all phases include Hamming and FSM distance heuristics [39, 40].

Other Algorithms. Similar to the case of safety properties *trail improvement* can also be used for lasso-shaped counterexamples [40, 76]. Assume, that a lasso-shaped counterexample $\pi = \pi_{stem} \circ \pi_{loop}^{\omega}$ to some ω-regular property is given. Directed model checking with Hamming or FSM distance heuristics is then used

---

[2] Note that finding a shortest counterexample (as opposed to only a shortest fair cycle in the product of model and property automaton) requires an appropriate translation of the property into a Büchi automaton [95, 98] or dedicated algorithms [70].

to shorten π as follows. Let s_l be the first state of π_{loop}. In a first step a potentially shorter trail π'_{stem} from the initial states to s_l is generated. Then a fair cycle π'_{loop} starting and ending in s_l is produced. Backtracking is used to guarantee fairness of π'_{loop}. As a further optimization, s_l can be replaced with any state s'_l that is equivalent to s_l in the sense that the sequence of transitions that leads from s_l to s_l in π'_{loop} also lead from s'_l to s'_l and hits a fair state in between.

Standard algorithms in BDD-based model checking, which are typically variants of the Emerson-Lei algorithm [46], perform a nested fixed point computation, which makes application of heuristics difficult. The idea of using hints has been extended to nested fixed points [20], though with less success than in [87]. CTL is covered in [21]. In the context of an SCC enumeration algorithm a prioritization was used based on the distance of states to the origin and on the number of fairness constraints they fulfill to select a state as the starting point for further SCC decomposition [108]. The approach by [50] extends to other least fixed point computations.

6   Partial Order Reduction

Partial order reduction (POR) [52, 80, 104] is one of the most important state-space reduction techniques in explicit state model checking. In this section we discuss how POR can be combined with directed model checking. The only essential difference with POR for standard model checking (for instance, as presented in [27]) is in the condition called the *cycle proviso*. Intuitively, this condition prevents ignoring parts of the system (state space) because of closing cycles during the search. The classical versions of the cycle proviso in standard model checking are closely dependent on the search order - usually DFS [52] or BFS [7]. Because of that they are not applicable in directed model checking. The proviso that we use to make POR compatible with directed model checking is inspired by the general search order proviso presented in [23]. In the rest of the section we introduce some basic terminology along the lines of [7] and state the new version of the cycle proviso for safety and liveness properties.

Let $\mathcal{M} = (\mathcal{S}, \mathcal{T}, \mathcal{I}, \mathcal{L}, \mathcal{F})$ be a model of the state space as introduced in Section 5. To improve readability, we write $s \xrightarrow{t}_\mathcal{M} s'$ for $(s, t, s') \in T$. When the model $\mathcal{M}$ is clear from the context we omit it. Further, we assume that the transition relation is deterministic in the sense that for each transition $t \in \mathcal{T}$ and each state $s \in \mathcal{S}$ there exists at most one $s' \in \mathcal{S}$ such that $s \xrightarrow{t} s'$. Thus, each transition can be seen as a partial function $t : \mathcal{S} \to \mathcal{S}$ which is defined if s' exists. We also say that s' is a *successor* of s. A transition $t \in \mathcal{T}$ is said to be $\mathcal{M}$-*enabled* in state $s \in \mathcal{S}$ iff $t(s)$ is defined. The set of all transitions $t \in \mathcal{T}$ enabled in state $s \in \mathcal{S}$ is denoted $enabled_\mathcal{M}(s)$.

The basic idea of state space reduction is to restrict the part of the state space of a concurrent system that is explored during verification in such a way that all properties of interest are preserved. To this end we define a function r which assigns to each state s a set of transitions $r(s)$. During the on-the-fly construction for each state s already included in the state set $\mathcal{S}_r$ of the reduced model $\mathcal{M}_r$, we add its successors obtained via transitions in $r(s)$. We start with an $\mathcal{S}_r$ that includes only the initial states $\mathcal{I}$ of the original model $\mathcal{M}$. Those states become also the initial states $\mathcal{I}_r$ of the reduced model $\mathcal{M}_r$. Then we iterate the above described extension of $\mathcal{S}_r$ $(\mathcal{M}_r)$ until a fixed point is reached. The construction of the reduced model is captured in the following definition:

For any *reduction* function $r : \mathcal{S} \rightarrow 2^{\mathcal{T}}$, we define the (partial-order) *reduction* of $\mathcal{M} = (\mathcal{S}, \mathcal{T}, \mathcal{I}, \mathcal{L}, \mathcal{F})$ with respect to r as the smallest model $\mathcal{M}_r = (\mathcal{S}_r, \mathcal{T}_r, \mathcal{I}_r, \mathcal{L}_r, \mathcal{F}_r)$ satisfying the following conditions: $\mathcal{S}_r \subseteq \mathcal{S}$, $\mathcal{I}_r = \mathcal{I}$; and for every $s, s' \in \mathcal{S}_r$ and $t \in r(s)$ if $s \xrightarrow{t}_{\mathcal{M}} s'$ then $s \xrightarrow{t}_{\mathcal{M}_r} s'$. We say that property ϕ is preserved by the reduction iff $\mathcal{M} \models \phi \Leftrightarrow \mathcal{M}_r \models \phi$. Depending on the properties that a reduction must preserve, we define additional restrictions on r. These sets of restrictions are well known in the POR theory (see [7, 27]).

Let $\mathcal{M}$ be a model with a reduction function r that is *persistent* in the sense of [7, 52] and let us first consider POR without DMC. The POR variation of the general model checking algorithm (GMCAPOR) is obtained by replacing in the algorithm in Fig. 2 the assignment $Succ \leftarrow \{s' \mid s \in S, (s, t, s') \in T\}$ with $Succ \leftarrow \{s' \mid s \in S, (s, t, s') \in T \wedge t \in r(s)\}$ where $r(s)$ satisfies — besides the well-known conditions C0a, C0b, C1 (see, e.g., [23]) — the condition

- C2c: For each $s \in \mathcal{S}_r$ there exists a transition $t \in r(s)$ such that $s' = t(s)$ and $s' \notin$ Closed. Otherwise $r(s) = enabled_{\mathcal{M}}(s)$.

Thus, we require that at least one new state which is explored via an action in $r(s)$ must not be in *Closed*. Otherwise the reduced set $r(s)$ must include all transitions which are enabled in s. The intuition behind C2c is that each transition t which is not in $r(s)$, i.e., it is temporarily ignored in s, will be considered in at least one successor s' of s. Since s' is not in *Closed*, it must be either in *Open* or a new unexplored state which will be put in *Open*. Thus, s' will be considered in some later iteration of the algorithm. Condition C1 ensures that t remains enabled also in s'. It could happen that t is ignored in s' too, but condition C2c will again ensure that it is considered later in some of its successors. As the set $\mathcal{S}_r$ is finite one can show that this ignoring cannot go forever and the action will be eventually included in some $r(s'')$ for some state s'' that is reachable in $\mathcal{M}_r$ from s' and therefore also from s.

Similarly as in [23], one can show that condition C2c implies the general ignoring prevention condition given by Lemma 2.2 of [7]. Although a stronger condition usually implies less reduction, in practice the advantage of C2c over Lemma 2.2 of [7] is that the former can be efficiently checked based only on local information, i.e., considering only state s and its successors. The correctness of the GMCAPOR algorithm does not depend on the order in which states are removed from *Open*, i.e., it is independent of the selection strategy implemented by Select$_{\mathcal{A}}$. Therefore, the correctness of the combination of POR with the directed model checking algorithm follows immediately. By requiring that S is a singleton we obtain the explicit state version of the general (directed) state exploring algorithm with POR in [23], while by putting $S = Open$ we get the POR algorithm for symbolic (breadth-first) search in [7].

To preserve liveness properties (LTL_{-X}, CTL^*_{-X}) with GMCAPOR one has to ensure that function r satisfies the liveness variant of the transition ignoring condition which requires that along each cycle c in the reduced model in at least one state s of c it holds $r(s) = enabled_{\mathcal{M}}(s)$. Intuitively, this condition ensures that a transition cannot be indefinitely postponed along c since it will be eventually included in $r(s)$. The drawback of this condition is that it is defined globally on the reduced state space. Like for safety properties, we give a stronger condition that might produce less reduction but it is locally checkable in an efficient manner:

- C2cl: For each $s \in \mathcal{S}_r$ for all transitions $t \in r(s)$ such that $s' = t(s)$ it holds $s' \notin Closed$. Otherwise $r(s) = enabled_{\mathcal{M}}(s)$.

7   Applications

To explore complex systems, the above algorithms have to be adapted.

Discrete Model Checking. Discrete edge costs are very common in model checking practice. In fact, most problem graphs considered are uniform, i.e., every edge has cost 1. As in this case the heuristic evaluation function estimates the remaining path length to the error, it is bounded by an upper-bound $\max_h$ on the optimal counterexample length. This allows to split the relation $\mathcal{H}$ into sets of states H_j, $j = 0, \ldots, \max_h$, that share the same heuristic value,

In Fig. 5 we have depicted the matrix implementation of the general directed model checking algorithm for uniform costs. Before expanding a state set (a.k.a. bucket) from the matrix, we eliminate possible duplicates by state set subtraction. Next we check for bad states, generate the successor set and distribute it according to the heuristic relation. For the sake of simplicity, we have assumed consistent estimates, for which each state is expanded at most once. For admissible but non-consistent estimates, we have to re-expand buckets and enlarge the range of j to $[0, \ldots, \max_h]$.

For disk-based (graph) search [94], the changes to the algorithm *Discrete-DirectedModelCheck* are moderate. For detecting duplicates in one bucket, it is sorted beforehand, and, instead of intersecting two sets internally, we scan the corresponding files (assuming they are already sorted). In external frontier search relay layers are not needed; the exploration fully resides on disk. There is one subtle problem: predecessor pointers are not available on disk. This is resolved by saving the predecessor together with every state, by scanning with decreasing depth the stored files, and by looking for matching predecessors. Any reached node that is a predecessor of the current node is its predecessor on an optimal solution path. This results in an I/O complexity that corresponds to a linear scan of at most all nodes visited.

To organize the communication between the processors in a parallel environment a working queue is maintained on disk [37]. The working queue contains the requests for exploring parts of a (g, h) bucket together with the part of the

Procedure DiscreteDirectedModelCheck
Input: Model $\mathcal{M} = (\mathcal{S}, \mathcal{T}, \mathcal{I}, \mathcal{L})$, set of bad states $\mathcal{B}$, estimate sets H_j, $0 \leq j \leq \max_h$
Output: *true* if property is satisfied or counterexample if not

```
1     for each i = 1,...,L for each j = 0,...,max_h
2         Open(-i, j) ← ∅
3     for each j = 0,...,max_h
4         Open(0, j) ← I ∩ H_j
5     f_min ← min{j ≥ 0 | Open(0, j) ≠ ∅}
6     while (f_min ≠ ∞)
7         g_min ← min{i | Open(i, f_min − i) ≠ ∅}
8         while (g_min ≤ f_min)
9             Min ← Open(g_min, f_min − g_min)
10            Min ← Min\ ⋃_{k=1}^{L} Open(g_min − k, f_min − g_min)
11            if (Min ∩ B ≠ ∅) then return GeneratePath(Min ∩ B)
12            Succ ← {s' | s ∈ Min, (s, t, s') ∈ T}
13            for each j = f_min − g_min − 1,...,max_h
14                Open(g_min + 1, j) ← Open(g_min + 1, j) ∪ (Succ ∩ H_j)
15            g_min ← g_min + 1
16        f_min ← min({i + j > f_min | Open(i, j) ≠ ∅} ∪ {∞})
```

Fig. 5. Directed Model Checking Algorithm for Uniform Costs

file that has to be considered. As processors may have different computational power and processes can dynamically join and leave the exploration, the number of state space parts does not necessarily have to match the number of processors.

Real-Time Model Checking. Timed automata (TA) extend finite labelled transition systems with real-valued variables called *clocks* to capture delays and timing constraints. Directed model checking for TAs was developed parallel to directed model checking for finite systems, and was coined *guided model checking* [13]. These techniques have been successfully applied to several case studies and were implemented in the directed model checker for timed automata MCTA [71, 73] and added to the existing model checker UPPAAL [13, 33, 84].

TA distinguish between delay and discrete edge transitions. Delay transitions increment all clock variables with the same amount, while the finite part of the state remains unchanged. Discrete edge transitions may change the finite part of the state and reset clock variables to zero. Guards and invariant conditions over clock variables are defined using clock constraints $\Psi(Cl)$, defined by $\psi := x \lhd c \mid x - y \lhd c \mid \psi \wedge \psi \mid \neg \psi$ with $x, y \in Cl$, $c \in \mathbb{Z}$, and $\lhd \in \{<, \leq\}$. This restriction to simple constraints on clocks, and constraints on differences between clocks is used in [8] to show that model checking TAs is decidable.

Common model checkers use symbolic semantics based on *zones*. A zone Z is a maximal set of clock valuations satisfying a constraint from $\Psi(Cl)$. A symbolic state s is a pair (l, Z) of a location and a zone. Symbolic state $s = (l, Z)$ represents a subset of $s' = (l', Z')$, denoted $s \subseteq s'$, if $l = l'$ and $v \models Z \Rightarrow v \models Z'$.

Procedure ModelCheck
Input: Model $\mathcal{M} = (\mathcal{S}, \mathcal{T}, \mathcal{I}, \mathcal{L})$, set of bad states $\mathcal{B}$, cost algebra $\mathcal{A}$
Output: *true* if property is satisfied or counterexample if not

```
1    Closed ← ∅; Open ← I
2    while (Open ≠ ∅)
3        S ← Select_A(Open)
4        Open ← Open \ S; Closed ← Closed ∪ S
5        if (S ∩ B ≠ ∅) return GeneratePath(S ∩ B)
6        Succ ← {s′ | s ∈ S, (s, t, s′) ∈ T}
7        Succ ← {s ∈ Succ| ∀s′ ∈ Closed. s ⊄ s′}
8        Open ← {s ∈ Open| ∀s′ ∈ Succ. s ⊄ s′} ∪ {s ∈ Succ| ∀s′ ∈ Open. s ⊄ s′}
9    return true
```

Fig. 6. General Model Checking Algorithm for Timed Automata

Necessary operations can be effectively realized, using a canonical representation of zones as weighted graph, known as Difference Bound Matrices [16].

Due to the nature of delay, it is possible to reach any reachable state by an alternation of delays and edge transitions (by inserting zero delays or merging successive delays). The length of a counterexample can and is in practice expressed in the number of discrete edge transitions. Cost and heuristic are typically defined over cost algebra $\mathcal{A} = (I\!N_0 \cup \infty, +, \leq, \infty, 0)$. If the goal is to minimize the length of the error trace, we assume for the cost that $c(t) = 0$ for delay transitions, and $c(t) = 1$ otherwise. The forward reachability algorithm presented in Fig. 2 can then be extended, as depicted in Fig. 6, to deal with TAs. We assume that set of bad states $\mathcal{B}$ is a pair of a location and zone (l_b, Z_b).

A consequence of the zone-semantics is that a symbolic state $s′$ may represent a subset of another symbolic state s. Model checking algorithms for TAs differ therefore in one important aspect from the general algorithm in Fig. 2. Rather than checking for equality between sets of states, they typically check for set inclusion. If symbolic state $s \in Closed$, then we can discard exploration of any subset $s′$ of s. Duplicate detection in Line 8 in Fig. 6 reflects the deletion of subsets. Similarly, a symbolic state will not be added to *Open* if it is the subset of some symbolic state in *Open*.

Although guided model checking as presented in [13] was aimed at cost optimal reachability, it also explored briefly heuristics for simple reachability. Heuristics in this area have traditionally been problem dependent, but Kupferschmid et al. introduced generic heuristics based on *monotonicity relaxations* and *automata-theoretic abstractions*[71, 72]. The *monotonicity relaxation* assumes that once a value of a variable is attained, it may keep this value forever. The semantics of a transition system under the monotonicity relaxation is set based, and the successors increase monotonously with respect to set inclusion. The *automata-theoretic abstraction* repeatedly replaces a pair of automata with an abstraction of their product. The size of these abstraction is limited by a given N; to reach this bound bisimilar states and states with a large heuristic value are merged.

This ensures that close to the error state, the abstraction is nevertheless accurate. For given benchmarks both heuristics reduced time and memory requirements, and furthermore found shorter error traces than Uppaal's random DFS [71, 73].

Stochastic Model Checking. integrates quantitative dependability analysis with model checking. In this context, systems are usually described as Markov models. The mostly used models are *discrete-time Markov chains* (DTMCs), *continuous-time Markov chains* (CTMCs) and *Markov Decision Processes* (MDPs) [102]. These models can be considered as a labelled transition system extended by transition probabilities. More concretely, in each state a probability distribution describes the probability of firing a particular transition as the next step of the system. Dependability requirements on such models are usually formulated in a stochastic temporal logic like PCTL [60] in the discrete-time case or CSL [9, 10] in the continuous-time case. Model checking of PCTL or CSL formulae relies mainly on numerical methods to solve linear equation systems [9, 10, 60, 102]. A weakness of these methods is their inability to provide counterexamples. This problem has been studied in the literature for a particular type of dependability properties, namely *probabilistic reachability*, [3, 4, 5, 57, 58]. A probabilistic reachability property is a claim that the probability to run into a bad state, i.e., a state from $\mathcal{B}$, does not exceed a particular probability bound p. Such a property is violated in the case that the accumulated probability of all *offending paths*, i.e., paths from an initial state to a state in $\mathcal{B}$, is higher than p. A counterexample in this context is then a set of offending paths such that its accumulated probability is higher than p. Since paths with high probability represent high probable system executions, we expect the human user to be more interested in counterexamples which include most probable offending paths.

In [3, 4], an approach based on directed model checking has been proposed to address this problem. The basic idea of that approach is to select the most probable offending path. This can be done by using the algorithm in Fig. 3 combined with the probabilistic cost algebra $\langle [0, 1], \cdot, \geq, 0, 1 \rangle$. The cost of a transition is its probability. This means that the cost of a path, i.e., the product of the costs of each transition along the path, is just the probability of that path. This setting results in selecting the offending path with the maximal probability. In [3, 4] the basic algorithm is extended to construct a whole counterexample by not only selecting one most probable offending path but a sufficient set of such paths. Since counterexamples in this context can contain a large number of paths, analysing them is a chellange for a human user. In [6], a method based on interactive visualization is proposed which makes analysing complex counterexamples easier.

Search for Schedules. The following is an overview of techniques to approach scheduling problems. [112] provides a more detailed discussion, comparing the tools SPIN, CADP and UPPAAL CORA. In recent years, model checkers have been applied to solving combinatorial optimization problems. In particular, scheduling problems have been considered often, e.g. [1, 13, 14, 24, 25, 48, 92, 103, 110, 111, 112]. The approach here is to interpret the problem as a reachability problem, where the question is, in a system where transitions have costs, what the minimal necessary cost is to reach a state in $\mathcal{B}$, where $\mathcal{B} \subseteq \mathcal{S}$ is a set of goal states (i.e. 'good' states where a complete schedule for the given problem has been achieved). A trace providing this minimal cost then represents a schedule for the problem at hand.

A scheduling problem is about processing a certain number of entities, e.g. products. The processing is usually done by a one or more resource, which can perform tasks, provided, that the accompanying constraints are met. Furthermore, each task has an execution time ([24] consider uncertain execution times). A certain goal should be reached, usually having completely processed a finite batch of entities. The question asked in scheduling is not mainly *if* this goal can be reached, but *how efficiently*. Using model checking tools, we are able to deal with complex industrial problems. We model tasks as transitions, meaning that performing task t_i in an execution appears as $s_i \xrightarrow{t_i} s_{i+1}$ in a state space model $\mathcal{M}$, where s_i and s_{i+1} are two states in the trace corresponding with the execution. In such state spaces, we can observe the following.

A function *progress*: $\mathcal{S} \rightarrow \mathbb{N}$ can be constructed, which accesses the state variables, using the specification of $\mathcal{M}$, and quantifies the progress made to reaching some predetermined goal, e.g. having completely processed a given batch of entities. In general, say we have $c_0, c_{end} \in \mathbb{N}$, $\forall s \in \mathcal{S}.c_0 \leq progress(s) \leq c_{end}$ and $progress(\mathcal{I}) = c_0$, i.e. c_0 is the initial (no) progress and c_{end} represents having reached the goal. Tasks may also lead a schedule further away from the goal.

For most scheduling problems, e.g. [1, 13, 14, 25, 48, 92, 112], typically $\mathcal{B} = \{s \in \mathcal{S} \mid progress(s) = c_{end}\}$. One technique is to iteratively search $\mathcal{M}$ using a set of formulas, written in a temporal logic, such as LTL or μ-calculus. Placed in the context of DMC; cost-bounded model checking algorithm (Fig. 3) can be used to search $\mathcal{M}$ for a schedule, cheaper than the provided cost upper bound U. Using this approach, one can iteratively search for increasingly good schedules. This has been done e.g. in SPIN [92] and CADP [112]. In the latter case, costs are modelled in μCRL by means of additional actions. Iterative searching can be very inefficient, though, depending on the number of iterations needed. Depth-first branch-and-bound is based on the iterative search. Here, the upper bound in the formula is updated on-the-fly. The benefit of using this technique is that $\mathcal{M}$ only needs to be searched once, although it can still take a lot of resources. In SPIN 4.0, this technique can be used by using C primitives [92]. An update section in the model, written in C, is fired each time a counterexample is found, which updates the (hidden) minimal cost variable, changing the property to check.

In state spaces of the most basic scheduling problems, a liveness property ϕ that always a state $e \in \mathcal{B}$ can be reached holds. In other words, every schedule, i.e. trace, eventually leads to a successful finish. This fact means that DMC algorithms which aggressively prune and are therefore usually less effective for functional model checking can be very useful for finding schedules. Examples of such algorithms are *nearest neighbour heuristic*, which follows a single trace based on cumulated costs, and *beam search* [77, 89], which follows up to β traces, using cumulated costs and estimations. In functional model checking, if such searches do not return a counterexample, it is no guarantee that the property holds. In 'basic' scheduling, the worst we get are near-optimal solutions.

In a more general setting, we consider the presence of unsuccessful termination, i.e. deadlocks e for which $progress(e) \neq c_{end}$. See e.g. [103, 111] for examples in this setting. Now, the aforementioned liveness property still holds, but $\mathcal{B} = \{s \in \mathcal{S} \mid progress(s) = c_{end} \vee enabled_{\mathcal{M}}(s) = \emptyset\}$. Here, let us call the goal states $\mathcal{G} = \{s \in \mathcal{S} \mid progress(s) = c_{end}\}$. The BnB technique for SPIN can be adapted to this setting by incorporating a secondary check in the C code, to ensure that a goal state has been found [110]. Pruning algorithms may lead to no solution at all, depending on the ratio $\mid \mathcal{G} \mid : \mid \mathcal{B} \setminus \mathcal{G} \mid$ and how promising the traces leading to states in $\mathcal{B} \setminus \mathcal{G}$ initially appear to be, based on the guiding function. Besides improving the guiding function, with beam search, we can also counter this problem by increasing β, but of course, the penalty of this is less pruning.

Beam search (BS) has been applied to a whole range of scheduling problems [31, 93, 100, 103, 111, 112]. Two variants of BS are considered most classic: *detailed* and *priority* BS. Both versions use a *beam width*, to indicate the maximum number of states which may be expanded in each level of $\mathcal{M}$. Detailed BS uses an evaluation function $f(s) = a \times b$, where $\mathcal{C}(s, a)$ and $\mathcal{H}(s, b)$, to select up to β states. In priority BS adapted for general state spaces [103], outgoing transitions of each state are ordered by means of a priority function $prio : \mathcal{T} \to \mathbb{Z}$. The beam width is represented by $\beta = \alpha^l$, where α is the maximum number of outgoing transitions explored per state in the first l levels of the search. In subsequent levels, only one transition is explored per state. One extension of BS is called *flexible* BS [103, 112], where the beam width is not strongly fixed. In flexible detailed BS, tie-breaking is avoided in cases where there are not clearly β best states, and all competent candidates are explored. In arbitrary state space structures, this can improve the search a lot, since selections beyond the influence of the guiding function are avoided [103, 110, 111, 112]. Another extension is a combination of Dijkstra's search and BS. The advantage of this extension over regular BS is that once a goal state has been found, the search can safely terminate [112].

Other settings which still largely remain to be investigated are multi-cost problems [14, 110], infinite scheduling problems with or without nondeterministic product input, where the main difficulty is to determine what we are looking for, e.g. a single cycle, and what actually constitutes a 'best' schedule, and parallel scheduling problems where concurrent executions of tasks cannot be represented in an interleaved fashion ([112] contains an example dealing with this).

8   Conclusion

In the survey we have illustrated the algorithmic essentials of direct model checking, a recently proposed bug-finding paradigm for mitigating the state explosion problem. We have shown that it applies in a wide number of verification areas, and pointed to recent advances in AI search. Algorithms were presented in a general set-theoretic manner and instantiated to specific needs.

Meanwhile, directed model checking has become major branch of the techniques to cope with very large state spaces. The survey thus fills the gap left open by directed model checking not being mentioned in the most visible books like "Model Checking" [27] and surveys like "25 Years of Model Checking" [53].

The currently envisioned future of directed model checking includes the design of refined heuristics [61, 62], relevance analysis to detect helpful and useless transitions [109], local search alternatives such as randomized guided search [90]. large-scale disk-based search with refined delayed duplicate elimination strategies [12, 47, 75], semi-external search incorporating space-efficient perfect hash function for a better time-space trade-off [42, 43], exploiting edges of current hardware technology such as addressing flash memory instead of magnetic devices [2, 11, 43], and parallel computation, especially the integration of multi-core processing [64] and GPU computation [44].

References

1. Abdeddaïm, Y., Asarin, E., Maler, O.: Scheduling With Timed Automata. Theoretical Computer Science 354(2), 272–300 (2006)
2. Ajwani, D., Malinger, I., Meyer, U., Toledo, S.: Characterizing the performance of flash memory storage devices and its impact on algorithm design. In: McGeoch, C.C. (ed.) WEA 2008. LNCS, vol. 5038, pp. 208–219. Springer, Heidelberg (2008)
3. Aljazzar, H., Hermanns, H., Leue, S.: Counterexamples for timed probabilistic reachability. In: Pettersson, P., Yi, W. (eds.) FORMATS 2005. LNCS, vol. 3829, pp. 177–195. Springer, Heidelberg (2005)
4. Aljazzar, H., Leue, S.: Extended directed search for probabilistic timed reachability. In: Asarin, E., Bouyer, P. (eds.) FORMATS 2006. LNCS, vol. 4202, pp. 33–51. Springer, Heidelberg (2006)
5. Aljazzar, H., Leue, S.: Counterexamples for model checking of markov decision processes. Technical Report soft-08-01, Chair for Software Engineering, University of Konstanz, Gemany (December 2007) (submitted for publication)
6. Aljazzar, H., Leue, S.: Debugging of dependability models using interactive visualization of counterexamples. In: QEST 2008. IEEE Computer Society Press, Los Alamitos (2008)
7. Alur, R., Brayton, R., Henzinger, T., Qadeer, S., Rajamani, S.: Partial-order reduction in symbolic state-space exploration. Formal Methods in System Design 18, 97–116 (2001)
8. Alur, R., Dill, D.L.: A theory of timed automata. Theoretical Computer Science 126(2), 183–235 (1994)
9. Aziz, A., Sanwal, K., Singhal, V., Brayton, R.: Model-checking continuous-time Markov chains. ACM Trans. Comput. Logic 1(1), 162–170 (2000)
10. Baier, C., Haverkort, B., Hermanns, H., Katoen, J.-P.: Model-checking algorithms for continuous-time Markov chains. IEEE Trans. Software Eng. 29(7) (2003)
11. Barnat, J., Brim, L., Edelkamp, S., Šimeček, P., Sulewski, D.: Can flash memory help in model checking? In: FMICS, pp. 159–174 (2008)
12. Barnat, J., Brim, L., Šimeček, P., Weber, M.: Revisiting resistance speeds up I/O-efficient LTL model checking. In: Ramakrishnan, C.R., Rehof, J. (eds.) TACAS 2008. LNCS, vol. 4963, pp. 48–62. Springer, Heidelberg (2008)

13. Behrmann, G., Fehnker, A., Hune, T., Larsen, K.G., Pettersson, P., Romijn, J.M.T.: Efficient guiding towards cost-optimality in UPPAAL. In: Margaria, T., Yi, W. (eds.) TACAS 2001. LNCS, vol. 2031, p. 174. Springer, Heidelberg (2001)
14. Behrmann, G., Larsen, K., Rasmussen, J.: Optimal scheduling using priced timed automata. SIGMETRICS Performance Evaluation Review 32(4), 34–40 (2005)
15. Bellman, R.: On a routing problem. Quaterly of Applied Mathematics 16(1), 87–90 (1958)
16. Bengtsson, J.E., Yi, W.: Timed Automata: Semantics, Algorithms and Tools. In: Desel, J., Reisig, W., Rozenberg, G. (eds.) Lectures on Concurrency and Petri Nets. LNCS, vol. 3098, pp. 87–124. Springer, Heidelberg (2004)
17. Biere, A.: μcke — efficient μ-calculus model checking. In: Grumberg, O. (ed.) CAV 1997. LNCS, vol. 1254. Springer, Heidelberg (1997)
18. Biere, A., Artho, C., Schuppan, V.: Liveness checking as safety checking. In: FMICS (2002)
19. Bisiani, R.: Beam search. In: Shapiro [99], pp. 1467–1568
20. Bloem, R., Ravi, K., Somenzi, F.: Efficient decision procedures for model checking of linear time logic properties. In: Halbwachs, N., Peled, D.A. (eds.) CAV 1999. LNCS, vol. 1633, pp. 222–235. Springer, Heidelberg (1999)
21. Bloem, R., Ravi, K., Somenzi, F.: Symbolic guided search for CTL model checking. In: DAC, pp. 29–34 (2000)
22. Bouajjani, A., Habermehl, P., Vojnar, T.: Abstract regular model checking. In: Alur, R., Peled, D.A. (eds.) CAV 2004. LNCS, vol. 3114, pp. 372–386. Springer, Heidelberg (2004)
23. Bošnački, D., Leue, S., Lluch-Lafuente, A.: Partial-order reduction for general state exploring algorithms. In: SPIN (2006)
24. Bozga, M., Kerbaa, A., Maler, O.: Scheduling Acyclic Branching Programs on Parallel Machines. In: RTSS, pp. 208–215. IEEE Computer Society Press, Los Alamitos (2004)
25. Brinksma, E., Mader, A.: Verification and Optimization of a PLC Control Schedule. In: Havelund, K., Penix, J., Visser, W. (eds.) SPIN 2000. LNCS, vol. 1885. Springer, Heidelberg (2000)
26. Clarke, E., Grumberg, O., Long, D.: Model checking and abstraction. ACM Trans. Program. Lang. Syst. 16(5), 1512–1542 (1994)
27. Clarke, E., Grumberg, O., Peled, D.: Model Checking. MIT Press, Cambridge (2000)
28. Courcoubetis, C., Vardi, M., Wolper, P., Yannakakis, M.: Memory efficient algorithms for the verification of temporal properties. Formal Methods in System Design 1, 275–288 (1992)
29. Cousot, P., Cousot, R.: Abstract interpretation: A unified lattice model for static analysis of programs by construction or approximation of fixpoints. In: POPL (1977)
30. Dechter, R., Pearl, J.: The optimality of A* revisited. In: AAAI (1983)
31. Della Croce, F., T'kindt, V.: A recovering beam search algorithm for the one-machine dynamic total completion time scheduling problem. J. of the Operational Research Society 53, 1275–1280 (2002)
32. Dial, R.: Shortest-path forest with topological ordering. Communications of the ACM 12(11), 632–633 (1969)
33. Dierks, H.: Time, abstraction and heuristics – automatic verification and planning of timed systems using abstraction and heuristics. Habilitation thesis (July 2005)
34. Dijkstra, E.: A note on two problems in connection with graphs. Numerische Mathematik 1, 269–271 (1959)

35. Dillenburg, J., Nelson, P.: Perimeter search. Artificial Intelligence 65(1), 165–178 (1994)
36. Edelkamp, S.: Symbolic pattern databases in heuristic search planning. In: AIPS (2002)
37. Edelkamp, S., Jabbar, S.: Large-scale directed model checking LTL. In: Valmari, A. (ed.) SPIN 2006. LNCS, vol. 3925, pp. 1–18. Springer, Heidelberg (2006)
38. Edelkamp, S., Jabbar, S., Lluch-Lafuente, A.: Cost-algebraic heuristic search. In: AAAI (2005)
39. Edelkamp, S., Leue, S., Lluch-Lafuente, A.: Directed explicit-state model checking in the validation of communication protocols. STTT 5, 247–267 (2004)
40. Edelkamp, S., Leue, S., Lluch-Lafuente, A.: Partial order reduction and trail improvement in directed model checking. STTT 6, 277–301 (2004)
41. Edelkamp, S., Lluch-Lafuente, A.: Abstraction in directed model checking. In: ICAPS-Workshop on Connecting Planning Theory with Practice (2004)
42. Edelkamp, S., Sanders, P., Šimeček, P.: Semi-external LTL model checking. In: Gupta, A., Malik, S. (eds.) CAV 2008. LNCS, vol. 5123, pp. 530–542. Springer, Heidelberg (2008)
43. Edelkamp, S., Sulewski, D.: Flash-efficient LTL model checking with minimal counterexamples. In: SEFM (2008)
44. Edelkamp, S., Sulewski, D.: Model checking via delayed duplicate detection on the GPU. Technical Report 821, Dortmund University of Technology (2008)
45. Emerson, A.: Temporal and modal logic. In: van Leeuwen, J. (ed.) Handbook of Theoretical Computer Science, Volume B: Formal Models and Sematics, pp. 995–1072. Elsevier and MIT Press (1990)
46. Emerson, E., Lei, C.: Efficient model checking in fragments of the propositional mu-calculus (extended abstract). In: LICS, pp. 267–278 (1986)
47. Evangelista, S.: Dynamic delayed duplicate detection for external memory model checking. In: Havelund, K., Majumdar, R., Palsberg, J. (eds.) SPIN 2008. LNCS, vol. 5156, pp. 77–94. Springer, Heidelberg (2008)
48. Fehnker, A.: Scheduling a Steel Plant with Timed Automata. In: Proc. RTCSA 1999, IEEE Computer Society Press, Los Alamitos (1999)
49. Felner, A.: Improving Search Techniques and using them in Different Environments. PhD thesis, Bar-Ilan University (2001)
50. Fraer, R., Kamhi, G., Ziv, B., Vardi, M., Fix, L.: Prioritized traversal: Efficient reachability analysis for verification and falsification. In: Emerson, E.A., Sistla, A.P. (eds.) CAV 2000. LNCS, vol. 1855. Springer, Heidelberg (2000)
51. Ginsberg, M., Harvey, W.: Iterative broadening. Artificial Intelligence 55, 367–383 (1992)
52. Godefroid, P. (ed.): Partial-Order Methods for the Verification of Concurrent Systems. LNCS, vol. 1032. Springer, Heidelberg (1996)
53. Grumberg, O., Veith, H. (eds.): 25 Years of Model Checking. LNCS, vol. 5000. Springer, Heidelberg (2008)
54. Hajek, J.: Self-synchronization and blocking in data transfer protocols. Technical Report THE-RC29286 (1977)
55. Hajek, J.: Automatically verified data transfer protocols. In: Proceedings 4th International Computer Communications Conference (1978)
56. Hajek, J. (2002), http://www.humintel.com/hajek/
57. Han, T., Katoen, J.-P.: Counterexamples in probabilistic model checking. In: Grumberg, O., Huth, M. (eds.) TACAS 2007. LNCS, vol. 4424, pp. 72–86. Springer, Heidelberg (2007)

58. Han, T., Katoen, J.-P.: Providing evidence of likely being on time: Counterexample generation for CTMC model checking. In: Namjoshi, K.S., Yoneda, T., Higashino, T., Okamura, Y. (eds.) ATVA 2007. LNCS, vol. 4762, pp. 331–346. Springer, Heidelberg (2007)

59. Hansen, E., Zhou, R., Feng, Z.: Symbolic heuristic search using decision diagrams. In: Koenig, S., Holte, R.C. (eds.) SARA 2002. LNCS, vol. 2371, p. 83. Springer, Heidelberg (2002)

60. Hansson, H., Jonsson, B.: A logic for reasoning about time and reliability. Formal Asp. Comput. 6(5), 512–535 (1994)

61. Helmert, M., Geffner, H.: Unifying the causal graph and additive heuristic. In: ICAPS, pp. 140–147 (2008)

62. Helmert, M., Haslum, P., Hoffmann, J.: Flexible abstraction heuristics in optimal sequential planning. In: ICAPS, pp. 176–183 (2007)

63. Holzmann, G.: The Spin Model Checker: Primer and Reference Manual. Addison-Wesley, Reading (2004)

64. Holzmann, G., Bosnacki, D.: The design of a multicore extension of the SPIN model checker. IEEE Trans. Software Eng. 33(10), 659–674 (2007)

65. Holzmann, G., Peled, D., Yannakakis, M.: On nested depth first search. In: SPIN (1996)

66. Jensen, R., Bryant, R., Veloso, M.: SetA*: An efficient BDD-based heuristic search algorithm. In: AAAI (2002)

67. Korf, R.: Depth-first iterative-deepening: An optimal admissible tree search. Artificial Intelligence 27(1), 97–109 (1985)

68. Korf, R., Zhang, W., Thayer, I., Hohwald, H.: Frontier search. Journal of the ACM 52(5), 715–748 (2005)

69. Kumar, V.: Branch-and-bound search. In: Shapiro [99], pp. 1468–1472

70. Kupferman, O., Sheinvald-Faragy, S.: Finding shortest witnesses to the nonemptiness of automata on infinite words. In: Baier, C., Hermanns, H. (eds.) CONCUR 2006. LNCS, vol. 4137, pp. 492–508. Springer, Heidelberg (2006)

71. Kupferschmid, S., Dräger, K., Hoffmann, J., Finkbeiner, B., Dierks, H., Podelski, A., Behrmann, G.: UPPAAL/DMC – abstraction-based heuristics for directed model checking. In: Grumberg, O., Huth, M. (eds.) TACAS 2007. LNCS, vol. 4424, pp. 679–682. Springer, Heidelberg (2007)

72. Kupferschmid, S., Hoffmann, J., Dierks, H., Behrmann, G.: Adapting an AI planning heuristic for directed model checking. In: Valmari, A. (ed.) SPIN 2006. LNCS, vol. 3925, pp. 35–52. Springer, Heidelberg (2006)

73. Kupferschmid, S., Wehrle, M., Nebel, B., Podelski, A.: Faster than UPPAAL? In: Gupta, A., Malik, S. (eds.) CAV 2008. LNCS, vol. 5123, pp. 552–555. Springer, Heidelberg (2008)

74. Kurshan, R.: Computer-Aided Verification of Coordinating Processes: The Automata-Theoretic Approach. Princeton University Press, Princeton (1994)

75. Lamborn, P., Hansen, E.A.: Layered duplicate detection in external-memory model checking. In: Havelund, K., Majumdar, R., Palsberg, J. (eds.) SPIN 2008. LNCS, vol. 5156, pp. 160–175. Springer, Heidelberg (2008)

76. Lluch-Lafuente, A.: Directed Search for the Verification of Communication Protocols. PhD thesis, Albert-Ludwigs-Universität Freiburg im Breisgau (2003)

77. Lowerre, B.T.: The HARPY speech recognition system. PhD thesis, CMU (1976)

78. McMillan, K.L.: Interpolation and SAT-based model checking. In: Hunt Jr., W.A., Somenzi, F. (eds.) CAV 2003. LNCS, vol. 2725, pp. 1–13. Springer, Heidelberg (2003)

79. Pearl, J.: Heuristics. Addison-Wesley, Reading (1985)
80. Peled, D.: Combining partial order reductions with on-the-fly model-checking. Formal Methods in System Design 8, 39–64 (1996)
81. Qian, K.: Formal Symbolic Verification Using Heuristic Search and Abstraction Techniques. PhD thesis, University of New South Wales (2006)
82. Qian, K., Nymeyer, A.: Heuristic search algorithms based on symbolic data structures. In: ACAI (2003)
83. Qian, K., Nymeyer, A.: Guided invariant model checking based on abstraction and symbolic pattern databases. In: Jensen, K., Podelski, A. (eds.) TACAS 2004. LNCS, vol. 2988, pp. 497–511. Springer, Heidelberg (2004)
84. Rasmussen, J.I., Larsen, K.G., Subramani, K.: Resource-optimal scheduling using priced timed automata. In: Jensen, K., Podelski, A. (eds.) TACAS 2004. LNCS, vol. 2988, pp. 220–235. Springer, Heidelberg (2004)
85. Ravi, K., Somenzi, F.: High-density reachability analysis. In: ICCAD (1995)
86. Ravi, K., Somenzi, F.: Efficient fixpoint computation for invariant checking. In: ICCD (1999)
87. Ravi, K., Somenzi, F.: Hints to accelerate symbolic traversal. In: Pierre, L., Kropf, T. (eds.) CHARME 1999. LNCS, vol. 1703, pp. 250–266. Springer, Heidelberg (1999)
88. Reffel, F., Edelkamp, S.: Error detection with directed symbolic model checking. In: Wing, J.M., Woodcock, J.C.P., Davies, J. (eds.) FM 1999. LNCS, vol. 1708, p. 195. Springer, Heidelberg (1999)
89. Rubin, S.: The ARGOS Image Understanding System. PhD thesis, CMU (1978)
90. Rungta, N., Mercer, E.G.: Generating counter-examples through randomized guided search. In: Bošnački, D., Edelkamp, S. (eds.) SPIN 2007. LNCS, vol. 4595, pp. 39–57. Springer, Heidelberg (2007)
91. Russell, S.: Efficient memory-bounded search methods. In: European Conference on Artificial Intelligence (ECAI). Wiley, Chichester (1992)
92. Ruys, T.C.: Optimal scheduling using branch and bound with SPIN 4.0. In: Ball, T., Rajamani, S.K. (eds.) SPIN 2003. LNCS, vol. 2648, pp. 1–17. Springer, Heidelberg (2003)
93. Sabuncuoglu, I., Bayiz, M.: Job shop scheduling with beam search. European Journal of Operational Research 118, 390–412 (1999)
94. Sanders, P., Meyer, U., Sibeyn, J.F.: Algorithms for Memory Hierarchies. Springer, Heidelberg (2002)
95. Schuppan, V.: Liveness Checking as Safety Checking to Find Shortest Counterexamples to Linear Time Properties. PhD thesis, ETH Zürich (2006)
96. Schuppan, V., Biere, A.: Efficient reduction of finite state model checking to reachability analysis. STTT 5(2-3), 185–204 (2004)
97. Schuppan, V., Biere, A.: Liveness checking as safety checking for infinite state spaces. In: INFINITY (2005)
98. Schuppan, V., Biere, A.: Shortest counterexamples for symbolic model checking of LTL with past. In: Halbwachs, N., Zuck, L.D. (eds.) TACAS 2005. LNCS, vol. 3440, pp. 493–509. Springer, Heidelberg (2005)
99. Shapiro, S. (ed.): Encyclopedia of Artificial Intelligence. Wiley Interscience, Hoboken (1992)
100. Si Ow, P., Smith, S.F.: Viewing scheduling as an opportunistic problem-solving process. Annals of Operations Research 12(1-4), 85–108 (1988)
101. Sobrinho, J.L.: Algebra and algorithms for QoS path computation and hop-by-hop routing in the internet. IEEE/ACM Transactions on Networking 10, 541–550 (2002)

102. Stewart, W.: Introduction to the Numerical Solution of Markov Chains. Princeton University Press, New Jersey (1994)
103. Torabi Dashti, M., Wijs, A.J.: Pruning State Spaces with Extended Beam Search. In: Namjoshi, K.S., Yoneda, T., Higashino, T., Okamura, Y. (eds.) ATVA 2007. LNCS, vol. 4762, pp. 543–552. Springer, Heidelberg (2007)
104. Valmari, A.: Eliminating redundant interleavings during concurrent program verification. In: Odijk, E., Rem, M., Syre, J.-C. (eds.) PARLE 1989. LNCS, vol. 366, pp. 89–103. Springer, Heidelberg (1989)
105. Valtorta, M.: A result on the computational complexity of heuristic estimates for the A* algorithm. Information Sciences 34, 48–59 (1984)
106. Vardi, M., Wolper, P.: An automata-theoretic approach to automatic program verification. In: LICS (1986)
107. Wah, B., Shang, Y.: Study of IDA*-style searches. Artificial Intelligence 3(4), 493–523 (1995)
108. Wang, C., Bloem, R., Hachtel, G., Ravi, K., Somenzi, F.: Compositional SCC analysis for language emptiness. Formal Methods in System Design 28(1), 5–36 (2006)
109. Wehrle, M., Kupferschmidt, S., Podelski, A.: Useful actions are useful. In: ICAPS, pp. 388–395 (2008)
110. Wijs, A.J.: What to Do Next: Analysing and Optimising System Behaviour in Time. PhD thesis, Vrije Universiteit Amsterdam (2007)
111. Wijs, A.J., Lisser, B.: Distributed Extended Beam Search for Quantitative Model Checking. In: Edelkamp, S., Lomuscio, A. (eds.) MoChArt IV. LNCS (LNAI), vol. 4428, pp. 165–182. Springer, Heidelberg (2007)
112. Wijs, A.J., van de Pol, J.C., Bortnik, E.: Solving Scheduling Problems by Untimed Model Checking. In: STTT (to appear, 2008)
113. Yang, C., Dill, D.: Validation with guided search of the state space. In: DAC (1998)
114. Zhou, R., Hansen, E.: Breadth-first heuristic search. In: ICAPS (2004)
115. Zhou, R., Hansen, E.: Beam-stack search: Integrating backtracking with beam search. In: ICAPS (2005)

Automated Testing of Planning Models

Klaus Havelund, Alex Groce, Gerard Holzmann,
Rajeev Joshi, and Margaret Smith

Jet Propulsion Laboratory*, California Institute of Technology
4800 Oak Grove Drive, Pasadena/Los Angeles, CA 91109
{klaus.havelund,alex.d.groce,gh,rajeev.joshi,margaret}@jpl.nasa.gov

Abstract. Automated planning systems (APS) are maturing to the
point that they have been used in experimental mode on both the NASA
Deep Space 1 spacecraft and the NASA Earth Orbiter 1 satellite. One
challenge is to improve the test coverage of APS to ensure that no unsafe plans can be generated. Unsafe plans can cause wasted resources or
damage to hardware. Model checkers can be used to increase test coverage for large complex distributed systems and to prove the absence of
certain types of errors. In this work we have built a generalized tool to
convert the input models of an APS to PROMELA, the modeling language
of the SPIN model checker. We demonstrate on a mission sized APS input
model, that we with SPIN can explore a large part of the space of possible
plans and verify with high probability the absence of unsafe plans.

1 Introduction

Automated Planning Systems (APS) have performed onboard planning and commanding in experimental mode for two NASA technology validation missions:
Deep Space 1 and Earth Orbiter 1. APS are also used to support ground planning
of sequences for both the Mars Exploration Rovers and the Phoenix missions.
Unlike traditional software, which executes a fixed sequence, an APS takes a
few high level goals, and an input model describing behavioral constraints, and
automatically generates a sequence of actions, called a *plan*, that achieves the
goals while satisfying the constraints. An APS can respond to unexpected situations and opportunities that a fixed sequence can not. The same flexibility that
makes it possible to respond to unanticipated situations also makes a planner far
more difficult to verify. If a mission manager is to trust an APS to autonomously
command, it must be shown to generate the correct plan for a vast number of
situations. Empirical test cases can cover only a handful of the most likely or
critical situations. Formal methods can in principle prove that every plan meets
certain properties and can prove the absence of a dangerous or undesirable plan.

In this work, we expand upon the results of our previous work [1] that demonstrated that it was possible to apply formal methods, and in particular, the SPIN

---

* The research described in this paper was carried out at the Jet Propulsion Laboratory, California Institute of Technology, under a contract with the National Aeronautics and Space Administration.

D. Peled and M. Wooldridge (Eds.): MOCHART 2008, LNAI 5348, pp. 90–105, 2009.

model checker [2,3,5] to improve test completeness when verifying APS input models. In particular, we have constructed a tool called MAP to automate the conversion of APS models to PROMELA, the language of the SPIN model checker. We have demonstrated that a large portion of the semantics of an APS model is expressible in the language of the model checker. As the subject of this work, we selected the ASPEN APS and its modeling language AML [11,13,14,15] developed by Jet Propulsion Laboratory (JPL) because it is currently successfully commanding the Earth Observer 1 (EO1) Autonomous Sciencecraft Experiment onboard the EO1 satellite.

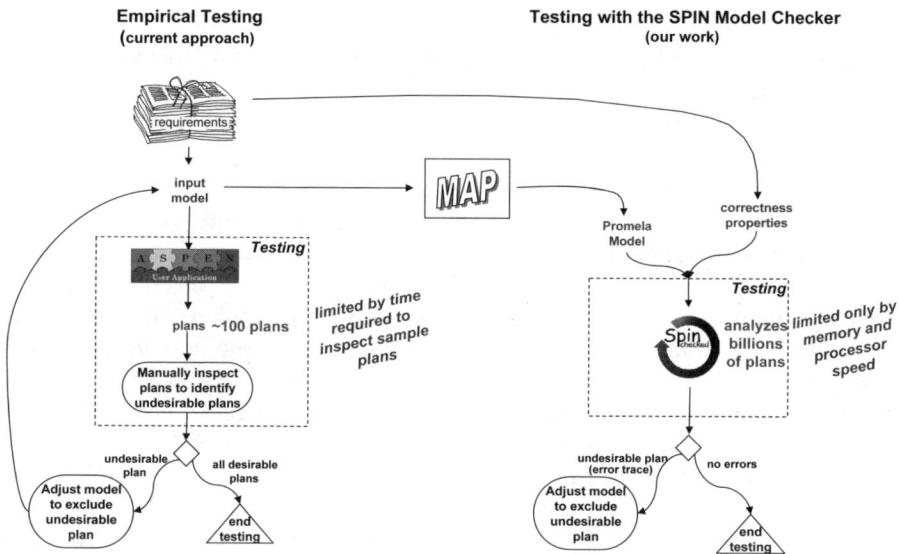

Fig. 1. MAP in context

The traditional approach to testing a plan model is to use ASPEN to exercise the model with various goals, and manually examine the generated plans, see Figure 1. The MAP conversion tool offers an alternative approach where an AML model is translated to a PROMELA model, such that the SPIN model checker can be used to test the plan model. The tool handles goals, activity decomposition, temporal constraints, and automated calculation of a cone of influence of variables (slicing) to reduce the search space. We demonstrate that the substantial increase in test coverage achieved through the use of model checking can work in practice and scale to a mission sized AML input model.

In work that predated publication of our previous paper [1], the real-time model checker UPPAAL was used to check for violations of mutual exclusion properties and to check for the existence of a plan meeting a set of goals [6]. In contrast, the work reported in this paper shows that for verification of a set of properties of interest, it is not necessarily required to reason about time. SPIN has also been used to verify plan execution engines [7,8]. Automatically generated test oracles have been used to assist in the interpretation of test plan outputs from APS [9]. A comparison of three popular model checkers, SPIN, SMV and Murphi showed that these model checkers can be used to check for the existence of a plan meeting a set of goals [10].

The rest of the paper is organized as follows. Section 2 briefly describes the ASPEN planner and the SPIN model checker. Section 3 presents an example of an AML model, and how SPIN is used to explore the PROMELA model generated by the MAP tool. Section 4 explains the principles of the translation from AML to PROMELA. Section 5 presents the results of analyzing the EO1 model. Finally, Section 6 concludes the paper and suggests future work.

2   The ASPEN Planner and the SPIN Model Checker

2.1   The ASPEN Planner

The ASPEN planner takes as input: an initial state, a goal, and a plan model describing allowable activities and constraints on their relationships; and produces a plan of activities that achieves the goal while satisfying the constraints in the model. In order to be efficient for on-board planning, the ASPEN planner performs a heuristics-based search, not exploring all possible paths, but instead only exploring a minimal search space. The objective of the planner is to find a single good plan, and the assumption is that such a plan exists. While this minimal search approach makes ASPEN efficient for finding plans quickly when they exist, it makes ASPEN's search incomplete, which is a drawback during testing. For instance, if ASPEN does not return a plan, one cannot conclude that there is no plan.

An AML model consists of a set of goals, activity specifications, resources, and states. C++ functions may be called from the model to calculate values used to determine resource requirements and states. The start of an activity is normally guarded so that the activity can only be scheduled if necessary resources are available and if the spacecraft is in a desired state. Activities typically modify states and resources at the beginning and/or end of the activity. Activities can be decomposed into lower level, sub-activities. A number of temporal relations can be defined to order the start and completion of sub-activities with respect to one another. States and resources are used in AML models to constrain the types of plans that are generated to a set that will be safe and feasible. For instance, an atomic resource such as a solid state recorder (SSR), that can only be safely accessed by one reader or writer at a given time, will be tracked by a mutex state. An activity that needs to write to the SSR will have a guard that prevents the activity from starting until the SSR lock is available. The activity needing to read or write to the SSR takes the lock upon entry and restores it upon exit.

A tightly constrained AML input model will have a smaller number of potential plans, and can be more completely tested, but will be less agile in responding to unexpected events during spacecraft operation. A less tightly constrained model exploits the strengths of the APS system to respond to the unexpected, but in order to be trusted, must be more thoroughly tested than is possible with standard test techniques.

2.2   The SPIN Model Checker

SPIN is a model checker and can analyze the correctness of finite state concurrent systems with respect to formally stated properties [3]. A particular concurrent system is formalized in the PROcess MEta LAnguage (PROMELA), and correctness properties to be verified can be formalized either in Linear Temporal Logic (LTL), in a visual tool such as the TimeEdit tool [12] that generates Buchi automata, or using assertions placed in the PROMELA model. The SPIN tool also provides a simulator, with which PROMELA models may be executed. This can in particular be used to re-run error traces generated by the model checker for properties that are not satisfied. SPIN's search attempts to be exhaustive, continuing until it finds an error, memory is exhausted, or the search completes. The correctness property can express a desired behavior, like a goal in ASPEN's AML language, or an undesired behavior, such as a unsafe plan that should be excluded from an AML input model.

PROMELA is SPIN's modeling language, supporting the declaration of process types, and instantiation (spawning) of instances of these types. The language can be thought of as a multi-threaded programming language. Processes communicate via shared variables and/or by message passing through communication channels. A process can block by waiting for a Boolean predicate over the global variables to become true, or it can block on waiting for a value to appear on an input channel. The execution of a PROMELA model consists of executing these parallel running processes in a non-deterministic interleaved manner until no process can continue, either because all processes have terminated normally, or they have deadlocked. A PROMELA model denotes the set of all such finite and infinite execution traces. The SPIN model checker conceptually explores all traces for conformance to or violation of a formal property.

3   Example

The following example is intentionally made as small as possible (and consequently rather artificial), but sufficiently complex to still illustrate the fundamental principles. The scenario is the operation of a planetary rover performing drilling activities. First an AML model is represented. Second, it is shown how SPIN is used to analyze the PROMELA model generated by MAP. In this section the generated PROMELA will be regarded as a black-box, not unlike how a user would perceive it. In Section 4 the translation will be explained.

3.1   AML Model of Drilling Rover

The rover can perform three activities: (i) *Drill*: the rover drills a hole of a certain depth, extracts some soil, and performs some analysis on the selected material, for

```
01   resource power {
02      type = depletable;
03      default_value = 75;
04      capacity = 100;
05      min_value = 10;
06   }
07
08   resource buffer { type = atomic; }
09
10   state_variable buffer_sv {
11      states = ("empty","full");
12      transitions = ("empty"->"full", "full" -> "empty");
13      default_state = "empty";
14   };
15
16   activity drill {
17      string hole;
18      int depth;
19      int power_use;
20      dependencies = power_use <- powerof(depth);
21      reservations =
22        buffer,
23        buffer_sv must_be "empty",
24        buffer_sv change_to "full" at_end,
25        power use power_use;
26   }
27
28   activity uplink {
29      reservations =
30        buffer,
31        power use 30;
32   }
33
34   activity charge {
35      reservations = power use -25;
36   }
37
38   activity experiment {
39      decompositions =
40        (drill with ("hole1" -> hole, 7 -> depth),uplink,charge
41          where charge ends_before end of drill)
42        or
43        charge;
44   }
```

Fig. 2. Aml model of drilling scenario

example using an oven. All these activities are here abstracted into the single drill action. (ii) *Uplink* : when the drilling (and included analysis) has been performed the results must be uplinked to a spacecraft (which subsequently transmits it to earth, not modeled). (iii) *Charge* : the drilling as well as the uplink both require power, represented by a power resource. This resource can be charged with new energy when becoming low. The AML model presented in Figure 2 formalizes this scenario. Our goal will be to generate plans that request drilling and uplink of the results, with charging occurring as needed. We shall illustrate how MAP can be used to detect various errors in the model to be presented.

The rover and the equipment on board the rover uses various resources. There are two types of resources: *atomic*, and *variable*. Atomic resources are physical devices that can only be used (reserved) by one activity at a time (for example a science instrument). A variable resource has at any point in time a value and can be used by more than one activity at a time, each reducing the quantity of the resource, as long as the minimum/maximum bounds are not exceeded. A variable resource is either depletable or non-depletable. A depletable resource's capacity is diminished after use (for example a battery), in contrast to a non-depletable resource, where the used quantity is automatically returned (for example solar power).

The model contains one variable depletable `power` resource (lines 01–06). The power resource has a current starting value of 75, a minimum value of 10 (it cannot go below) and a maximum capacity of 100. Digital results collected during drilling are stored in a data `buffer` before being uplinked. The data buffer is modeled as an atomic resource (line 08) and will be reserved by the `drill` and the `uplink` activities to ensure mutual access. In addition, a state variable `buffer_sv` is introduced (lines 10–14) to model the status of the buffer: whether it is empty or full. The state machine has two states (`"empty"` and `"full"`) and two transitions: one from `"empty"` (the initial state) to `"full"`, and one from `"full"` back to `"empty"`.

The `drill` activity (lines 16–26) declares three local variables: `hole`, `depth` and `power_use` (lines 17–19). Any local variable in AML can function as a parameter. The first two will function as parameters (what hole to drill and what depth), while the third is a real local variable holding how much power to consume, being assigned a value in a dependency clause (line 20) as a function of the depth. The `drill` activity reserves a collection of resources (lines 21–25): the data `buffer` (line 22, ensuring mutual exclusion during use), which must be `"empty"` (line 23), and will transition to `"full"` after (line 24); and `power` as a function of the `depth` of the hole (line 25). The `uplink` activity (lines 28–32) reserves the `buffer` from where data are uplinked and uses 30 `power` units. The `charge` activity (lines 34–36) adds 25 units back to the `power` resource (using AMLs semantics of providing negative numbers when adding, and positive numbers when subtracting).

The main activity is called `experiment` (lines 38–44) and is decomposed into the three activities: `charge`, `drill` and `uplink`. The decomposition consists of *either* (lines 40–41) performing a drill, an uplink and a charge, where the charge is required to end before the end of the drill (to save time); *or*, if there is not power enough, just charging the rover with new energy (line 43). Note the constraint: 'charge ends_before end of drill'. AML allows for several kinds of constraints , 'A *constraint* B', between two activities A and B (that can occur in any order if no constraints are given): contains, contained_by, starts_before, ends_before, starts_after, ends_after, all further followed by one of start of, end of, or all of. Examples are: A starts_before start of B, A starts_after end of B, and A contains all of B (the B activity occurs during the A activity, not before and not after).

An initialization file outlines what activities should be instantiated. In this case one instance of the experiment activity is initiated:

```
experiment exp {}
```

Note that the experiment activity itself launches the charge, drill and uplink activities through decomposition.

3.2 Analyzing the Model with SPIN

Verification 1. In order to verify LTL properties with SPIN, atomic conditions (PROMELA macros using #define) are introduced by MAP. For example, the event e_uplink will become true when the uplink activity terminates. For each activity A, there will be a b_A (begin A) and a e_A (end A) event, which can be referred to in SPIN. The first property we will verify is that eventually an *end of uplink* is observed. This is achieved by asking SPIN to prove that there is no execution satisfying the LTL property <>e_uplink (see Figure 3).

The property states that eventually the end of an uplink occurs. A trace satisfying this property should constitute in a good plan. By making SPIN attempt to verify that an execution satisfying this property does *not exist*, we use SPIN to generate an error trace (a plan) that achieves such a state in case it exists. Note that we have chosen the "*No Executions*" option in XSPIN in order to get an error trace (plan). The verification causes XSPIN to generate the message sequence diagram shown in Figure 4.

The message sequence diagram shows for each activity (a PROMELA process, see Section 4) a vertical time line, showing when it begins and when it ends. In this case it is observed that there is an uplink before any drilling has taken place. This is an error according to our informal requirements. By studying the model it is detected that the uplink activity does not check the status of the data buffer to see whether it contains data before the uplink takes place. The buffer must be full before uplink (a check on the buffer state variable), and after the uplink it must be set to empty. To fix this we modify the uplink activity as follows:

```
activity uplink {
    reservations =
        buffer,
        buffer_sv must_be "full",    // added
        buffer_sv change_to "empty", // added
        power use 30;
}
```

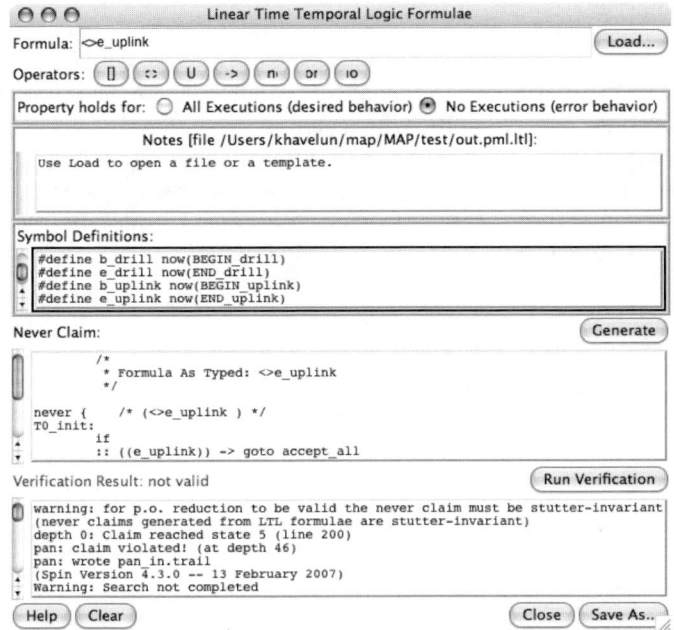

Fig. 3. XSPIN – generate a plan ending in an uplink

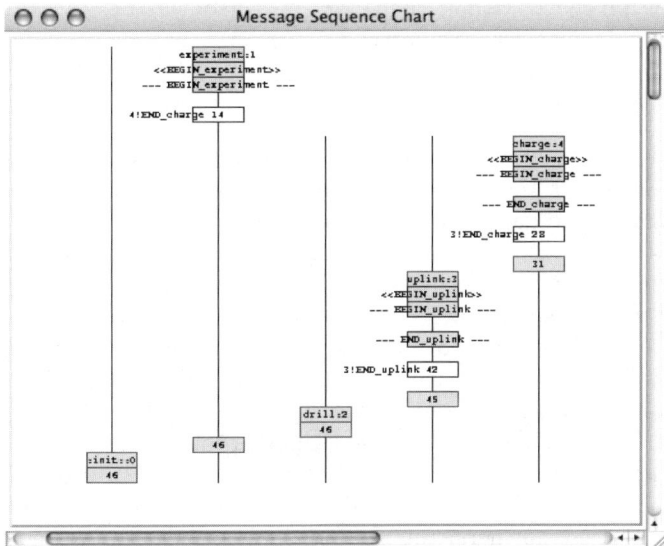

Fig. 4. XSPIN – an error trace equals a plan

3.3   Verification 2

Retrying the verification after this modification yields *no errors*. However, no errors means no plan. Recall that SPIN is asked to prove that there is no execution leading to an `uplink`. After further examination it is discovered that even though the `charge` activity adds 25 units, which should be enough to cover the combined usage of 70 (`drill`) plus 30 (`uplink`) with an initial resource value of 75, another 10 needs to be added since the minimal value of the resource is set to 10 (cannot go below). The maximum capacity must consequently also be increased. The `power` resource therefore needs to be modified as follows:

```
resource power {
    type = depletable;
    default_value = 85; // changed from 75 to 85
    capacity = 110;     // changed from 100 to 110
    min_value = 10;
}
```

This time an acceptable sequence of events is generated: first drilling, then a charge, and then uplink.

3.4   Verification 3

We have now demonstrated that there is a plan that ends in an uplink preceded with a drill. The question is whether there are any plans that end in an uplink without being preceded with an drill. We can verify this by searching for a plan satisfying the following LTL property:

```
!e_drill U e_uplink
```

That is: no drill until an uplink. The until operator of LTL is strong, hence this means that an uplink must occur (and no drill before that). Since we want to show that there is no such plan, we enter this property with *"No Executions"* set. The verification shows that there are no such executions (errors : 0), which is a satisfactory result.

All our properties so far have been stated as the LTL property `<>goal`, using the *"No Executions"* option to make SPIN attempt finding just one execution that makes the goal true. It turns out that for verification of plan models this seems to be the most natural verification style: to postulate the non-existence of an execution (plan) that satisfies a particular property. It is, however, possible also to use the *"All Executions"* option in XSPIN. That is, to prove that for all execution traces some property is true. Note though that a plan model denotes executions that lead nowhere. Such blind alleys are simply part of the search problem. Hence, one has to be careful when stating properties to be true on all executions. One has to limit the verification to only those executions that achieve some meaningful goal. In our last case we can state the property that: every uplink is preceded by a drill as the following property to be true on all traces,

knowing that there is only one uplink possible: `<>e_uplink -> <>(e_drill &`
`<>e_uplink)`. That is, "for all traces, if the trace is a good plan (eventually from
the beginning of the trace there is an uplink), then (also from the beginning of
the trace) there is a drill, followed by a (the) uplink". This is, however, a slightly
complicated way of stating our desired property.

4   Translation from AML to PROMELA

Planning in principle can be regarded as the following problem: given is a model
$M = (\Sigma, A)$ consisting of a state Σ (resources and state machines), and a finite
set of activities $A = A_1, A_2, A_3, \ldots, A_n$ that access variables in the state Σ.
Each activity A_i has a precondition $pre-A_i$ on the state Σ that has to be true
before that activity can execute (or "*be put down on a time-line*", using planning
terminology), and a post-condition $post-A_i$, defining a side-effect on the state Σ.
The activities can be thought of as guarded commands. A planning problem is a
triple (I, G, M) consisting of an initial state I and a goal state G to be achieved
from the initial state while obeying the model M (obeying the pre-conditions
essentially). The planning problem is obviously more complicated, in particular
in the case of AML, which allows for dynamically created activities and time
constraints.

However, this view of the planning problem directly leads to a process view
of planning: given a set of processes (activities), find an execution of these that
leads from the initial state to the goal state, without deadlocking or otherwise failing in between. This is the view underlying the MAP translator. It
translates an AML model into a PROMELA model of concurrent processes, one
for each activity, with a pre-condition and a post-condition. Concurrency is
normally regarded as a hard problem for users to get right, and the above
argumentation suggests that the planning problem is equally difficult to get
right.

More specifically, an AML model is translated into a PROMELA model, which
contains a process type (`proctype`) for each activity. The body of each such
process type consists of two sequentially composed statements $S_1; S_2$: a beginning
S_1 and an ending S_2, each of which is an atomic statement (encapsulated with
PROMELAs `atomic{...}`-construct). The basic idea is that the scheduling of an
AML activity A over a time period starting at time t_1 and ending at time t_2 in
SPIN will result in the corresponding process executing its first atomic statement
S_1 at a point corresponding to time t_1 and its second atomic statement S_2 at
a point corresponding to time t_2. However, since SPIN does not model real-
time, time periods are not measured, only the relative ordering of events is
modeled. Planning in SPIN consists of finding an execution trace that executes
the processes (respecting the guards) in such a manner that a specific end state
is reached, with the expected processes executing in a desired order, and such
that the state satisfies some invariants during the execution.

Resources are declared as state variables that get written to and read from
during the "execution" of the PROMELA model:

```
int power;
bool buffer;
byte buffer_sv;
int buffer_sv_reserve_count;
```

The **power** variable holds current power level. The **buffer** variable represents a semaphore, which is either taken (value 1) or free (value 0). The buffer state variable (**buffer_sv**) holds the current state of the buffer state machine. The **buffer_sv_reserve_count** is increased each time a process performs a **must_be** request, as for example the drill action in line 23 of Figure 2. The **drill** action requires the state variable to have this value throughout its execution. Several activities can require this to be true, and all be able to execute at the same time. Each process will count this variable up at entry and down on exit, and the state variable (**buffer_sv**) itself cannot change unless this counter is 0.

As already mentioned, an activity is modeled as a process. SPIN attempts to "execute" processes, thereby producing an execution trace, which becomes the sought plan. In the example, the **experiment** activity starts the three sub-activities **drill**, **uplink**, and **charge**, with the constraint that the charge should end before the end of the drill action. In addition, the three sub-activities should all terminate before the end of the experiment activity since they are created as sub-activities (AML semantics). These constraints are illustrated in Figure 5.

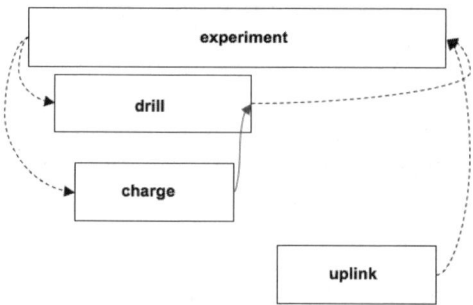

Fig. 5. Activity constraints. Stipled lines are constraints imposed by AML semantics. The fully drawn constraint comes from the model constraint: "**charge ends_before end of drill**".

These constraints are imposed in the PROMELA model by passing two sets (collections) of events to each process: those that it should wait for before it starts, and those it should wait for before it terminates. In the above case, for example, the drill process should be passed the sets: ∅ (don't wait to start) and {end_charge} (wait for charge to terminate before terminating). In order to know what events actually happened in the context (parent) in which a process exists, it takes a third parameter, a reference to a set that is continuously updated with events as they happen. The generated process declaration in Figure 6 contains these parameter definitions.

```
proctype drill(set begin_events; set end_events;
               set external_events; short sigstart; short sigend;
               int depth)
{
  byte _e_;
  int power_use;
  atomic {
    subset(begin_events,external_events);
    power_use = powerof(depth);
    (buffer==1 && buffer_sv==ENUM_empty &&
     (power-power_use)<=110 && (power-power_use)>=10 ) ->
    buffer = buffer-1;
    buffer_sv_reserve_count = buffer_sv_reserve_count+1;
    power = power-power_use;
    addorlog(external_events,sigstart)
  };
  atomic {
    subset(end_events,external_events);
    (buffer_sv==ENUM_empty &&
      (buffer_sv_reserve_count==1 || buffer_sv==ENUM_full)) ->
    buffer = buffer+1;
    buffer_sv_reserve_count = buffer_sv_reserve_count-1;
    buffer_sv = ENUM_full;
    addorlog(external_events,sigend)
  }
}
```

Fig. 6. PROMELA model of drill activity

The first two parameters are the sets of events to wait for before starting (begin_events) respectively ending (end_events). Sets are not available in PROMELA as a built in data type, so they are modeled as channels (the PROMELA model contains a macro definition of the form: '#define set chan'). The external_events parameter is a reference (pointer) to the set of actual events that happen, to be updated by the context. The process itself can add events to this set when starting and when ending such that other processes can be made aware thereof. The events to add are the last two parameters of the process: sig_start and sig_end. Whether these events should be added or not really depends on the context, whether some other process needs to know. If no process needs to know the parameter is negative, and it will not be added.

The last parameter (depth) to the process is an AML model-parameter, introduced by the user in the drill activity (line 18). Recall that any local "variable" of an activity in AML can be a parameter in case an instantiating activity passes a value to this variable. The drill activity has 3 local variables: hole, depth, and power_use, but only the first two of these are real parameters instantiated at call time in the experiment activity:

```
drill with ("hole1" -> hole, 7 -> depth)
```

However, only the `depth` parameter influences planning since it impacts how much power is used (lines 20 and 25). MAP performs abstraction by applying data flow analysis of the AML model in order to determine which variables are not used in planning, and which can therefore be abstracted away. The string variable `hole` does not influence the planning, and hence is abstracted away.

The body of the drilling process is divided into two atomic statements, representing respectively the beginning and the end of the activity. The explanations of the two blocks are similar. The beginning block starts by waiting for the events in the `begin_events` set to become a subset of the `external_events` set (`subset(begin_events,external_events)`). The various operations on sets are really operations on channels, modeling set addition, set membership test, and subset test. It then performs checks on and assignments to various resource, state and semaphore variables. A conditional statement *"condition -> statement"* causes the process to block until the condition becomes true (PROMELA semantics). Finally, it is signaled to the `external_events` set that the process has started (if the `sigstart` value is not negative). The `addorlog(set,signal)` function adds the signal to the set, if the signal is not negative, and furthermore stores the signal in a global variable `_event_` (such that LTL formulas can refer to it) of an enumerated type of all the possible events, one for the beginning and end for each activity:

```
mtype {
  BEGIN_drill, END_drill,
  BEGIN_uplink, END_uplink,
  BEGIN_charge, END_charge,
  BEGIN_experiment, END_experiment
}
local mtype _event_;
```

The `experiment` activity is similarly translated into the PROMELA process shown in Figure 7. This process declares two variables. The set-valued variable `events` will be updated continuously during execution and will contain the events that occur during an experiment (it becomes the `external_events` parameter to the sub-activities). The set-valued variable `end_drill` is initialized once to contain the set of events that the drill activity has to wait for before it can end. The required sizes of these sets (3 and 1) are calculated at translation time. For example, 3 events will need to be recorded: end of `charge` (needed by the `drill`), and end of `drill` and `uplink` (needed by the `experiment` that cannot terminate before these have terminated, see Figure 5).

The first atomic block contains a conditional `if ... fi` statement, having two entries (each preceded by `::`) that are chosen non-deterministically, corresponding to the `or` operator occurring in line 42 of the AML model in Figure 2. The form of the two choices are similar. In the first case, corresponding to lines 40-41 of Figure 2, the set `end_drill` is created to contain the event

END_charge by: `mustwaitfor(end_drill,END_charge)`, which adds its second argument to the first argument set. This set is then passed as the second argument to the `drill` activity in the subsequent line to indicate that the drill activity has to wait for the charge to end before it can end itself. The other event sets passed around are empty (`nullset`). The events passed as arguments, for example the negative `-BEGIN_charge` and the positive `END_charge` to the `charge` activity, indicate that no activity cares about when a charge begins (negative so it will not be added to the events set), whereas for example the `drill` activity needs to know when the charge ends. Finally, the `experiment` will not continue before the sub-activities spawned in each branch have terminated (`isin(...)`).

The AML model contains in line 20, Figure 2, a call of the function `powerof`, which must have been defined as a C++ function in a separate file. MAP does not translate these C++ functions. Instead, their occurrence in the AML model is marked by the translator, and a user has to program these as macros: `#define powerof(depth) (depth*10)`.

5   The Earth Orbiter 1 Application

ASPEN has successfully commanded (and is still at the time of writing commanding) the Earth Observer 1 (EO1) Autonomous Sciencecraft Experiment onboard the EO1 earth orbiting satellite. The EO1 satellite orbits earth, taking photos of the surface and comparing recent images with previous images to detect changes due to, for instance, flooding, fire and other natural events. Upon detecting a change, the spacecraft software generates a new goal to take a more detailed follow-up image and ASPEN generates a plan to achieve that goal.

Our original goal was to enable MAP to convert the EO1 AML model into PROMELA. The EO1 model features the most commonly used AML constructs, and therefore, a tool that can convert this model will be capable of converting a very broad set of realistic AML models, a non-trivial achievement. With well over 100 activities in the EO1 AML model, and an ever changing set of goals, EO1 also illustrates that an automated conversion tool is necessary to make the logic model checking of APS input models practical.

EO1 has two imaging instruments that can read from and write to a solid state recorder. The designers of the AML model were concerned about a possible data race on the state recorder, violating that reads and writes must mutually exclude each other. This property was formulated in PROMELA using a semaphore access counter that was shown not to go beyond 1 on a very large state space, although not the complete state space. The AML model analyzed is approximately 7300 lines of code, causing approximately 4000 lines of PROMELA code to be generated. Two experiments were performed, each applying SPINs bit-state hashing where not all of the state space is explored. Each experiment was performed comparing single core (1 CPU) and multi-core (8 CPUs) runs, using a recently developed multi-core version of SPIN [4]. In the first experiment 10 million states were explored using 11.6 minutes on 1 CPU and 89 seconds on 8 CPUs. In the

```
proctype experiment(set begin_events; set end_events;
                set external_events; short sigstart; short sigend)
{
  byte _e_;
  set events = [3] of {mtype};
  set end_drill = [1] of {mtype};
  atomic {
    subset(begin_events,external_events);
    addorlog(external_events,sigstart);
    if
    ::
      mustwaitfor(end_drill,END_charge);
      run drill(nullset,end_drill,events,-BEGIN_drill,END_drill,7);
      run uplink(nullset,nullset,events,-BEGIN_uplink,END_uplink);
      run charge(nullset,nullset,events,-BEGIN_charge,END_charge);
      isin(END_drill,events) && isin(END_uplink,events) &&
          isin(END_charge,events)
    ::
      run charge(nullset,nullset,events,-BEGIN_charge,END_charge);
      isin(END_charge,events)
    fi
  };
  atomic {
    subset(end_events,external_events);
    addorlog(external_events,sigend)
  }
}
```

Fig. 7. PROMELA model of experiment activity

second experiment, with more aggressive bit-state hashing, 2.5 billion states were explored, using 2.6 days on 1 CPU and 8 hours on 8 CPUs.

6   Conclusion and Future Work

The translator translates a large subset of AML relatively faithfully by attempting to map AML source constructs to PROMELA target constructs, which are supposed to yield a behavior in SPIN similar to the behavior of the source in ASPEN. However, some parts of AML are not translated, in some cases as an optimization mechanism. The main constructs of AML that are not translated include time values and durations, reals and floats, priorities, and a special form of call-by-reference parameter passing that PROMELA does not support. Of the omitted concepts, some are generally hard to translate, such as time, real numbers, and call-by-reference of activities. The remaining omissions could be handled more easily. The MAP tool shall be seen as an aid in examining the utility of model checking in testing plan models. Future work includes examining exactly what forms of verification can be performed with the presented tool that cannot easily be performed with ASPEN.

References

1. Smith, M., Holzmann, G., Cucullu, G., Smith, B.: Model Checking Autonomous Planners: Even the Best Laid Plans Must be Verified. In: IEEE Aerospace Conference, Big Sky, Montana (March 2005)
2. Holzmann, G.: The Model Checker Spin. IEEE Transactions on Software Engineering 23(5), 279–295 (1997)
3. Holzmann, G.: The Spin Model Checker: Primer and Reference Manual 2003, 608 pgs. Addison-Wesley, Reading (2003)
4. Holzmann, G., Bosnacki, D.: The Design of a Multi-Core Extension of the Spin Model Checker. IEEE Transactions on Software Engineering 33(10), 659–674 (2007)
5. http://www.spinroot.com
6. Khatib, L., Muscettola, N., Havelund, K.: Verification of Plan Models using UP-PAAL. In: First Goddard Workshop on Formal Approaches to Agent-Based Systems (March 2000)
7. Havelund, K., Lowry, M., Penix, J.: Formal Analysis of a Space Craft Controller using Spin. IEEE Transactions on Software Engineering 27(8) (August 2001)
8. Havelund, K., Lowry, M., Park, S., Pecheur, C., Penix, J., Visser, W., White, J.L.: Formal Analysis of the Remote Agent - Before and After Flight. In: The Fifth NASA Langley Formal Methods Workshop, Virginia (June 2000)
9. Feather, M., Smith, B.: Automatic Generation of Test Oracles: From Pilot Studies to Applications. In: Proceedings of the Fourteenth IEEE International Conference on Automated Software Engineering (ASE 1999), Cocoa Beach, FL, October 1999, pp. 63–72. IEEE Computer Society, Los Alamitos (1999)
10. Penix, J., Pecheur, C., Havelund, K.: Using Model Checking to Validate AI Planner Domain Models. In: 23 Annual NASA Goddard Software Engineering Workshop, Goddard, Maryland (December 1998)
11. Cichy, B., Chien, S., Schaffer, S., Tran, D., Rabideau, G., Sherwood, R.: Validating the Autonomous EO-1 Science Agent. In: International Workshop on Planning and Scheduling for Space (IWPSS 2004), Darmstadt, Germany (June 2004)
12. Smith, M., Holzmann, G., Ettessami, K.: Events and Constraints: a Graphical Editor for Capturing Logic Properties of Programs. In: 5th International Symposium on Requirements Engineering, Toronto, Canada, August 2001, pp. 14–22 (2001)
13. Chien, S., Knight, R., Stechert, A., Sherwood, R., Rabideau, G.: Using Iterative Repair to Improve Responsiveness of Planning and Scheduling. In: International Conference on Artificial Intelligence Planning Systems (AIPS 2000), Breckenridge, CO (April 2000)
14. Fukunaga, A., Rabideau, G., Chien, S.: ASPEN: An Application Framework for Automated Planning and Scheduling of Spacecraft Control and Operations. In: Proceedings of International Symposium on Artificial Intelligence, Robotics and Automation in Space (i-SAIRAS 1997), Tokyo, Japan, pp. 181–187 (1997)
15. Smith, B., Sherwood, R., Govindjee, A., Yan, D., Rabideau, G., Chien, S., Fukunaga, A.: Representing Spacecraft Mission Planning Knowledge in Aspen. In: AIPS 1998 Workshop on Knowledge Engineering and Acquisition for Planning (June 1998); Workshop notes published as AAI Technical Report WS-98-03

Towards Partial Order Reduction
for Model Checking Temporal Epistemic Logic

Alessio Lomuscio[1], Wojciech Penczek[2], and Hongyang Qu[1]

[1] Department of Computing, Imperial College London, UK
{A.Lomuscio,Hongyang.Qu}@imperial.ac.uk
[2] Institute of Computer Science, PAS, and University of Podlasie, Poland
penczek@ipipan.waw.pl

Abstract. We introduce basic partial order reduction techniques in a
temporal-epistemic setting. We analyse the semantics of interpreted systems
with respect to the notions of trace-equivalence for the epistemic
linear time logic $LTLK_{-X}$.

1   Introduction

In recent years there has been growing attention to the area of verification
of multi-agent systems (MAS) by automatic model checking. Differently from
standard reactive systems where plain temporal logics are often used, MAS are
specified by using rich, intensional logics such as epistemic and deontic logics in
combination with temporal logic. To accommodate for these needs several techniques
for model checking have been suitably extended. For instance in [4, 20]
OBDD-based techniques for temporal epistemic logic were introduced. Similar
analysis were carried out previously for SAT-based approaches, including
bounded and unbounded model checking [10, 18]. These approaches have now
been implemented [1, 4, 13] and experimental results obtained in a variety of areas
such as verification of security protocols, web-services, etc. Several extensions
to other logics, including ATL, real-time, and others, have also been analysed.

It is surprising however that two mainstream techniques in symbolic verification,
i.e., *predicate abstraction* and *partial order reduction* have not so far been
applied to the verification of MAS logics. In this paper we begin the analysis of
partial order reduction for temporal epistemic logic. Specifically, we look at the
case of the linear temporal logic $LTLK_{-X}$ (i.e., the standard LTL [14] without
the X next-time operator in which an epistemic modality is added [3]). The
main contributions of this research note are the notions of weak and strong path
equivalence defined on MAS semantics, the corresponding dependency relations,
and a proof showing that these equivalences preserve the satisfaction of $LTLK_{-X}$
formulas.

The rest of the paper is organised as follows. In Section 2 we introduce syntax,
semantics of our setting together with some basic notions. In Section 3 we present
the definitions of path equivalence and dependency which are used in Theorem 1,
the key result of the paper, showing that strongly equivalent paths preserve

D. Peled and M. Wooldridge (Eds.): MOCHART 2008, LNAI 5348, pp. 106–121, 2009.

LTLK$_{-X}$ formulas. We exemplify the methodology in Section 4 while discussing an example, and present our conclusions in Section 5.

2   Preliminaries

We introduce here the basic technical background to the present paper. In particular we discuss the semantics of interpreted systems, properly augmented with suitable concepts for our needs, and the basic syntax we shall be using in the rest of the paper.

2.1   Interpreted Systems

The semantics of interpreted systems provides a setting to reason about MAS. Interpreted systems were originally developed independently by Parikh and Ramanujam [16], Halpern and Moses [8] and Rosenschein [21]. Their adoption as a semantics of choice for several MAS concept follows the publication of [3]. Although several valuable extensions have been proposed, in their basic settings interpreted systems offer a natural synchronous semantics for linear time and an external account of knowledge of the agents in the system. The following is a brief summary of the fundamental concepts needed for the rest of the paper; we refer to [3] for more details.

We begin by assuming a MAS to be composed of n agents $\mathcal{A} = \{1, \ldots, n\}$[1]. We associate a finite set of *possible local states* $L_i = \{l_i^1, l_i^2, \ldots, l_i^{nl_i}\}$ and *actions* $Act_i = \{a_i^1, a_i^2, \ldots, a_i^{na_i}\}$ to each agent $i \in \mathcal{A}$. In the interpreted systems model the actions of the agents are selected and performed synchronously according to each agent's *local protocol* $P_i : L_i \to 2^{Act_i}$; the local protocol effectively models the program the agent is executing. A *global state* $g = (l_1, \ldots, l_n)$ is a tuple of local states for all the agents in the MAS corresponding to an instantaneous snapshot of the system at a given time. Given a global state $g = (l_1, \ldots, l_n)$, we denote $g_i = l_i$ as the local component of agent $i \in \mathcal{A}$ in g. Global transitions are executed by means of joint actions on global states. In a nutshell, the *global evolution function* $t : G \times Act_1 \times \cdots \times Act_n \to G$ defines the target global state from a global state when a joint action $(a_1, \ldots, a_n) \in Act_1 \times \cdots \times Act_n$ is selected and performed by all agents in the system. More details can be found in [3].

In the following analysis we differ from the standard presentation by abstracting from the actual protocols and actions being performed and focus on the transitions only. For this reason we simply focus on the set of all possible *global transitions* $\mathcal{T} = \{(g, g') \mid \exists (a_1, \ldots, a_n) \in Act_1 \times \cdots \times Act_n$ such that $t(g, a_1, \ldots, a_n) = g'\}$. For simplicity we shall often use lower case letters $t_1, t_2, \ldots$ to denote elements of $\mathcal{T}$. Given the set $\mathcal{T}$ of global transitions we denote by $\mathcal{T}_i, i \in \mathcal{A}$, the set of all *local transitions* of the form $t_i = (l_i^k, l_i^{k+1})$ for an agent $i \in \mathcal{A}$. The set of all local transitions can be obtained by projecting $\mathcal{T}$ over the corresponding dimension for the agent in question; more formally $(l_i^k, l_i^{k+1}) \in \mathcal{T}_i$ if there

---

[1] Note in the present study we do not consider the environment component. This may be added with no technical difficulty at the price of heavier notation.

exists a joint action $(a_1, \ldots, a_n)$ such that $t(g^k, a_1, \ldots, a_n) = g^{k+1}$, where the local component for agent i in g^k (respectively g^{k+1}) is l_i^k (respectively l_i^{k+1}). With slight abuse of notation for any global transition $t = (g, g') \in \mathcal{T}$ we write $t = (t_1, \ldots, t_n)$, where each $t_i \in \mathcal{T}_i, i \in \mathcal{A}$ is such that $t_i(g_i, g_i')$, and say that all $t_i, i = 1, \ldots, n$, are the local transitions in t.

With respect to the above we use the following notations. Given a local transition $t_i = (l_i, l_i')$ we write $source(t_i) = l_i$ and $target(t_i) = l_i'$. Further, if $l_i = l_i'$, we denote t_i as ϵ. We use similar notation for global transitions too with obvious meaning in terms of source and target on global states. A sequence of global states $\rho = g^0 g^1 g^2 \ldots$ is called a path (or a run) if for every $g^k, g^{k+1} \in \rho$ ($k \geq 0$) we have that $(g^k, g^{k+1}) \in \mathcal{T}$. Given a path ρ we say $\rho|_i = g_i^0 g_i^1 g_i^2 \ldots$ is the local path for agent i in ρ. Given a path $\rho = g^0 g^1 g^2 \ldots$, $\rho(k) = g^k$, and $\rho\langle k \rangle = (g^k, g^{k+1}) = t^k$. Similarly, the k-th state and k-th transition in $\rho|_i$ are denoted as $\rho|_i(k)$ and $\rho|_i\langle k \rangle$ respectively. Let $\rho[0..k] = g^0 g^1 \ldots g^k$ (respectively $\rho|_i[0..k] = g_i^0 g_i^1 \ldots g_i^k$) be the prefix of ρ (respectively $\rho|_i$) and $\rho[k] = g^k g^{k+1} \ldots$ (respectively $\rho|_i[k] = g_i^k g_i^{k+1} \ldots$) the suffix. The set of paths originating from g is denoted as $\Pi(g)$.

We express synchronisation of transitions as follows. Local transitions are synchronised if they are always performed jointly by the system; this is formally expressed as follows.

Definition 1 (Synchronisation). *For any $i, j \in \mathcal{A}$ ($i \neq j$), a local transition t_i is said to be* semi-synchronised *to a local transition t_j if whenever t_i appears in a global transition $t = (t_1, \ldots, t_n)$ so does t_j. Two local transitions t_i, t_j are* synchronised *if t_i is semi-synchronised to t_j and t_j is semi-synchronised to t_i.*

We write $t_1 \rightarrow t_2$ to denote the fact that t_1 is semi-synchronised to t_2 and $t_1 \leftrightarrow t_2$ denote t_1 is synchronised to t_2. Figure 1 shows an interpreted system composed of three agents. The dotted lines represents synchronised transitions, i.e., the local transitions t_1^2 and t_2^2 are synchronised.

Definition 2 (Interpreted Systems). *Given a set of atomic propositions P, an* interpreted system *(or simply a* model*) is a tuple $M = (G, G_0, \Pi, h)$, where G is a set of global states, $G_0 \subseteq G$ is a set of initial (global) states, $\Pi = \bigcup_{i \in G_0} \Pi(i)$ is the set of paths originating from all states in G_0, and $h : P \rightarrow 2^G$ is an*

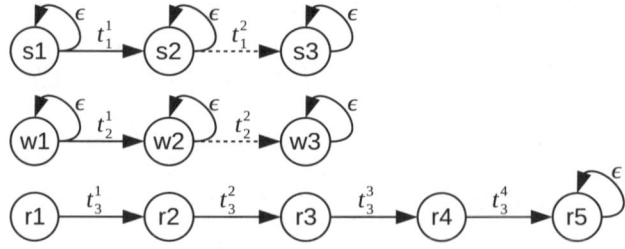

Fig. 1. A synchronous system

interpretation for the atomic propositions. Particularly, we define a local atomic proposition p_i^j for each local state l_i^j of the agent $i \in \mathcal{A}$ such that $h(p_i^j) = \{g \mid g \in G \text{ and } g_i = l_i^j\}$. We assume G to be the set of states reachable from G_0 by any path in Π.

We can now define the syntax and interpretation of our language.

2.2   Syntax

Combinations of linear time and knowledge have long been used in the analysis of temporal epistemic properties of systems [3, 7]. In partial order reduction for LTL one typically excludes from the syntax the next time operator X as the preservation results [12] do not hold when X is present. Given this we consider LTLK$_{-X}$ in this paper.

Definition 3 (Syntax). *Let PV be set of atomic propositions to be interpreted over the global states of a system. The syntax of LTLK$_{-X}$ is defined by the following BNF grammar:*

$$\phi ::= true \mid false \mid p \mid \neg p \mid \phi \wedge \phi \mid \phi \vee \phi \mid \phi \mathcal{U} \phi \mid \phi \mathcal{R} \phi \mid K_i \phi \mid \overline{K}_i \phi,$$

where $p \in PV$.

The temporal operators $\mathcal{U}$ and $\mathcal{R}$ are named as usual *until* and *release* respectively. The formula $K_i \phi$ represents "agent i knows ϕ" and $\overline{K}_i \phi$ is the corresponding dual representing "agent i does not know whether or not ϕ holds". The epistemic modalities are defined by means of the following relations as standard.

Definition 4 (Epistemic relation). *For each agent $i \in \mathcal{A}$, $\sim_i \subseteq G \times G$ is an epistemic indistinguishably relation over global states defined by $g \sim_i g'$ if $g_i = g_i'$.*

Given a model $M = (G, G_0, \Pi, h)$, where $h(p)$ is the set of global states where p holds. Let $\overline{\Pi}$ denote the suffix-closure of Π, i.e., the set of all the paths in Π and their suffices. The formal semantics of an LTLK$_{-X}$ formula ϕ being satisfied by M and $\rho \in \overline{\Pi}$, denoted as $M, \rho \models \phi$, is recursively defined as follows.

Definition 5 (Satisfaction)

- $M, \rho \models true$ for each $\rho \in \overline{\Pi}$;
- $M, \rho \not\models false$ for each $\rho \in \overline{\Pi}$;
- $M, \rho \models p$ iff $\rho(0) \in h(p)$;
- $M, \rho \models \neg p$ iff $M, \rho \not\models p$;
- $M, \rho \models \phi_1 \wedge \phi_2$ iff $M, \rho \models \phi_1$ and $M, \rho \models \phi_2$;
- $M, \rho \models \phi_1 \vee \phi_2$ iff $M, \rho \models \phi_1$ or $M, \rho \models \phi_2$;
- $M, \rho \models \phi_1 \mathcal{U} \phi_2$ iff $M, \rho[k] \models \phi_2$ for some $k \geq 0$ and $M, \rho[j] \models \phi_1$ for all $0 \leq j < k$;
- $M, \rho \models \phi_1 \mathcal{R} \phi_2$ iff either $M, \rho[k] \models \phi_2$ and $M, \rho[k] \not\models \phi_1$ for all $k \geq 0$, or $M, \rho[k] \models \phi_1$ for some $k \geq 0$ and $M, \rho[j] \models \phi_2$ for all $0 \leq j \leq k$;

- $M, \rho \models K_i\phi$ iff all paths $\rho' \in \overline{\Pi}$ we have that $\rho'(0) \sim_i \rho(0)$ implies $M, \rho' \models \phi$.
- $M, \rho \models \overline{K}_i\phi$ iff for some path $\rho' \in \overline{\Pi}$ we have that $\rho'(0) \sim_i \rho(0)$ and $M, \rho' \models \phi$.

Given a global state g of M and an LTLK$_{-X}$ formula ϕ, we use the following notations:

- $M, g \models \phi$ iff $M, \rho \models \phi$ for all the paths $\rho \in \Pi(g)$.
- $M \models \phi$ iff $M, g \models \phi$ for all $g \in G_0$.
- $Props(\phi) \subseteq PV$ is the set of atomic propositions that appear in ϕ.

In order to define partial order reduction for LTLK$_{-X}$, we transform each formula $\neg p$ into a fresh atomic proposition q such that $h(q) = G \setminus h(p)$. Next, we present the main notions used for our reduction.

Definition 6 (Simple State Expression). *Let $I \subseteq \mathcal{A}$. A set $L_I \subseteq \bigcup_{i \in I} L_i$ is said to be* simple *if it contains exactly one element from each set L_i. Given a simple set L_I, a* simple state expression *$\mathcal{P}$ for an atomic proposition p is a Boolean formula of the form:*

$$\mathcal{P} = \bigwedge_{l_i^j \in L_I} p_i^j, \tag{1}$$

where p_i^j is the local atomic proposition corresponding to l_i^j and for all $g \in G$ and $i \in I$: $g_i \in L_I$ implies $g \in h(p)$.

In the above definition, each local atomic proposition in $\mathcal{P}$ denotes a local state which "forces" any global state in which it appears to satisfy p. Given any $I \subseteq \mathcal{A}$, let $[p]$ denote the set of all valid simple state expressions for p. Given an atomic proposition p, a set $I \subseteq \mathcal{A}$ and a simple state expression $\mathcal{P}$, we write $\overline{[\mathcal{P}]}$ for L_I and $\mathcal{A}|_{\mathcal{P}}$ for I.

Let $G|_{\mathcal{P}} \subseteq G$ be the set of global states in which $\mathcal{P}$ holds. Given two simple state expressions $\mathcal{P}_k, \mathcal{P}'_k \in [p]$, we write $\mathcal{P}_k \leq \mathcal{P}'_k$ iff $G|_{\mathcal{P}_k} \subseteq G|_{\mathcal{P}'_k}$ and $\mathcal{P}_k < \mathcal{P}'_k$ iff $\mathcal{P}_k \leq \mathcal{P}'_k$ and $\mathcal{P}_k \neq \mathcal{P}'_k$. Clearly, $([p], \leq)$ is a poset. Let $Max[p]$ be the set of the maximal elements in $[p]$. Note that the maximal elements intuitively correspond to the "smallest" simple state expressions.

Definition 7 (Full State Expression). *The* full state expression *E_p for an atomic proposition p is a Boolean formula of the form:*

$$E_p = \bigvee_{\mathcal{P} \in Max[p]} \mathcal{P}, \tag{2}$$

In other words, E_p encodes the set of global states where p holds, i.e., $h(p)$. In what follows we also use the following shortcuts: $\mathcal{A}|_p = \bigcup_{\mathcal{P} \in Max[p]} \mathcal{A}|_{\mathcal{P}}$ ($\mathcal{A}|_p$ denotes the set of agents appearing in the full state expression of p), and $\mathcal{A}|_\phi = \bigcup_{p \in Props(\phi)} \mathcal{A}|_p$.

3   Partial Order Reduction on Interpreted Systems

In the literature, partial order reduction has been studied intensively for asynchronous systems, e.g., [5, 6, 9, 11, 15, 17, 19, 22]. The technique permits the exploration of a portion of the state space when checking for satisfaction of a formula in a system. The basic idea consists in observing that two consecutive independent transitions in a path can sometimes be interchanged with no effect to the satisfaction of a formula. Because of this, the set of all the paths in a system can be partitioned into subsets, named *traces* [2]. In this section, we aim to define a dependency relation between transitions in order to be able to partition paths into traces. We begin with the notion of *stuttering* [12].

Definition 8. *The* stuter normal form *of a path ρ is a sequence $\#\rho$ such that each consecutive repetition of states in ρ is replaced by a single state. Two paths are said to be* equivalent up to stuttering *if they have the same stutter normal form.*

For example, two paths $g^1 g^2 g^2 g^3 g^3$ and $g^1 g^2 g^2 g^2 g^3$ are equivalent up to stuttering since their stutter normal form is $g^1 g^2 g^3$. The same definition applies to local paths $\rho|_i$.

Definition 9 (Weak equivalence). *Two paths ρ and ρ' are* weakly equivalent *iff $\rho|_i$ and $\rho|'_i$ are equivalent up to stuttering, for all agents $i \in \mathcal{A}$.*

Figure 2 and 3 display two weakly equivalent paths in the system of Figure 1 based on the above definition.

Observe that even if two paths are weakly equivalent, they may not satisfy the same LTLK$_{-X}$ formula. For example, consider the system in Figure 1 and two atomic propositions p and q such that p holds in all the global states containing $s1$ while q holds in all the global states containing $w2$. The formula

$$p \mathcal{U} q \tag{3}$$

holds in the path in Figure 3, but does not hold in the one in Figure 2.

Now we start to define dependency relations between transitions to strengthen weak equivalence in order to get strong equivalence preserving the LTLK$_{-X}$ formulae.

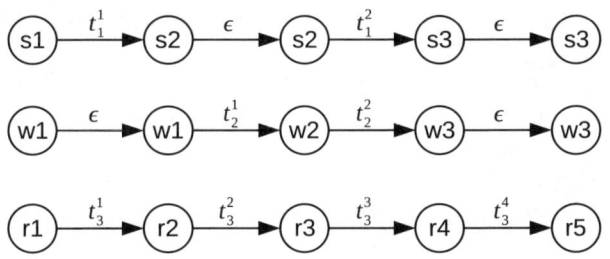

Fig. 2. A path ρ

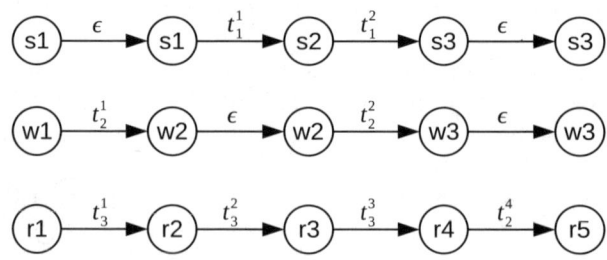

Fig. 3. A path weakly equivalent to ρ

Definition 10 (Basic dependency relation). *For any agent $i \in \mathcal{A}$, the dependency relation D_i is the symmetric closure of the relation:*

$$d_i = \{(t_i, t_i') \mid t_i, t_i' \in \mathcal{T}_i \text{ and } (\text{ either } (t_i \neq \epsilon, t_i' \neq \epsilon) \text{ or}$$
$$(t_i \neq \epsilon \text{ and } \exists t_j \in \mathcal{T}_j, t_j \neq \epsilon, t_i' \rightarrow t_j \text{ or } t_j \rightarrow t_i') \text{ or}$$
$$((\exists t_j \in \mathcal{T}_j, t_j \neq \epsilon, t_i \rightarrow t_j \text{ or } t_j \rightarrow t_i) \text{ and } (\exists t_k \in \mathcal{T}_k, t_k \neq \epsilon, t_i' \rightarrow t_k \text{ or } t_k \rightarrow t_i')))\}.$$

The basic dependency relation relates two local transitions if either they cause an effective change of local states or they do not but they are (semi-)synchronised to other local transitions that do so.

Definition 11 (Dependency relation for synchronisation). *The dependency relation D_{syn} is the symmetric closure of the following relation:*

$$d_{syn} = \{(t_i, t_j) \mid t_i \in \mathcal{T}_i, t_j \in \mathcal{T}_j \text{ and } t_i \rightarrow t_j\}.$$

We now define the dependency relation for an LTLK_{-X} formula. We begin with the dependency relation for an atomic proposition.

Definition 12 (Dependency relation for atomic propositions). *For an atomic proposition p with corresponding full state expression $E_p = \bigvee_{\mathcal{P} \in Max[p]} \mathcal{P}$, the dependency relation D_p for p is*

$$D_p = \{(t_i, t_j) \mid t_i \in \mathcal{T}_i, t_j \in \mathcal{T}_j, i \neq j, \mathcal{P} \in Max[p], \mathcal{P}' \in Max[p],$$
$$target(t_i) \in \overline{[\mathcal{P}]} \text{ and } t_i \neq \epsilon \text{ and } source(t_j) \in \overline{[\mathcal{P}']} \text{ and } t_j \neq \epsilon\}.$$

D_p requires that each non-ϵ transition t_i entering a local state in $\overline{[\mathcal{P}]}$ is dependent on every non-ϵ transition t_j leaving a local state in any $\overline{[\mathcal{P}']}$. The reason for this is that p may become satisfied after t_i is executed and become unsatisfied after t_j is executed. For example, consider an atomic proposition p with full state expression $s2 \wedge r2$ (as shown in Figure 1). We have $D_p = \{(t_1^1, t_3^2), (t_3^2, t_1^2), (t_3^2, t_1^1), (t_1^2, t_3^2)\}$.

To define the dependency relation for an arbitrary LTLK_{-X} formula ϕ, we need to preform some pre-processing on ϕ. Firstly, we need to make sure that each atomic proposition p occurs only once in ϕ. If there is more than one occurrence for p, we generate a fresh atomic proposition p' for each occurrence and define $h(p') = h(p)$. It follows that $E_{p'} = E_p$. For example, we transform $\phi = K_i p \vee K_j p$ into $K_i p_1 \vee K_j p_2$ with $h(p_1) = h(p_2) = h(p)$. Secondly, we define the *epistemic nesting depth* $\{\psi\}_K$ for every sub-formula ψ of ϕ. The epistemic nesting of a sub-formula corresponds to the "epistemic depth" of a sub-formula in a formula. Intuitively, the "deeper" a sub-formula is in an epistemic formula the higher its nesting will be. To calculate the nesting we assign a level 0 of nesting to the whole formula and increase it by 1 every time we find an epistemic operator while exploring the parse tree of the formula. More formally, we proceed as follows.

Definition 13 (Epistemic nesting depth). *Given a formula ϕ, the epistemic nesting $\{\psi\}_K$ of a sub-formula ψ of ϕ is defined as follows.*

- *If $\psi = \phi$, then $\{\phi\}_K = \{\psi\}_K = 0$;*
- *If $\psi \in \{\psi_1 \wedge \psi_2, \psi_1 \vee \psi_2, \psi_1 \mathcal{U} \psi_2, \psi_1 \mathcal{R} \psi_2\}$, then $\{\psi_1\}_K = \{\psi_2\}_K = \{\psi\}_K$;*
- *If $\psi \in \{K_i \psi_1, \overline{K}_i \psi_1\}$, then $\{\psi_1\}_K = \{\psi\}_K + 1$;*
- *If $\psi = p$, then $\{p\}_K = \{\psi\}_K$.*

Let $|\phi|_K = \max\{\{p\}_K \mid p \in Props(\phi)\}$ be the maximum epistemic nesting depth of ϕ. Let AP_ϕ^m be the subset of $Props(\phi)$ such that for each $p \in AP_\phi^m$, $\{p\}_K = m$, and $AP_\phi = \bigcup\limits_{0 \le m \le |\phi|_K} AP_\phi^m$. Assume $i_1, i_2, \ldots, i_m$ is the sequence of indexes for the epistemic modalities scoping p (e.g., for $\phi = K_1 q \wedge K_2(EF(K_1 p))$, the sequence of indexes for p is $(2, 1)$). Then we perform the following two steps on AP_ϕ:

1. For each $p \in AP_\phi^m$ for all $m > 0$, we generate the set of propositions

$$\Sigma_p = \{p_{j_1, j_2, \ldots, j_m} \mid l_{i_1}^{j_1} \in L_{i_1}, \ldots, l_{i_m}^{j_m} \in L_{i_m} \text{ and } E_{p_{j_1, j_2, \ldots, j_m}} = p_{i_1}^{j_1} \wedge \cdots \wedge p_{i_m}^{j_m} \wedge E_p\},$$

   where $p_{i_k}^{j_k}$ is the local atomic proposition for $l_{i_k}^{j_k}$. For example, consider $\phi = EF(K_2 p)$ with $E_p = s_2 \wedge r_2$ in the system of Figure 1. Since $\{p\}_K = 1$, we generate the propositions p_1, p_2, p_3 with $E_{p_1} = w_1 \wedge s_2 \wedge r_2$, $E_{p_2} = w_2 \wedge s_2 \wedge r_2$ and $E_{p_3} = w_3 \wedge s_2 \wedge r_2$. Let $AP_\phi' = \bigcup\limits_{0 < m \le |\phi|_K} (\bigcup\limits_{p \in AP_\phi^m} \Sigma_p)$ be the set of the newly generated atomic propositions.

2. For each pair of atomic propositions p and q in $AP_\phi^0 \cup AP_\phi'$, we define a fresh atomic proposition r with $h(r) = h(p) \cup h(q)$. Let AP_ϕ^r be the set of atomic propositions generated in this step.

Definition 14 (Dependency relation for an LTLK$_{-X}$ formula ϕ). *The dependency relation D_ϕ for ϕ is defined as follows:*

$$D_\phi = \bigcup\limits_{p \in AP_\phi^0 \cup AP_\phi' \cup AP_\phi^r} D_p.$$

Consider the example $\phi = EF(K_2 p)$ with $E_p = s_2 \wedge r_2$ again. D_ϕ is the symmetric closure of the following set: $\{(t_2^1, t_1^1), (t_2^1, t_3^1), (t_1^1, t_3^2), (t_3^1, t_1^2), (t_2^2, t_1^1), (t_2^1, t_3^1), (t_2^1, t_1^2), (t_2^1, t_3^2), (t_2^2, t_1^2), (t_2^2, t_3^2)\}$. The above dependency relation is used to avoid inconsistencies among weakly equivalent paths where a formula holds in one path but does not hold in the other. For example, the paths in Figure 2 and Figure 3 can be distinguished now with respect to Formula (3). Since $D_{p\mathcal{U}q} = \{(t_1^1, t_2^1), (t_2^1, t_1^1)\}$, t_1^1 and t_2^1 are not interchangeable and the execution order between them has an impact on the satisfaction of the formula.

Definition 15 (Extended Formula). *For any LTLK$_{-X}$ formula ϕ, an extended formula ϕ' for ϕ is defined by replacing each subformula $\psi = K_i \varphi$ with*

$$\psi' = K_i((p_i^1 \wedge \varphi) \vee \ldots \vee (p_i^{nl_i} \wedge \varphi)),$$

where p_i^j is the local atomic proposition corresponding to l_i^j ($1 \le j \le nl_i$). The substitution is carried out bottom-up in the parse tree.

Note that obviously $D_\phi = D_{\phi'}$. So in what follows we assume to be dealing with extended formulae only.

Given an LTLK$_{-X}$ formula ϕ, let

$$D = (\bigcup_{i \in \mathcal{A}} D_i) \cup D_{syn} \cup D_\phi. \tag{4}$$

For a path ρ containing two specific occurrences t_i and t_j ($i, j \in \mathcal{A}$) of local transitions, we write $t_i <_\rho t_j$ if t_i happens earlier than t_j in ρ. We write $t_i =_\rho t_j$ if they are executed together in a global transition. We use $t_i \le_\rho t_j$ to denote either $t_i <_\rho t_j$ or $t_i =_\rho t_j$.

Now we are ready to present the main result of this note. To this aim we first define strong equivalence, and then show that it preserves the LTLK$_{-X}$ formulae.

Definition 16 (Strong equivalence). *Two paths ρ and ρ' are strongly equivalent with respect to an LTLK$_{-X}$ formula ϕ iff the following two conditions hold:*

(1) ρ and ρ' are weakly equivalent,
(2) for any two occurrences t and t' of local transitions in ρ and $(t, t') \in D$, $t <_\rho t'$ implies $t <_{\rho'} t'$, and $t =_\rho t'$ implies $t =_{\rho'} t'$.

Given the above equivalence, we formulate two auxiliary lemmas.

Lemma 1. *The following two conditions hold:*

A) For a path ρ and an LTLK$_{-X}$ formula ϕ, if $M, \rho \models \phi$ and $M, \rho[1] \not\models \phi$, then there exists $p \in Props(\phi)$ such that $M, \rho \models p$ and $M, \rho[1] \not\models p$,
B) if $M, \rho \not\models \phi$ and $M, \rho[1] \models \phi$, we can find an atomic proposition $p \in Props(\phi)$ such that $M, \rho \not\models p$ and $M, \rho[1] \models p$.

Proof. We prove A) by induction on the structure of ϕ. The condition B) can be shown similarly.

1. $\phi = p$. This case is obvious.
2. $\phi = \psi_1 \wedge \psi_2$. We have $M, \rho \models \psi_1 \wedge \psi_2$ and $M, \rho[1] \not\models \psi_1 \wedge \psi_2$. If $M, \rho[1] \not\models \psi_1$, given that $M, \rho \models \psi_1$, it follows that there exists an atomic proposition p in ψ_1 such that $M, \rho \models p$ and $M, \rho[1] \not\models p$.
3. $\phi = \psi_1 \vee \psi_2$. This case is similar to the previous one.
4. $\phi = \psi_1 \mathcal{U} \psi_2$. We have $M, \rho \models \psi_1 \mathcal{U} \psi_2$ and $M, \rho[1] \not\models \psi_1 \mathcal{U} \psi_2$. So $M, \rho \models \psi_2$ and $M, \rho[1] \not\models \psi_2$. Therefore, by induction the case holds.
5. $\phi = \psi_1 \mathcal{R} \psi_2$. We have $M, \rho \models \psi_1 \mathcal{R} \psi_2$ and $M, \rho[1] \not\models \psi_1 \mathcal{R} \psi_2$. If ψ_2 holds in all states in ρ and ψ_1 does not holds in any states, then $M, \rho[1] \models \phi$. Thus there exists k such that ψ_1 holds in $\rho(k)$ and ψ_2 holds in $\rho(j)$ for all $0 \leq j \leq k$. Similarly to the $\mathcal{U}$ case, $k = 0$, and ψ_1 or ψ_2 does not hold in $\rho(1)$. Then there exists p in ψ_1 or ψ_2 satisfying the lemma.
6. $\phi = K_i \psi$. We have $M, \rho \models K_i \psi$ and $M, \rho[1] \not\models K_i \psi$. So $\rho|_i(0) \neq \rho|_i(1)$. Since ϕ is an extended formula, we know that $M, \rho \models K_i((p_i^1 \wedge \psi) \vee \ldots \vee (p_i^{nl_i} \wedge \psi))$, and there exists a $1 \leq j \leq nl_1$ such that p_i^j is the local atomic proposition corresponding to $\rho|_i(0)$. We have $M, \rho \models p_i^j$ and $M, \rho[1] \not\models p_i^j$.
7. $\phi = \overline{K}_i \psi$. This case is similar to the one above. $\square$

Lemma 2. *Let ϕ be an LTLK$_{-X}$ formula and paths $\rho, \rho' \in \Pi$ be strongly equivalent. Then there exist $k, k' \geq 0$ such that the following two conditions hold:*

A) If $M, \rho[k] \models \phi$, then $M, \rho'[k'] \models \phi$;
B) There exists an $i \in \mathcal{A}|_\phi$ such that the paths $\rho|_i[0..k]$ and $\rho'|_i[0..k']$ are equivalent up to stuttering, and if $M, \rho[k-1] \not\models \phi$ and $M, \rho[k] \models \phi$, then $\rho|_i\langle k \rangle \neq \epsilon$.

Proof. A) By induction on the structure of ϕ.

The base case: $\phi = p$.

Assume $M, \rho[k] \models p$ for some $k \geq 0$. Given that $\rho(k) \in h(p)$, we have that there exists a simple state expression $\mathcal{P} \in Max[p]$ for some simple set $L_I, I \subseteq A$ and $\rho(k) \in G|_{\mathcal{P}}$. For any $i \in I$, consider the shortest and longest prefixes of the projections of ρ' onto i that are equivalent to $\rho|_i[0..k]$ up to stuttering. Call $\rho'|_i[0..j_i]$ the shortest and $\rho'|_i[0..\overline{j}_i]$ the longest. Given ρ and ρ' are strongly equivalent, they are weakly equivalent and therefore, we have $\rho'|_i(j_i) = \rho'|_i(\overline{j}_i) = \rho|_i(k)$. Consider the following two cases, which may arise.

1. $\bigcap_{i \in I} [j_i, \overline{j}_i] \neq \emptyset$. Then, there is a $k' \geq 0$ such that $k' \in \bigcap_{i \in I} [j_i, \overline{j}_i]$. Given that $\rho'|_i(k') = \rho|_i(k)$ for all $i \in I$, we have that $M, \rho'[k'] \models p$.
2. $\bigcap_{i \in I} [j_i, \overline{j}_i] = \emptyset$. Then, there must exist $x, y \in I$ such that $j_x > \overline{j}_y$. This implies that the transitions $t_x^{j_x - 1}$ and $t_y^{\overline{j}}$ are dependent. However, by the inductive hypothesis ρ, ρ' are strongly equivalent and therefore we have $t_y^{\overline{j}} \leq_{\rho'} t_x^{j_x - 1}$. This is a contradiction. So, we have $\bigcap_{i \in I} [j_i, \overline{j}_i] \neq \emptyset$.

The induction steps.

1. $\phi = \psi_1 \wedge \psi_2$. Assume $M, \rho[k] \models \psi_1 \wedge \psi_2$, therefore $M, \rho[k] \models \psi_1$ and $M, \rho[k] \models \psi_2$. By the inductive assumption there exist $k', k'' \geq 0$ such that $M, \rho'[k'] \models \psi_1$ and $M, \rho'[k''] \models \psi_2$. If $k' = k''$, then $M, \rho'[k'] \models \psi_1 \wedge \psi_2$. So, we are done. Without loss of generality, assume now that $k' < k''$. Let $\bar{k}' \geq k'$ be the biggest natural number such that $M, \rho'[j] \models \psi_1$ for $k' \leq j \leq \bar{k}'$ and $M, \rho'[\bar{k}' + 1] \not\models \psi_1$. Similarly let $\bar{k}''$ be the smallest natural number such that $M, \rho'[j] \models \psi_2$ for $\bar{k}'' \leq j \leq k''$ and $M, \rho'[\bar{k}'' - 1] \not\models \psi_2$. If $\bar{k}'' \leq \bar{k}'$ then there exists a k''' such that $M, \rho'[k'''] \models \psi_1 \wedge \psi_2$.

   Otherwise, we have $\bar{k}' < \bar{k}''$. By Lemma 1, there exists an atomic proposition p in ψ_1 such that $M, \rho'[\bar{k}'] \models p$ and $M, \rho'[\bar{k}' + 1] \not\models p$, and an atomic proposition q in ψ_2 such that $M, \rho'[\bar{k}'' - 1] \not\models q$ and $M, \rho'[\bar{k}''] \models q$. Assume p is satisfied by the simple state expression $\mathcal{P}_1 \in Max[p]$ for some $I \subseteq \mathcal{A}$ and q by $\mathcal{P}_2 \in Max[q]$ for some $I' \subseteq \mathcal{A}$. Therefore, there exist an agent $i \in I$ such that $t_i^{\bar{k}'} = \rho'|_i \langle \bar{k}' \rangle$ ($t_i^{\bar{k}'} \neq \epsilon$) leaves the local state $\rho'|_i(\bar{k}') \in \overline{[\mathcal{P}_1]}$, and an agent $j \in I'$ such that $t_j^{\bar{k}'' - 1} = \rho'|_j \langle \bar{k}'' - 1 \rangle$ ($t_j^{\bar{k}'' - 1} \neq \epsilon$) enters the local state $\rho'|_j(\bar{k}'') \in \overline{[\mathcal{P}_2]}$ (note that $i \neq j$, otherwise we would have $k' = k''$.). According to the construction of D_ϕ, $t_i^{\bar{k}'}$ and $t_j^{\bar{k}'' - 1}$ are dependent. So we have $t_i^{\bar{k}'} \leq_{\rho'} t_j^{\bar{k}'' - 1}$ and $t_j^{\bar{k}'' - 1} <_\rho t_i^{\bar{k}'}$. But ρ and ρ' are strongly equivalent by the inductive hypothesis, so we get a contradiction.

2. $\phi = \psi_1 \vee \psi_2$. This case is immediate.

3. $\phi = \psi_1 \mathcal{U} \psi_2$. Assume $M, \rho[k] \models \psi_1 \mathcal{U} \psi_2$. By definition we have that there exists a $k' \geq k$ such that $M, \rho[k'] \models \psi_2$ and $M, \rho[j] \models \psi_1$ for $k \leq j \leq k'$. Then by induction, we have that there exists a k'' such that $M, \rho'[k''] \models \psi_2$. So we have $M, \rho'[k''] \models \psi_1 \mathcal{U} \psi_2$.

4. $\phi = \psi_1 \mathcal{R} \psi_2$. According to the semantics of $\mathcal{R}$, we know that $M, \rho[k] \models \psi_2$ and thus there exists k' such that $M, \rho'[k'] \models \psi_2$. If for all $j > k$, $M, \rho[j] \not\models \psi_1$, then for all $j' > k'$, $M, \rho'[j'] \not\models \psi_1$ (otherwise, there exists $\bar{j} > k$ such that $M, \rho[\bar{j}] \models \psi_1$). If there exists j ($j \geq k$), $M, \rho[j] \models \psi_1$, then $\psi_1 \mathcal{R} \psi_2 = \psi_2 \mathcal{U}(\psi_1 \wedge \psi_2)$ and the case may be shown similarly to the above.

5. $\phi = K_i \psi$. Assume $M, \rho[k] \models K_i \psi$. Since ρ, ρ' are strongly equivalent, $\rho|_i[0..k]$ and $\rho'|_i[0..k']$ are equivalent up to stuttering for some k'. So $\rho|_i(k) = \rho'|_i(k')$. Therefore $M, \rho'[k'] \models \phi$.

6. $\phi = \overline{K}_i \psi$. It is the same as the K_i case.

B) A proof of this condition follows from the above proof.   □

Strong equivalence for an LTLK$_{-X}$ formula ϕ naturally partitions Π into traces of strongly equivalent paths. We have the following theorem.

Theorem 1. *For any LTLK$_{-X}$ ϕ and any two strongly equivalent paths $\rho, \rho' \in \Pi$, we have $M, \rho \models \phi$ iff $M, \rho' \models \phi$.*

Proof. By induction on the structure of ϕ.
The base case $\phi = p$ is obvious given $\rho(0) = \rho'(0)$.
The induction steps $\phi = \psi_1 \wedge \psi_2$, $\phi = \psi_1 \vee \psi_2$, $\phi = K_i \psi$ and $\phi = \overline{K}_i \psi$ can be obtained similarly. In the following, we prove the case $\phi = \psi_1 \mathcal{U} \psi_2$. A similar proof can be obtained for $\phi = \psi_1 \mathcal{R} \psi_2$.

$\phi = \psi_1 \mathcal{U} \psi_2$. Assume $M, \rho \models \psi_1 \mathcal{U} \psi_2$. If $M, \rho \models \psi_2$, then $M, \rho' \models \psi_2$ and therefore $M, \rho' \models \phi$. Assume there exists a $k \geq 0$ such that $M, \rho[k] \models \psi_2$ and $M, \rho[j] \models \psi_1$ for $0 \leq j < k$. By Lemma 2, there exists a smallest $k' > 0$ such that $M, \rho'[k'] \models \psi_2$; we need to show that $M, \rho'[j] \models \psi_1$ for all $0 \leq j < k'$. Assume that $M, \rho'[j] \not\models \psi_1$ for the smallest $0 \leq j < k'$. Note that $M, \rho'[0] \models \psi_1$; so this implies that $M, \rho'[j-1] \models \psi_1$. So there must exist a set of agents $I \subseteq \mathcal{A}$ such that $\rho'|_i(j-1) \neq \rho'|_i(j)$ for all $i \in I$. Similarly observe there exists a set of agents $I' \subseteq \mathcal{A}$ such that $\rho'|_i(k') \neq \rho'|_i(k'-1)$ for all $i \in I'$. So by observing there are atomic propositions changing values from $\rho'(k'-1)$ to $\rho'(k')$ and from $\rho'(j-1)$ to $\rho'(j)$, and reasoning similarly to the case of conjunction in the proof of Lemma 2, we can reach a contradiction with hypothesis of ρ, ρ' being strongly equivalent.   □

Theorem 1 implies that partial order reduction based on the relation of strong equivalence preserves $LTLK_{-X}$ properties.

4   Example

We exemplify the technique above on the system of three agents $\mathcal{A} = \{1, 2, 3\}$ of Figure 1 with respect to the formula

$$\phi = \Diamond K_3\, p.$$

We assume p is an atomic proposition that holds in the global state $(s2, w2, r5)$, i.e., its full state expression is

$$E_p = s2 \wedge w2 \wedge r5.$$

Before we start to explore the state space, we need to generate the dependency relation according to the formula 4.

- The basic dependency relation is defined as follows.

$$D_1 = \{(t_1^1, t_1^1), (t_1^2, t_1^2), (t_1^1, t_1^2), (t_1^2, t_1^1)\}$$
$$D_2 = \{(t_2^1, t_2^1), (t_2^2, t_2^2), (t_2^1, t_2^2), (t_2^2, t_2^1)\}$$
$$D_3 = \{(t_3^1, t_3^1), (t_3^2, t_3^2), (t_3^3, t_3^3), (t_3^4, t_3^4), (t_3^1, t_3^2), (t_3^1, t_3^3), (t_3^1, t_3^4), (t_3^2, t_3^3), (t_3^2, t_3^4),$$
$$(t_3^3, t_3^4), (t_3^2, t_3^1), (t_3^3, t_3^1), (t_3^4, t_3^1), (t_3^3, t_3^2), (t_3^4, t_3^2), (t_3^4, t_3^3)\}$$

- The dependency relation for synchronisation is as follows.

$$D_{syn} = \{(t_1^2, t_2^2), (t_2^2, t_1^2)\}$$

- The dependency relation for atomic propositions is as follows.

$$D_p = \{(t_1^2, t_3^4), (t_2^2, t_3^4), (t_3^4, t_1^2), (t_3^4, t_2^2)\}$$

– The dependency relation for the formula is defined as follows. For $K_3\, p$, we construct a new atomic proposition p' such that

$$E_{p'} = \bigvee_{l_3 \in L_3} (l_3 \wedge s2 \wedge w2 \wedge r5)$$

$$= (r1 \wedge s2 \wedge w2 \wedge r5) \vee (r2 \wedge s2 \wedge w2 \wedge r5) \vee (r3 \wedge s2 \wedge w2 \wedge r5) \vee$$
$$(r4 \wedge s2 \wedge w2 \wedge r5) \vee (r5 \wedge s2 \wedge w2 \wedge r5) \vee$$
$$= s2 \wedge w2 \wedge r5$$
$$= E_p.$$

Therefore, we have $D_\phi = D_p$.

By means of the technique discussed, to check the validity of the formula above we do not need to explore the full state space shown in Figure 4. Since p does not hold in the state $(s1, w2, r5)$ (nor in $(s1, w1, r5)$, $(s2, w1, r5)$, $(s3, w3, r5)$) and $(s1, w2, r5) \sim_3 (s2, w2, r5)$, $K_3\, p$ does not hold in the model.

After applying partial order reduction, we are able to check that $K_3\, p$ does not hold. Figure 5 illustrates the reduced state space, clearly showing the potential of this technique.

It is easy to see that any path in Figure 4 has a strongly equivalent path in Figure 5. For example, the path

$$(s1, w1, r1)(s1, w1, r2)(s2, w2, r3)(s2, w2, r4)(s2, w2, r5)(s3, w3, r5)$$

is equivalent to

$$(s1, w1, r1)(s1, w1, r2)(s1, w1, r3)(s1, w1, r4)(s1, w1, r5)(s2, w2, r5)(s3, w3, r5).$$

We can use similar considerations to check any LTLK_{-X} formulae effectively.

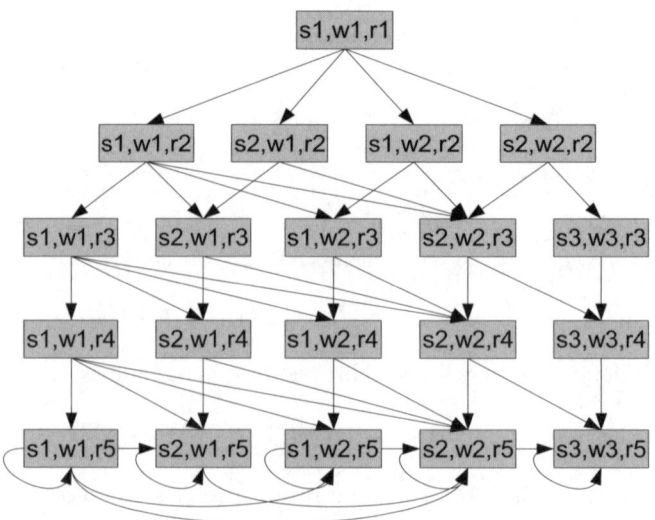

Fig. 4. The full state space

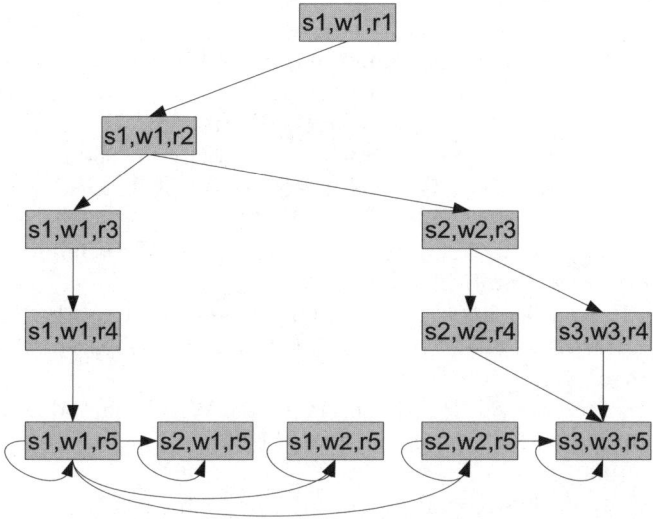

Fig. 5. The reduced state space

5 Conclusions

In this research note we have extended a partial order reduction technique to a basic logic for knowledge and linear time. Our main result concerns the preservation of satisfaction of LTLK$_{-X}$ formulae on equivalent paths on synchronous interpreted systems semantics.

The dependency relation we defined is quite general, as we do not impose any restrictions on the underlying models. While this makes it easier to design an algorithm ans test its effectiveness, we believe we can further enhance its effectiveness by exploring particular properties in the temporal epistemic logic.

We are currently investigating the feasibility of an algorithm to verify satisfiability on reduced traces and plan to test its implementation against known results for temporal epistemic specification available in the multi-agent systems literature.

Acknowledgements

The research described in this paper is partly supported by the European Commission Framework 6 funded project CONTRACT (IST Project Number 034418) and by the Polish Ministry of Science and Higher Education under grant 3T11C01128.

References

1. Dembinski, P., Janowska, A., Janowski, P., Penczek, W., Półrola, A., Szreter, M., Woźna, B.z., Zbrzezny, A.: VerICS: A tool for verifying Timed Automata and Estelle specifications. In: Garavel, H., Hatcliff, J. (eds.) TACAS 2003. LNCS, vol. 2619, pp. 278–283. Springer, Heidelberg (2003)
2. Diekert, V., Rozemberg, G. (eds.): The Book of Traces. World Scientific Publishing Co. Pte. Ltd., Singapore (1995)
3. Fagin, R., Halpern, J.Y., Moses, Y., Vardi, M.Y.: Reasoning about Knowledge. MIT Press, Cambridge (1995)
4. Gammie, P., van der Meyden, R.: MCK: Model checking the logic of knowledge. In: Alur, R., Peled, D.A. (eds.) CAV 2004. LNCS, vol. 3114, pp. 479–483. Springer, Heidelberg (2004)
5. Gerth, R., Kuiper, R., Peled, D., Penczek, W.: A partial order approach to branching time logic model checking. Information and Computation 150, 132–152 (1999)
6. Godefroid, P.: Using partial orders to improve automatic verification methods. In: Clarke, E.M., Kurshan, R.P. (eds.) CAV 1990. ACM/AMS DIMACS Series, vol. 3, pp. 321–340 (1991)
7. Halpern, J., van der Meyden, R., Vardi, M.Y.: Complete axiomatisations for reasoning about knowledge and time. SIAM Journal on Computing 33(3), 674–703 (2003)
8. Halpern, J., Moses, Y.: Knowledge and common knowledge in a distributed environment. Journal of the ACM 37(3), 549–587 (1984); A preliminary version appeared in Proc. 3rd ACM Symposium on Principles of Distributed Computing (1984)
9. Holzmann, G., Peled, D.: Partial order reduction of the state space. In: First SPIN Workshop, Montréal, Quebec (1995)
10. Kacprzak, M., Lomuscio, A., Penczek, W.: From bounded to unbounded model checking for temporal epistemic logic. Fundamenta Informaticae 63(2,3), 221–240 (2004)
11. Kurbán, M.E., Niebert, P., Qu, H., Vogler, W.: Stronger reduction criteria for local first search. In: Barkaoui, K., Cavalcanti, A., Cerone, A. (eds.) ICTAC 2006. LNCS, vol. 4281, pp. 108–122. Springer, Heidelberg (2006)
12. Lamport, L.: What good is temporal logic? In: IFIP Congress, pp. 657–668 (1983)
13. Lomuscio, A., Raimondi, F.: MCMAS: A model checker for multi-agent systems. In: Hermanns, H., Palsberg, J. (eds.) TACAS 2006. LNCS, vol. 3920, pp. 450–454. Springer, Heidelberg (2006)
14. Manna, Z., Pnueli, A.: The temporal logic of reactive and concurrent systems, vol. 1. Springer, Berlin (1992)
15. McMillan, K.L.: A technique of a state space search based on unfolding. Formal Methods in System Design 6(1), 45–65 (1995)
16. Parikh, R., Ramanujam, R.: Distributed processes and the logic of knowledge. In: Parikh, R. (ed.) Logic of Programs 1985. LNCS, vol. 193, pp. 256–268. Springer, Heidelberg (1985)

17. Peled, D.: All from one, one for all: On model checking using representatives. In: Courcoubetis, C. (ed.) CAV 1993. LNCS, vol. 697, pp. 409–423. Springer, Heidelberg (1993)
18. Penczek, W., Lomuscio, A.: Verifying epistemic properties of multi-agent systems via bounded model checking. Fundamenta Informaticae 55(2), 167–185 (2003)
19. Penczek, W., Szreter, M., Gerth, R., Kuiper, R.: Improving partial order reductions for universal branching time properties. Fundamenta Informaticae 43, 245–267 (2000)
20. Raimondi, F., Lomuscio, A.: Automatic verification of multi-agent systems by model checking via OBDDs. Journal of Applied Logic (2007) (to appear in Special issue on Logic-based agent verification)
21. Rosenschein, S.J.: Formal theories of ai in knowledge and robotics. New Generation Computing 3, 345–357 (1985)
22. Valmari, A.: A stubborn attack on state explosion. In: Clarke, E., Kurshan, R.P. (eds.) CAV 1990. LNCS, vol. 531, pp. 156–165. Springer, Heidelberg (1991)

Model Checking Driven Heuristic Search for Correct Programs

Gal Katz and Doron Peled

Bar Ilan University,
Ramat Gan 52900, Israel

Abstract. Genetic programming and model checking were combined recently to generate correct-by-construction programs. Unlike other synthesis methods, this approach is based on a search in the state space of syntactically-restricted programs. This search can be seen as a probabilistic and heuristic search. In this paper we discuss the connection between program synthesis and heuristic search.

1 Introduction

Formal methods suggest various techniques to enhance the reliability of software, including the automatic verification of finite state programs, called model checking [3,9]. Model checking compares a given system with formal specification, written in some formalism, e.g., linear temporal logic [13]. It is of course tempting to try to convert the specification directly into a working code. In this way, one should obtain code that is "correct by construction". There are several obstacles for the automatic generation of code:

- In order to synthesize code from specification, the specification needs to be *complete*, i.e., include all possible requirements from the code. This is usually difficult to achieve. To begin with, providing formal specification is hard enough. Specification for model checking is usually incomplete, and usually only *some* aspects of the software are checked.
- The complexity of synthesizing correct code can be very high or, even undecidable [14,15] (depending on the architecture). Practically, most of the work on synthesis is devoted to either generating synchronized systems [10,14,1], or to imposing controlled (and centralized) restrictions on existing systems, such that they will satisfy further requirements [16].
- Automatically synthesizing a program from specification assumes also that one can first synthesize some abstract machine, usually a collection of finite state automata, and then transfer them into a program in some programming language. This does not take into account various restrictions and typical behavior of programming constructs and physical systems. Such restrictions can include timing constraints (which may be transformed sometimes into fairness constraints, in the sense that one process does not wait indefinitely to another independent process). Another restriction can be related to the

D. Peled and M. Wooldridge (Eds.): MOCHART 2008, LNAI 5348, pp. 122–131, 2009.
© Springer-Verlag Berlin Heidelberg 2009

granularity of atomicity, taking into account the capabilities of doing some collection of testing and setting variable values, without the possibility of intermediate results.

A common way of looking for a solution for a problem in a discrete system is performing a *search*, typically Depth First Search or Breadth First Search. A search makes sense when there is a relation between elements, usually a graph, were immediately related elements are connected by edges. One reason for performing a search is the ability to systematically cover the possible candidates for a solution. A search can use a hash table, a stack, or some other structure, to maintain that elements that were already found are not repeated, e.g., in a non-progressing search cycle. When the search space is huge, it may be pointless to make just a systematic search. An exhaustive search in the space of syntactically restricted programs for mutual exclusion programs was reported in [2], and for a security protocol was reported in [17].

Heuristic search is employed in order to attempt to direct the search quickly in the direction of the correct solution. Directing the search is done by providing some weight for each node that is reached during the search and using a search strategy and some priority-based selection process in order to choose directions that seem to be most promising on the way to the search goal. For example, the A* search [12] assigns an estimated cost to reach the goal from the current state and a cost to reach the current state. It selects the successor node, from which the search will continue, as the one which minimizes the sum of these two values. The intuition behind this search is that if the estimate was accurate, it would indicate in which direction (i.e., edge from some node at the current boundary of the search) one will find the shortest path to the goal.

To some extent, genetic programming [7] can be seen as a heuristic search. Each node is provided with a *fitness* value. A selection of candidate programs is chosen (randomly or based on fitness), some mutations of these candidates are generated, sometimes even a combination of candidates (in an operation that combines existing candidate programs, called *crossover*), and then the fitness of the newly generated candidates can be used to select those that replace the old candidates.

The main challenge is then to design a fitness function for candidate programs generated during the GP search that provides a good prediction on progress. That is, candidates with high fitness value have at least a qualitative, if not quantitative, high expectation to develop, through the mutation operations, into an appropriate solution. There should also be a correlation between the mutation (and crossover) operation and the fitness function: applying a mutation operation on a candidate with high fitness should have a reasonably high probability of generating a new candidate with a high fitness value. If this is not the case, the genetic search, is not more meaningful than generating random candidates and checking them.

The fitness function that we use in [4,5] to automatically generate solutions for the mutual exclusion problem is based on the result of applying model checking on the candidate programs, with respect to a fixed set of properties. In a previous attempt, Johnson [8] suggested basing the fitness function on model checking, such that one ascribes a value related to the number of properties that hold in a candidate program. This approach turned out to produce too coarse fitness scheme. We deviated from straightforward model checking by providing contributing fitness value even if a property was not *completely* satisfied by a program. This was based on a deeper decision procedure, that checks situations where e.g., some *bad* executions were not satisfying the specification, but from every point they could be extended by the program into *good* executions, satisfying the specification. A logic that allows providing various relaxed criteria for satisfying a linear temporal property was introduced in [11].

1.1 Preliminaries

1.2 Genetic Programming

Genetic programming [7] is a branch of Genetic algorithms that attempts to develop programs by means of evolution principles. The genetic search involves generations of candidate programs. Iteratively, one selects some portion of the currently available candidate programs, applies some mutation operations that produces new candidates. Then, some mutations, selected based on fitness values, are returned to the list of candidate programs, replacing some existing candidates. The initial generation of candidates, the selection of candidates for applying the mutation operations to candidates, or crossover operations, that combine and mutate several candidates, and the selection of the kind of mutation to perform, all employ probabilistic decision process.

One can describe the basic search loop as follows:

Initialization. Create a set of N initial candidates S at random.

Pre-mutation selection. Select some portion $f(S)$ of S for mutation and crossover operation.

Applying mutating operations. Apply transforming operations to the elements in $f(S)$ to obtain the elements $g(f(S))$. Note that it is not compulsory that $|g(f(S))| = |f(S)|$.

Evolution through fitness. The fitness value for the elements $g(f(S))$ is calculated.

Obtaining next generation. Using the fitness values, the N elements for the next generation are selected, out of the elements $S \cup g(f(S))$, forming the new set S of candidates. Note that this does not mean necessarily that the N elements have the best fitness values; alternatively, we may select the best candidates out of $f(s) \cup g(f(S))$, leaving the elements $S \setminus f(S))$ intact for the next generation.

Repeat. If no perfect solution was found, and the predefined limit on the number of iterations was not exceeded, we return to the *Pre-mutation selection* stage.

One applies a random choice in the choices made in the stages of *Initialization*, *Pre-mutation selection* and *Applying mutation operation*.

Each candidate program is represented using its syntactic tree. The syntax of the programming language used strictly dictates the type of subtrees that each node can have. For example, a while node, representing a while loop in the code, will have a left subtree that corresponds to the while condition, and a right subtree that corresponds to the loop body. The mutation operations can be the following:

Replacement. Replacing some subtree in the tree representing the candidate program with another randomly generated subtree.

Insertion. Add an immediate parent to some node in the subtree. Create additional offsprings needed by the type of node added.

Reduction. Replace a selected node by one of its offspring, when the types of the replacing node is the same as the original.

Deletion. Delete some subtree. Update the ancestors recursively in an appropriate manner.

1.3   Model Checking

Model Checking [3,9] is a method for automatically checking the correctness of finite state systems. The system (here, a program) is translated into an automaton, and some graph algorithms are applied to it. Specification is given using a formalism called Temporal Logic. In essence, there are two main dichotomies for temporal logics used in verification: linear time [13], which asserts about the valid execution sequences, and branching time [3], which asserts also about the availability of choices from various given points. For our purposes, it is usually possible to use linear time temporal logic. However, in some cases, an adaptation that corresponds to branching time logics is needed.

An *execution* is a sequence accepted by the automaton representing the system $\mathcal{A}$. The set of executions of $\mathcal{A}$, i.e., the *language* of the automaton representing the system is denoted $L(\mathcal{A})$. For linear temporal logic, we look at the set of sequences satisfying a property φ, i.e., the *language* of φ, denoted $L(\varphi)$. Then, the correctness criterion is that $L(\mathcal{A}) \subseteq L(\varphi)$.

There is often more than a single temporal property that needs to hold in the generated program (albeit one can conjoin all such properties), related to different requirements and aspects of the systems. Some properties, e.g., represent the "safety" of the code (in mutual exclusion, that only one process can enter a critical section at the same time), and other are "liveness" properties (in mutual exclusion, that when a process wants to enter a critical section, it will eventually be able to do so). One can sometimes define a hierarchy between such properties, e.g., making the safety properties more basic than the liveness properties (in the sense that a solution that satisfies only the safety properties is more accepted than a solution that satisfies the liveness but not the safety properties).

A genetic programming search based on model checking, where the fitness is calculated directly by counting the number of temporal properties that hold for a candidate program was reported in [8]. In [4,5], we used a more refined fitness measures (which were formalized in a logic called $EmCTL^*$, described in [11]). Under this approach, we sometimes provide positive fitness measure for properties that do not fully satisfy the above correctness criteria, but rather a *relaxed* criterion. For example, we may still provide some fitness value when part of the executions are "good", i.e., when $L(\mathcal{A}) \cap L(\varphi) \neq \emptyset$. An even higher fitness value will be given when infinite "bad" executions must require infinitely many choices to avoid becoming "good" executions. In other words, each infinite sequence in $L(\mathcal{A}) \setminus L(\varphi)$ satisfies that each of its finite prefixes can be extended into a "good" execution.

The fitness calculated in [4,5] takes into account both the various relaxed correctness criteria described above, and a hierarchy between the temporal properties, which gives different weights to the various specification properties.

2   Why Does It Work?

In this section, we will try to justify the reasons that one can expect a genetic search, as performed in [4,5] to find correct programs, and explain what makes this approach different than others. The kind of search we adopt is influenced by the fact that the search space is enormous (or even infinite). We look at several parameters.

Genetic search differs from other common ways of attempting to obtain correct programs for a given task automatically. It is not based on learning the desired task as in machine learning [6]. It does not make deductions from a collected database or knowledge base. There is no refinement from the abstract into the concrete implementation. Koza [7] argues that the kind of search performed in genetic programming resembles the process of inventions, which appears somewhat instantaneous, and then is refined, by checking related variants. Another related approach is that of simulated annealing [18], which takes its metaphoric description from physics: one produces some "heating" around existing candidate solutions, in order to perform variants, and a "controlled cooling", when it seems that a solution is within reach. Accordingly, the genetic programming process also selects some instances of candidate solutions, performs some limited amount of changes ("heating") and attempts to control the variables ("controlled cooling") by using fitness metrics.

Randomization

The genetic search is probabilistic. It starts with some random instances, and, progress is partially random. The relevant observation is that in searching for a correct program there is no known "correct" or "preferred" initial state. An important situation that one wants to avoid is "hill climbing". In this situation, one progresses in the search towards a deceptively promising local optimum, which does not provide a path to the actual goal. The GP search is not strictly greedy, and not only the most promising candidate programs are selected for future rounds of the search. Also, the initial random selection of programs also allows us to jump directly into several distinct points in the search graph. In addition, if the search does not progress after some predefined amount of time, or number of generations, we start from scratch, with new random instances.

No Need for Saving Programs

There is no mechanism in our genetic search for saving elements that were already discovered. This task is typically performed using a hash table. We do not use a hash table here. This is because the search space of programs is infinite, and even when restricted to some size, it is still huge. Only a small portion of the possible candidates are covered before we abandon the current attempt and start from scratch. Due to the nature of the genetic mutation operator, it is quite possible that the same candidate is regenerated again and again. In fact, a loop of size two is quite plausible, using two complementary mutations. Even if such loops may exist, the random choice provides ample chance of getting rid of such loops.

Correlation between Fitness and Successors

There is no apriory relation between different versions of programs. An edge between two nodes in the graph of programs, corresponds to the application of a particular mutation operation. A multi-edge (edge between more than two nodes) from a pair (or more) nodes to another node, corresponds to the crossover operation. If the search could be comprehensive we would just need to wait until a solution, if exists, will be found. This is obviously not the case here, where the state space is enormous.

This makes it extremely important to have a correlation between fitness and programs that are obtained from one other by mutation or crossover. That is, if some candidate programs are ranked higher than most others, the search will have a good chance of success if there is a nontrivial probability that, by applying a sequence of mutation and crossover operations, the search will progress through a sequence of well fitted candidates, into a program that satisfies all of the specification properties. In particular, we conjecture the following relation on pairs of programs that are related through the mutation operations:

> There is a significant probability that by transforming a program with a high fitness value using the mutation and crossover operations (once or a small number of times), we obtain another program with a high fitness value.

This works since the process, in some sense, mimics program debugging, where some of the changes are local, and have a limited affect on the behavior of the program. Tsay [19] explains how some of the mutual exclusion algorithms are discovered. His description of the mental process of discovering new algorithms resembles, to some extent, the genetic mutation approach. Some of the changes include switching the order of some assignments, combining parts that take care of complimentary goals from different algorithms and adding tests or assignments to shared variables. It is quite a challenging task to obtain correct code for such an intricate problem as mutual exclusion, especially when practical constraints such as limitations on the access of certain variables are added. We claim that for obtaining optimized algorithms, it becomes more practical to use an automatic programming process, as our GP with model checking approach, than to attempt to discover such an algorithm manually.

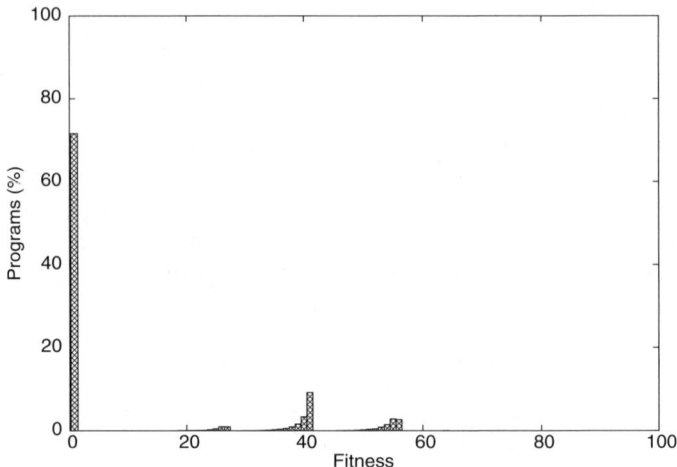

Fig. 1. Fitness distribution of random programs

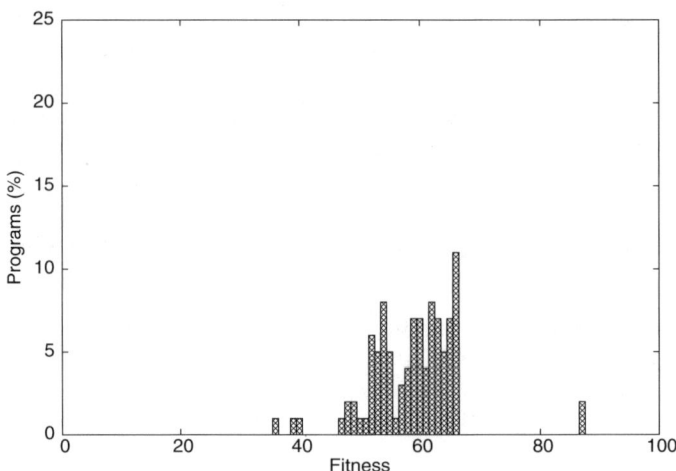

Fig. 2. Fitness distribution during round 500 of a GP run

Fitness That Is Based on Trial and Error

Our fitness function is not fixed. That is, not only that the specification is changed from one programming problem to another, but the fine-tuning of the actual function is done separately for each programming problem.

It is quite natural that for different applications we will need to make many changes in order to provide a fitness value that gives a good heuristics for the

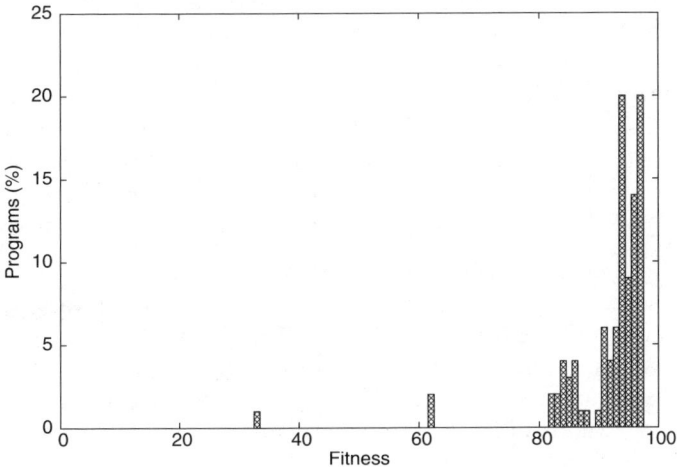

Fig. 3. Fitness distribution during the last round of a GP run

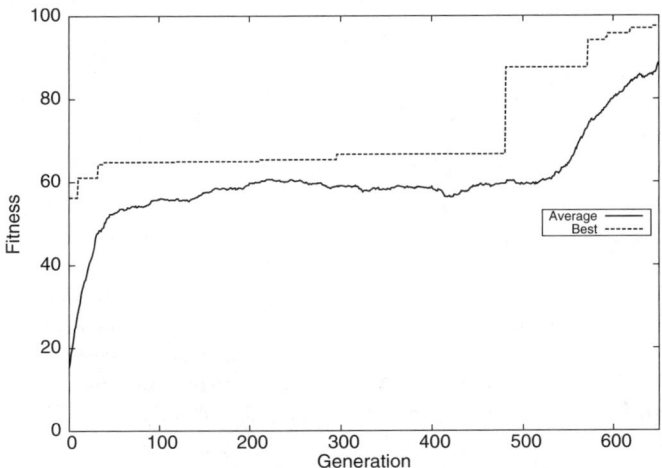

Fig. 4. Fitness distribution of random programs

search. In fact, it is mostly a trial-and-error process, where the fitness function is refined. There are several factors in evaluating the fitness function:

- The properties used for the specification are given.
- Unlike [8], we may assign *different weights* to the properties.
- We may choose some priority order among the specification properties. If a higher priority property (say a safety property) does not hold, there is no point or value in checking the candidate solution further (say for satisfying liveness properties).

– Sometimes it is beneficial to use some additional properties even if they are implied by existing ones. For example, in mutual exclusion, there is a requirement that each process that wants to enter its critical section will succeed to do so. We used also a weaker property: that a process that wants to enter its critical section while the other does not attempt to do so will be able to enter. Obviously, the first property implies the second, weaker one. However, adding the second property, and giving it a higher priority than the first one did help the search to converge into correct solutions.

The following figures compare the performance of a GP run with this of a simple random search. Figure 1 shows the distribution of fitness values of 1,000,000 randomly generated programs. More than 70% of the programs do not satisfy even the most basic property, and thus receive a fitness value of 0. Other programs succeeded in satisfying one or more properties, and received higher fitness values. However, none of the programs was able to satisfy enough properties in order to get a significant fitness value.

In a typical GP run, the population usually contain a few hundreds or thousands of program. Therefore, the chances that the first generation will contain "good" programs, is very low. However, after some generations, the combination of the genetic operations, and the selection mechanism, usually improves the average fitness of the population, and the fitness values are gradually shifted towards the right side of the distribution graph. Figure 2 shows the fitness distribution at the 500th generation of a successful GP run, while Figure 3 shows the fitness distribution at the last generation.

Figure 4 shows the best and average fitness values throughout the entire run.

References

1. Abadi, M., Lamport, L., Wolper, P.: Realizable and unrealizable specifications of reactive systems. In: Ronchi Della Rocca, S., Ausiello, G., Dezani-Ciancaglini, M. (eds.) ICALP 1989. LNCS, vol. 372, pp. 1–17. Springer, Heidelberg (1989)
2. Bar-David, Y., Taubenfeld, G.: Automatic discovery of mutual exclusion algorithms. In: Fich, F.E. (ed.) DISC 2003. LNCS, vol. 2848, pp. 136–150. Springer, Heidelberg (2003)
3. Emerson, E.A., Clarke, E.M.: Characterizing correctness properties of parallel programs using fixpoints. In: de Bakker, J.W., van Leeuwen, J. (eds.) ICALP 1980. LNCS, vol. 85, pp. 169–181. Springer, Heidelberg (1980)
4. Katz, G., Peled, D.: Model checking-based genetic programming with an application to mutual exclusion. In: Ramakrishnan, C.R., Rehof, J. (eds.) TACAS 2008. LNCS, vol. 4963, pp. 141–156. Springer, Heidelberg (2008)
5. Katz, G., Peled, D.: Genetic programming and model checking: Synthesizing new mutual exclusion algorithms. In: Cha, S(S.), Choi, J.-Y., Kim, M., Lee, I., Viswanathan, M. (eds.) ATVA 2008. LNCS, vol. 5311, pp. 33–47. Springer, Heidelberg (2008)
6. Kearns, M., Vazirani, U.: An Introduction to Computational Learning Theory. MIT Press, Cambridge (1994)
7. Koza, J.R.: Genetic Programming: On the Programming of Computers by Means of Natural Selection. MIT Press, Cambridge (1992)

8. Johnson, C.G.: Genetic programming with fitness based on model checking. In: Ebner, M., O'Neill, M., Ekárt, A., Vanneschi, L., Esparcia-Alcázar, A.I. (eds.) EuroGP 2007. LNCS, vol. 4445, pp. 114–124. Springer, Heidelberg (2007)
9. Quielle, J.P., Sifakis, J.: Specification and verification of concurrent systems in CE-SAR. In: Dezani-Ciancaglini, M., Montanari, U. (eds.) Programming 1982. LNCS, vol. 137, pp. 337–350. Springer, Heidelberg (1982)
10. Manna, Z., Wolper, P.: Synthesis of communicating processes from temporal logic specifications. ACM Transactions on Programming Languages and Systems 6, 68–93 (1984)
11. Niebert, P., Peled, D., Pnueli, A.: Discriminative model checking. In: Gupta, A., Malik, S. (eds.) CAV 2008. LNCS, vol. 5123, pp. 504–516. Springer, Heidelberg (2008)
12. Pearl, J.: Heuristics. Addison-Wesley, Reading (1984)
13. Pnueli, A.: The temporal logic of programs. In: FOCS 1977, Providence, Rhode Island, pp. 46–57. IEEE, Los Alamitos (1977)
14. Pnueli, A., Rosner, R.: On the synthesis of reactive systems. In: POPL 1989, Austin, Texas, pp. 179–190 (1989)
15. Pnueli, A., Rosner, R.: Distributed Reactive Systems are Hard to Synthesize. In: FOCS 1990, St. Louis, Missouri, vol. II. IEEE, Los Alamitos (1990)
16. Rammage, P., Wonham, M.: The control of discrete event systems. Proceedings of the IEEE 77, 81–98 (1989)
17. Song, D.X., Perrig, A., Phan, D.: Agvi – automatic generation, verification, and implementation of security protocols. In: Berry, G., Comon, H., Finkel, A. (eds.) CAV 2001. LNCS, vol. 2102, pp. 241–245. Springer, Heidelberg (2001)
18. Kirkpatrick, S., G. Jr., D., Vecchi, M.P.: Optimization by simulated annealing. Science 220(4598), 671–680 (1983)
19. Tsay, Y.K.: Deriving a scalable algorithm for mutual exclusion. In: Kutten, S. (ed.) DISC 1998. LNCS, vol. 1499, pp. 393–407. Springer, Heidelberg (1998)

Experimental Evaluation of a Planning Language Suitable for Formal Verification*

Radu I. Siminiceanu[1], Rick W. Butler[2], and César A. Muñoz[1]

[1] National Institute of Aerospace, Hampton, Virginia, USA
[2] NASA Langley Research Center, Hampton, Virginia, USA

Abstract. The marriage of model checking and planning faces two seemingly diverging alternatives: the need for a planning language expressive enough to capture the complexity of real-life applications, as opposed to a language simple, yet robust enough to be amenable to exhaustive verification and validation techniques. In an attempt to reconcile these differences, we have designed an abstract plan description language, ANMLite, inspired from the Action Notation Modeling Language (ANML). We present the basic concepts of the ANMLite language as well as an automatic translator from ANMLite to the model checker SAL (Symbolic Analysis Laboratory). We discuss various aspects of specifying a plan in terms of constraints and explore the implications of choosing a robust logic behind the specification of constraints, rather than simply propose a new planning language. Additionally, we provide an initial assessment of the efficiency of model checking to search for solutions of planning problems. To this end, we design a basic test benchmark and study the scalability of the generated SAL models in terms of plan complexity.

1 Introduction

Historically, the fields of planning and formal verification have had very little interaction. As branches of Artificial Intelligence, planning and scheduling have mainly focused on developing powerful search heuristics for efficiently finding solutions to extremely complex, specialized problems that take into account intricate domain specific information. Traditionally, this field and has been heavily influenced by the goals of one of the major sponsoring agencies (NASA, Ames Center) and its affiliated institutes (RIACS, JPL). The planning software produced is in a perpetual process of expansion to include the latest and fanciest capabilities: re-planning, on-the-fly reconfiguration, resource allocation, etc.

These goals are often contrasting with the main purpose of our field of formal verification. To make the planning software ready for space missions and pass the certification process, the main thrust of our activities are in a completely opposite direction: simplify, reduce complexity, understand the concepts, make software amenable to exhaustive verification.

---

* Research funding was provided by the National Aeronautics and Space Administration under the cooperative agreement NCC-1-02043.

D. Peled and M. Wooldridge (Eds.): MOCHART 2008, LNAI 5348, pp. 132–146, 2009.

To this end, we seek to define a simple language that can be used to describe planning problems. Hopefully, by drastically restricting the constructs in the language, two benefits accrue: (1) the language will be easy to understand and write, and (2) the language will lend itself to formal verification.

We have named the language ANMLite [4] because it was developed to support the analysis of planning domains described in the Action Notation Modeling Language (ANML) [20] under development at NASA Ames[12]. ANML succeeds other planning languages, such as PDDL [15] and NDDL, that have been used in the software package EUROPA2 [2].

In ANMLite, a planning problem consists of a finite set of disjoint timelines, a set of valid actions for each timeline, and a set of temporal constraints that govern the correct scheduling of the actions. The constraints can be broadly categorized into two groups. The first group is specified by a *transition relation* and only involves actions on the same timeline. These constraints express the valid succession of actions along the timeline. The transition relation disallows overlapping actions and gaps on a timeline. The second category are general constraints, expressed in some logic of choice, which specify cross-timeline relationships between actions. The temporal logic must be chosen with care. It has to be rich enough to cover all the significant relations that can occur (such as Allen temporal operators [1], a popular logic in planning), but simple enough to avoid inconsistencies and ambiguities. Furthermore, since we seek to develop a framework for formal verification, it must be translatable into a form suitable for model checking or theorem proving. We are currently targeting the SAL model checker [7].

SAL is a framework for combining different tools to calculate properties of concurrent systems. The SAL language is designed for specifying concurrent systems in a compositional way. It is supported by a tool suite that includes state of the art symbolic (BDD-based) and bounded (SAT-based) model checkers, and a unique "infinite" bounded model checker based on SMT solving. Auxiliary tools include a simulator, deadlock checker, and an automated test case generator.

2 Related Work

The idea of using symbolic model checking techniques for planning problems is relatively recent. A seminal line of work was initiated by Cimatti et al [5], which generated a series of articles applied to a variety of planning domains. In [9], Edelkamp applies symbolic model checking techniques for finding a sequence of actions that always has a possibility to lead to a goal state in non-deterministic domains. SPUDD [13] introduces the use algebraic decision diagrams for stochastic planning. More recently, approaches applying SAT based techniques to planning in non-deterministic domains under null and partial observability have been proposed [11]. Model checking has been applied in the context of logics with actions [17] and knowledge representation [14]. The symbolic model checker of choice in this case is NuSMV.

The avenue of using constraint solvers for planning problems has been explored in [19], based on temporal interval logic and attributes, and [18], by solving a particular class of disjunctive temporal problems via SAT techniques.

Test case generation for planning has been attempted in [10]. While testing is not an exhaustive verification technique, it is always seen as complementary and is mostly motivated by the need of low cost and performance. Finally, runtime monitoring, a lightweight version of verification, has been applied to the fault protection engine of the Deep-Impact spacecraft flight software [8].

3   ANMLite Language Concepts

We briefly describe the basic ANMLite concepts. For further information, an extensive discussion of the ANMLite language syntax and semantics is given in the NASA Technical Memorandum [4].

3.1   Timelines and Actions

Discovering a suitable sequence of actions on a timeline is fundamental to solving a planning problem. The first step in defining the problem is to identify all the actions that can be scheduled on a timeline. In ANMLite, this is declared as in the following example:

```
TIMELINE A ACTIONS
    A0
    A1:  [_,10]
    A2:  [2,_]
```

This specification defines the timeline A and its three actions: A0, A1, and A2. Actions A1 and A2 have time duration constraints: A1 takes at most 10 time units and A2 takes at least 2 time units. Usually, there are also constraints on the sequence of actions, so an intuitive, unambiguous specification of these constraints is highly desirable. There are two different approaches to the specification of these constraints:

- Assume that all action sequences are possible unless specifically forbidden and then specify the sequences that are *not* allowed.
- Assume that no sequences are allowed and then systematically add the allowed sequences.

We have currently opted for the second approach. This is different from many AI planning systems, but it follows the approach frequently used in the formal methods community. We currently believe that this leads to a clearer specification, though we recognize that we may be biased by the historic conventions of our discipline.

3.2   Transitions

The transition relation on a timeline is similar to state-transition systems. Here, the states are the actions and a directed edge represents a valid transition between states. We have used the same construction deployed in the Abstract Plan Preparation Language (APPL) [3]. Hence, the transition relation is a set of pairs of actions, which can be declared by listing for each action the (complete) set of its successors, as in the following example:

```
TRANSITIONS
    A0 -> A1 -> A2 -> (A0 | A1 | A3)
    A3 -> A2
```

The flexibility of the language is increased by allowing parametrization of actions. For example, the following

```
A1(x,y: animal): [10,_]
```

defines an action `A1` with two parameters of type `animal` that takes at least 10 units of time.

We allow more restrictive forms of transitions to be defined using a simple parameter matching scheme, with implicitly declared variables. For example,

```
A1(cat,u) -> A2(u,_)
```

states that only `A1` actions with a first parameter equal to `cat` are to be followed by an `A2` action and that the first parameter of `A2`, represented by the variable u, must be equal to the second parameter of `A1`. Unless explicitly specified on a different constraint, no other transition from `A1` is allowed.

Multiple timeline instances are defined using a `VARIABLE` section:

```
VARIABLES
    t1, t2: A
    t3: B
```

This specification declares two distinct instances, `t1` and `t2`, defined by `TIMELINE A`, and one instance `t3` defined by `TIMELINE B`.

The variables of the same `TIMELINE` share the transition relation, but might still behave differently, in case specific constraints are declared in the general constraint section. This is beneficial in terms of keeping the model compact, and it is frequently seen in practice.

3.3   Goal Statements and Initialization

In ANMLite, goals can be specified by an action name. Initial states can also be specified using an `INITIAL-STATE` declaration though they are not necessary.

```
INITIAL-STATE
|-> t1.A0
|-> t2.A1
```

This specifies that A0 is the first scheduled action on timeline t1 and that A1 is the first scheduled action on timeline t2. A generic form is also allowed

```
INITIAL-STATE
|-> A.A0
```

This means that on *every* timeline of type A, A0 is the first scheduled action.

4   Constraints

The transition statements are adequate to specify the allowed sequences of actions on a timeline, but they cannot be used to specify constraints between actions on different timelines. The constraint section is used to accomplish this. The ANMLite constraints are built upon a simple but powerful foundation: linear inequations between the start and end timepoints of actions. Expressions may contain at most one variable on each side of the relational operator, e.g.

```
A1.start + 16 < B2.end
```

Restricting the constraint language to these simple linear relationships enables a very natural translation into the SAL model checking language (see Sec. 5).

4.1   Repetitive Actions

It is often the case that the same action is scheduled several times on a timeline. For example, crew activities on a space station are mostly routine tasks repeated every day, intertwined with other specific activities. Two occurrences of the same action are distinct because they are scheduled at different time intervals. There is a clear need to distinguish between these intervals when writing a set of constraints, which can refer to all or just one of these instances. We consider two approaches: (1) provide a new construct to establish a reference point for a constraint (called the **at** expression) and (2) introduce the qualifier **next** for a second occurrence of an action in the same constraint.

Neither of these two constructs were previously considered in planning languages, yet there is an obvious risk of ambiguities in their absence.

The at Expression. In the following example

```
at A0.start:  B0.end < next A0.start
```

all actions that are active at the timepoint A0.start are the current ones. The next instance after the completion of the current one is the **next** one. For example

If the action is not active at the reference point, then the "current" is the last completed one and the next is the first occurrence after the reference point.

	A0	A1	A0	A2	
B1	B0	B1	B0	B1

↑ B1.start   ↑   ↑ next B1.start

↑ reference point

It should also be noted that there is an implicit universal quantifier in every constraint. If the reference point involves action **A1** and **A1** can occur multiple times on a timeline, then this constraint applies every time **A1** is scheduled.

4.2 Timeline Instance Specific Constraints

Constraints can be specialized by using a timeline variable in the constraint. Suppose we have

```
VARIABLES
    t1,t2: A
    t3,t4: B
```

```
CONSTRAINTS
    t1.A1.start < t4.B1.end
```

This constraint only affects timelines **t1** and **t4**. But the constraint

```
    A1.start < B1.end
```

is equivalent to four constraints:

```
    t1.A1.start < t3.B1.end      t1.A1.start < t4.B1.end
    t2.A1.start < t3.B1.end      t2.A1.start < t4.B1.end
```

4.3 Vacuous Solutions

Consider the Allen logic operator **A1 contains B1**. A constantly debated issue is whether the constraint can be satisfied by the following timeline

A0	A2		
B0	B1	B2

Because the Allen operator has the implicit quantifiers **FORALL A1: EXISTS B1: A1 contains B1**, this constraint can be vacuously met in case **A1** is never scheduled. Whether this is desirable or not is a recurring theme in the plan specification domain. A non-ambiguous semantics should be chosen for all these situations.

4.4 Summary of Constraint Semantics

There are two major issues that need to be resolved when interpreting a constraint in ANMLite:

- Determination of the time point from which the current and next instances of an action can be disambiguated.
- Determination of which actions are universally quantified and which ones are existentially quantified.

These issues are orthogonal and hence the most general solution allows an independent specification of them. The first issue is handled by the at expression. The second issue is handled by a syntactic convention, namely, that the last term in the chain of inequalities determines the universally quantified action. This choice is justified by the way the constraint checking has to performed (efficiently) in the SAL models. The other alternative, of attaching the universal quantifier to the first term, is equally valid from the theoretical point of view.

5 Translating ANMLite to SAL

Although using a model checker might not be the most efficient means of finding a solution to a planning problem, building a translator has provided a sanity check on the meaning of the language constructs.

5.1 Simple Example

We will begin our look at the technique for translating ANMLite to SAL with a very simple two timeline example:

```
PLAN ex1
TIMELINE A                      TIMELINE B
ACTIONS                         ACTIONS
    A0: [2,_]                       B0: [2,_]
    A1                              B1: [1,10]
    A2
TRANSITIONS                     TRANSITIONS
    A0 -> A1 -> A2                  B0 -> B1
END A                           END B

INITIAL-STATE                   GOALS
|-> A.A0                            A.A2
|-> B.B0                            B.B1
END ex1
```

Corresponding to the timeline and action declarations, the following types are generated:

```
  A_actions: TYPE = {A0, A1, A2, A_null};
  B_actions: TYPE = {B0, B1, B_null};
```

In addition to the declared actions, a null state is created for each of the timelines. There are two purposes for these extra states. They provide a means for the completion of an action when the action has no successor and also a convenient mechanism for recording when a goal state has been reached and completed on each timeline.

The generated SAL model consists of three modules: module A_m, corresponding to timeline A. module B_m to timeline B, and module Clock, which advances time.

5.2   Multiple Variables

If there are multiple variables of a timeline, say

```
VARIABLES
    t1,t2: A
```

then a variable identifier type is generated,

```
A_ids: TYPE = {t1,t2};
```

and the module A_m is parametrized with the variable id

```
A_m[i: A_ids]   : MODULE =
```

Furthermore, since each instance of the timeline is a separate module, all the local and global variables in the parametrized module have to be arrays. For example, a non-parametrized module A_m might include a variable for A0_start:

```
GLOBAL
    A0_start: TM_rng;
```

The parametrized version has to be

```
GLOBAL
    A0_start: ARRAY A_ids OF TM_rng;
```

This way, the start of A0 for instance t1 is referred to as A0_start[t1].

5.3   Modeling Time

Time is governed by the generic clock module. We have experimented with various implementations of this module. The most straightforward approach is to have the clock module increment the current time by one time unit at each step. This approach is very simple but is not scalable, because the system would traverse a very large number of states that are identical with the exception of the clock value. This state explosion problem is exacerbated by problems with large planning horizons. A possible alleviation of problem is to allow the clock to advance by larger amounts. However, this still does not rule out the traversal of multiple states in an interval of time when nothing interesting happens (from the point of view of action change). The best solution in this case is to use the concept of timeouts [16] that model the *event driven* clocks. In this approach, each timeline maintains a future clock value where an event is scheduled to occur, and time jumps directly to the next interesting event. The timeouts are stored in an array of timepoints and the clock module determines the next (minimum value in the future) timeout.

The modules are composed asynchronously.

```
System: MODULE = A_m [] B_m [] Clock;
```

The SAL model checker will be used to search through all possible sequences of actions on the timelines to find sequences which satisfy all of the constraints specified in the ANMLite model. These constraints fall into two broad categories:

- Timing constraints that impact durations and start/stop times of actions.
- Simple relationships between `start` and `end` variables.

The search is started at time 0 and proceeds forward in time until the planning horizon `TM_rng` is reached.

5.4   Model Variables

The `GLOBAL` sections of all of the timeline modules contain variables which record the action that is scheduled during the current time:

```
GLOBAL
    A0_start: TM_rng,
    B0_start: TM_rng,
    B1_start: TM_rng,
    B_state: B_actions,
    A_state: A_actions,
```

The `_state` variables store the current action and the `_start` and `_end` variables record the start and end times of the actions.

5.5   Transitions

The ANMLite `TRANSITIONS` section is the major focus of the translation process. The SAL `TRANSITIONS` section is constructed from this part of the ANMLite model. When a transition occurs, an action is completed and another transition is initiated. No empty time slots are allowed. For example, the following

```
TRANSITIONS
    A0 -> A1 -> A2
```

is translated into three SAL transitions, which are labeled as follows:

```
A0_to_A1:      %% A0 -> A1
A1_to_A2:      %% A1 -> A2
A2_to_A_null:  %% A2 -> A_null
```

The first transition is guarded by the following expression:

```
A_state = A0
AND time >= A0_start + 2
```

The first conjunct ensures that this transition only applies when the current action on the timeline is A0 and the second conjunct insures that the duration of the action is at least 2 time units. This corresponds to the fact that A0 was declared as A0: [2,_].

The GOALS statement is translated into the following SAL specification:

```
sched_sys: THEOREM
    System |- AG(NOT(A_state = A_null AND B_state = B_null));
```

Since the "null" states can only be reached from the goal states (i.e., A2 and B1), these efficiently record the fact that the appropriate goal has been reached and completed on each timeline. Note that the ANMLite goal statement has been negated. Therefore when the model checker is instructed to establish the property, any counterexample provided by SAL will serve as a feasible realization of the plan.

5.6 Translating Constraints

There are major conceptual differences between *specifying* constraints and *checking* constraints that need to be reconciled. In principle, the specification is declarative by nature and the modeler usually looks "forward" in time in expressing what needs to happen in order for the plan to complete. The checking of the plan is operational by nature, because start and end variables are assigned values as they occur, hence testing that a constraint is valid cannot be performed until the last timepoint has occurred. Therefore, in the checking of the constraints the modeler has to look "backwards" in time.

For example, the constraint A.start < B.end < C.start cannot be established when A starts. Even if B has not ended yet, its relationship to the start of C cannot be established.

The mechanism of checking constraints with a model checker is based on assigning and updating the values of timeline state and each action start and end variables. This is performed at the timepoints when a timeline transitions from one action to another, according to the TRANSTIONS section.

Repetitive actions require special care, as multiple occurrences of the same actions will overwrite the values of the corresponding start and end variables, so only the most recent one is actually available (and possibly the previous occurrence, given that we allow the next qualifier).

For example, if there is a transition A1 -> A2 on timeline A, the following updates are necessary:

- A_state' = A2
- A1_end' = time
- A2_start' = time

A constraint is, in principle, applicable to all the transitions that affect the variables present in the constraint expression. That is, a start variable is relevant to *entering* an action, while the `end` variable is relevant to *exiting* an action. Transition guards are generated for the events that are involved.

The general approach of translating constraints into transition guards consists of determining the last timepoint in the chain and substituting that term with the value of the system variable `time`. For example, in the constraint

```
A1.start + 4 < B1.start <  C1.end
```

the last timepoint is `C1_end`. The transitions of relevance to this timepoint are from a predecessor of `C1` to `C1`.

6   Experiments

To instrument a scalability study for the model checker, we have explored two options. On the one hand, we have already accumulated a small benchmark of ANML models used for basic checks of the ANML operator semantics against the EUROPA2 [2] implementation. On the other hand, the model checker is not able to solve even moderately complex problems, with no more than a handful of timelines. Therefore, we took the path of generating random models to fit into the current range of capabilities of SAL.

6.1   Real Models

The small suite of examples includes 73 models designed to investigate the basic Allen operators that are at the core of the EUROPA2 [2] logic. The main purpose was not the study of performance but to expose semantics issues, inconsistencies in the solutions, and insights into the subtleties of the logic (such as vacuous solutions, repetitive actions, the need for quantifiers, etc). Additionally, a space station crew activities and a dock worker robots models have been developed. Even though not nearly as sophisticated as necessary for practical purposes, they were still too complex to model check with SAL.

6.2   Random Models

The major challenge in using the "real" models is that it is very tedious and time consuming to manually scale up the models (e.g. increase the number of timelines, actions, constraints) in a meaningful way.

Instead, from the statistical point of view, it might be better to just generate random models. They are obviously meaningless form the planning point of view, but they are better from the experimental point of view, since they are completely "unbiased".

In our experiments, we used $3,900$ random models, generated by a C program which takes in a few parameters:

- the number of timelines, T;
- the number of actions on a timeline, A;

- the number of transitions in a timeline, R;
- the number of constraints/Allen operators in the constraint section, C;

The transition graph is generated randomly. The program picks a source and target action (without self loops) and adds an edge. For simplicity, the constraints are all of the form *endpoint + constant < endpoint*, where endpoints are randomly selected from the set: *action.{start/end}*.

A completely random generator would most likely produce a large number of planning problems with no solution, as is the case of disconnected transition graphs. Therefore, the random generation is "steered" towards more meaningful setups. Instead of completely random graphs (which are likely to contain unreachable goal states), we always add the backbone chain $A_0 \to A_1 \to \ldots \to A_{n-1}$ and make A_{n-1} the goal state. This gives the model checker something useful to work with and increases the probability of an existing solution.

The set of sample parameters is the following:

- $T \in \{1, 2, 3, 4, 5\}$;
- $A \in \{3, 4, \ldots, 10\}$;
- R takes sample values between the minimal (backbone) graphs with $A - 1$ edges and the full graph with $\frac{A(A-1)}{2}$ edges. The test harness covers values for the fraction of "fullness" $f \in \{0, \frac{1}{4}, \frac{1}{3}, \frac{1}{2}, \frac{2}{3}, \frac{3}{4}, 1\}$, that is

$$R = (A - 1) + f \cdot \left(\frac{A(A-1)}{2} - (A - 1) \right);$$

- C takes sample values from "nothing" to "a lot": $\{0, \frac{A}{4}, \frac{A}{3}, \frac{A}{2}, A, 2A\}$.

6.3   Results

We ran our batch of experiments using SAL version 3.0 on a 64bit, 3.2 GHz machine with 8GB of memory running RH Enterprise Linux version 2.6.9-5ELsmp. We collected the runtime for each model with the `time` command, using a timeout of 30 minutes (after which the SAL instance was aborted).

Outcome.   The analysis has to take into account the outcome of a run: a solution is found, no solution is found, or the run is aborted when reaching the timeout cutoff. Since the model checking query was set up as a negation of the statement "no solution exists", in case a counterexample is found, it is then displayed (which is a time-consuming operation for a model checker). Figure 1 shows the outcome breakdown for the runs, function of the four parameters in the experiment.

We observe a few natural trends. The number of timeouts increases dramatically with the number of timelines, which is the largest contributor to the complexity of a SAL model. The number of timeouts also increases with the number of actions, but more interestingly, for the number of constraints, it first peaks for an intermediate value, before dipping. We attribute this to the fact that increasing the number of constraints is likely to reduce the chances of an existing solution.

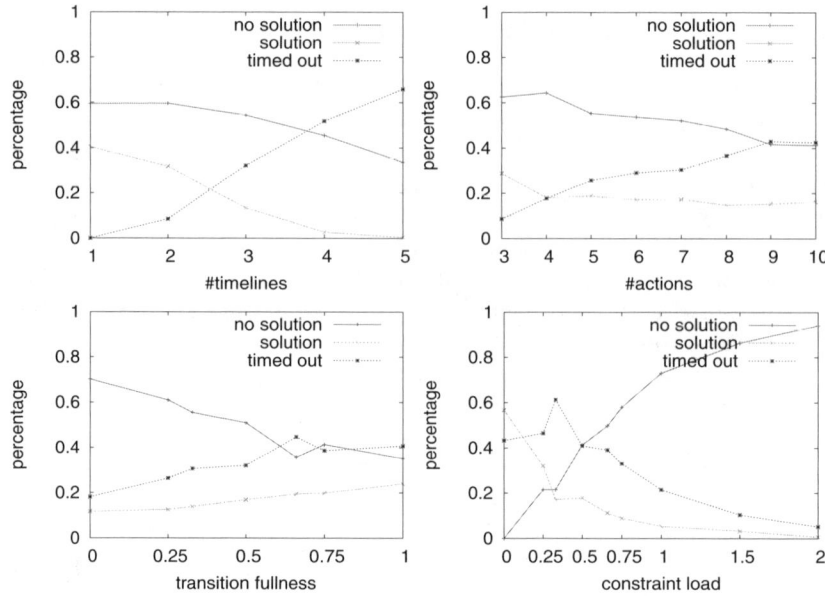

Fig. 1. Outcome breakdown

In terms of finding a solution, there is a mix of results. As seen above, more timelines and more constraints decrease the possibility of a solution. The number of actions has a small effect, while the number of transitions seems to favor the existence of a solution. This can be attributed to the fact that more edges in the transition graph would allow the reach of a goal state by "bypassing" actions that are tied into unfeasible constraints.

In general, the generated models seem to be more likely to lack a solution rather than have one. This is probably due to the "random" (that is often meaningless) nature of the models.

Runtimes. Figure 2 shows the average runtime for six combinations of parameters. The trends are also mixed. While it is obvious that the runtime will grow with the increase in the number of timelines and actions, the number of transitions seems to have a negligible effect on the runtime. Also, the number of constraints produces a peak in the middle and decreases for larger values.

The dependency on the number of timelines can be illustrated by the total runtime of the script for the approximately 800 models for each value of T. It took less than a day (23 hours) to finish the models with $T = 1$, more than two days (51 hours) for $T = 2$, six and a half days (156 hours) for $T = 3$, ten days (240 hours) for $T = 4$, and nearly two weeks (320 hours) for $T = 5$.

We also computed the averages in subcategories, corresponding to the existence of a solution or not. Both due to lack of space and also to the fact that the comparison is unfair to the case when a solution exists (given that the model checker spends more time constructing the counterexample), we left those graphs

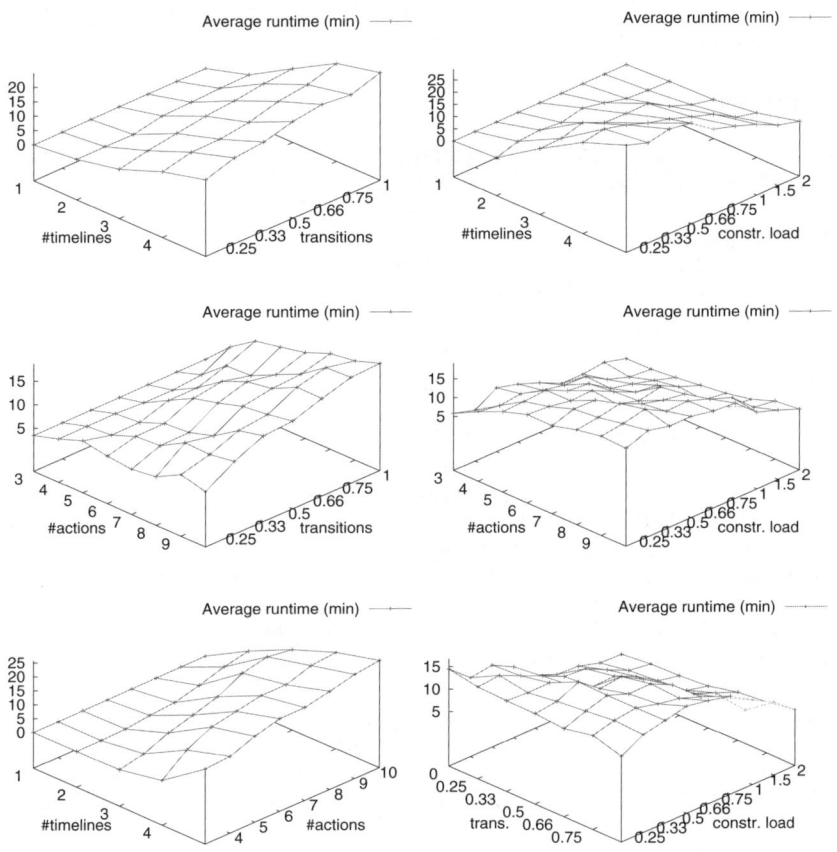

Fig. 2. Average runtimes

out of this paper. The profile of the graphs is largely similar to the overall averages, but is roughly scaled (down for no solution, up for an existing solution) by a constant factor.

7 Conclusions

We are just making small steps in this area. Traditional symbolic model checking technology is not mature enough to handle complex applications. Yet, with the help of more advanced techniques (timeout automata and other deductive approaches, such as SMT solvers [6]), more progress can be made.

In general, we believe that there is a clear role for formal methods in designing planning languages. While the powerful heuristics of the AI software are more suited to efficiently find a solution, exhaustive techniques, such as model checking, are obviously the only alternative to prove the lack of a solution. Moreover, in safety-critical applications, eliminating ambiguities in the specification language is a strong requirement. Our comparative study with EUROPA2 has provided valuable insight and feedback to the designers to help them make the planning language more robust and safe.

References

[1] Allen, J.F., Ferguson, G.: Actions and Events in Interval Temporal Logic. Technical Report TR521, University of Rochester (1994)

[2] Bedrax-Weiss, T., McGann, C., Bachmann, A., Edington, W., Iatauro, M.: EUROPA2: User and Contributor Guide. Technical report, NASA Ames Research Center, Moffett Field, CA (February 2005)

[3] Butler, R.W., Muñoz, C.A.: An Abstract Plan Preparation Language. Report 214518, NASA Langley, Hampton VA 23681-2199, USA (2006)

[4] Butler, R.W., Siminiceanu, R.I., Muño, C.A.: The ANMLite language and logic for specifying planning problems. Report 215088, NASA Langley, Hampton VA 23681-2199, USA (November 2007)

[5] Cimatti, A., Giunchiglia, F., Giunchiglia, E., Traverso, P.: Planning via model checking: a decision procedure for AR. In: Steel, S. (ed.) ECP 1997. LNCS (LNAI), vol. 1348, pp. 130–142. Springer, Heidelberg (1997)

[6] de Moura, L., Dutertre, B.: Yices 1.0: An Efficient SMT Solver. Technical report, SRI International, SMCOMP (2006), http://yices.csl.sri.com

[7] de Moura, L., Owre, S., Shankar, N.: The SAL Language Manual. Technical Report SRI-CSL-01-02, CSL Technical Report (2003)

[8] Drusinsky, D., Watney, G.: Applying Run-Time Monitoring to the Deep-Impact Fault Protection Engine. In: 28th IEEE/NASA Software Engineering Workshop, p. 127 (2003)

[9] Edelkamp, S.: Heuristic search planning with BDDs. In: PuK (2000)

[10] Feather, M.S., Smith, B.: Automatic Generation of Test Oracles – From Pilot Studies to Application. Automated Software Eng. 8(1), 31–61 (2001)

[11] Ferraris, P., Giunchiglia, E.: Planning as satisfiability in nondeterministic domains. In: AAAI, pp. 748–753 (2000)

[12] Frank, J., Jonsson, A.: Constraint-based Attribute and Interval Planning. Journal of Constraints 8, 339–364 (2003)

[13] Hoey, J., St-Aubin, R., Hu, A., Boutilier, C.: SPUDD: Stochastic planning using decision diagrams. In: Uncertainty in Artificial Intelligence (UAI 1999), pp. 279–288 (1999)

[14] Lomuscio, A., Pecheur, C., Raimondi, F.: Automatic Verification of Knowledge and Time with NuSMV. In: IJCAI, pp. 1384–1389 (2007)

[15] Drew McDermott and AIPS 1998 IPC Committee. PDDL – the Planning Domain Definition Language. Technical report, Yale University (1998)

[16] Owre, S., Shankar, N.: Formal Analysis Methods for Spacecraft Autonomy, Final Report. Technical Report SRI-17625, SRI International (2007)

[17] Pecheur, C., Raimondi, F.: Symbolic model checking of logics with actions. In: Edelkamp, S., Lomuscio, A. (eds.) MoChArt IV. LNCS, vol. 4428, pp. 113–128. Springer, Heidelberg (2007)

[18] Sheini, H.M., Peintner, B., Sakallah, K.A., Pollack, M.E.: On solving soft temporal constraints using SAT techniques. In: van Beek, P. (ed.) CP 2005. LNCS, vol. 3709, pp. 607–621. Springer, Heidelberg (2005)

[19] Smith, D.E., Frank, J., Jonsson, A.K.: Bridging the Gap between Planning and Scheduling. The Knowledge Engineering Rev. 15(1), 113–128 (2000)

[20] Smith, D.E., Frank, J., McGann, C.: The ANML Language. Technical report, NASA Ames, unpublished report (2006)

Relaxation Refinement: A New Method to Generate Heuristic Functions

Jan-Georg Smaus[1] and Jörg Hoffmann[2]

[1] University of Freiburg, Germany
smaus@informatik.uni-freiburg.de
[2] SAP Research, Karlsruhe, Germany
joe.hoffmann@sap.com

Abstract. In artificial intelligence, a *relaxation* of a problem is an overapproximation whose solution in every state of an explicit search provides a heuristic solution distance estimate. The heuristic guides the exploration, potentially shortening the search by exponentially many search states. The big question is how a good relaxation for the problem at hand should be derived. In model checking, overapproximations are called *abstractions*, and *abstraction refinement* is a powerful method developed to derive approximations that are sufficiently precise for *verifying* the system at hand. In our work, we bring these two paradigms together. We pioneer the application of (predicate) abstraction refinement for the generation of heuristic functions that are intelligently adapted to the problem at hand. We investigate how an abstraction refinement process for generating heuristic functions should differ from the process used in the verification context. We do so in the context of DMC of timed automata. We obtain a variety of interesting insights about this approach.

Keywords: Directed model checking, abstraction refinement, predicate abstraction, timed automata.

1 Introduction

In artificial intelligence (AI), a *relaxation* of a problem is an overapproximation of the problem. During an explicit search in the state space of the problem, in each state s the relaxed problem is solved starting from s, and the length of the relaxed solution is used as a heuristic distance estimate, i.e., an estimate of the distance from s to the nearest solution state. States with lower estimated distance are explored first. It is well known that this strategy can exponentially decrease the explored part of the state space (e.g. [22]). Recently, the same idea has been applied for *falsification*, namely in *directed model checking* (*DMC*) [11], which is the search for errors using a heuristic function.

Both in AI and in DMC, the main question to be addressed is how to define the approximation that underlies the heuristic function. Different definitions yield different heuristics, and this makes all the difference between being and

D. Peled and M. Wooldridge (Eds.): MOCHART 2008, LNAI 5348, pp. 147–165, 2009.

not being able to find an error. Intuitively, the heuristic function should capture sufficient information for predicting whether a state is likely to lead to an error. Doing so requires knowledge about the reasons for the error in the particular system considered. The "hot trail" we follow is to use methods coming from the field of model checking to learn this kind of knowledge.

In model checking, overapproximations are called *abstractions*, and have been used for *verification*. Applying the formalism of *abstract interpretation* [7], an abstraction of a system is designed so that if some undesirable state is unreachable in the abstraction, then it is surely unreachable in the original system. A highly successful method in this context is *abstraction refinement* [2,6,23]: starting from some trivial abstraction, the abstract state space is computed. If there is no path to the undesirable state (error path), the system is safe and one can stop. Otherwise, one determines if the path is *spurious*, i.e., if it does not correspond to a path in the original system. If it is spurious, one examines the path and tries to refine the abstraction in order to exclude this spurious error path in the next iteration. If the path is not spurious, an error has been found. The process of repeated refinement iterations is called *refinement loop*.

Given these facts, the obvious question that springs to mind is: can, and how can, we use abstraction refinement to devise heuristic functions that are intelligently adapted to the system at hand? This question may be of relevance in many different contexts, ranging from DMC in various model checking formalisms to the various search problems traditionally considered in AI. Here, we investigate this question in the context of DMC of timed automata.

In our own previous work [16], we have shown how one can use predicate abstraction [14] to generate heuristic functions for DMC of timed automata using UPPAAL [4]. Following the *pattern database* approach [8], the abstract state space is built before the actual search for an error starts; during the search, the abstract state space is used as a look-up table for retrieving the heuristic values. The abstraction predicates in that work were mostly generated by reading the predicates directly off transition guards in the system. We also made an initial experiment with abstraction refinement, realised via the *abstraction refinement model checker (ARMC)* [23]. The conclusion from the latter experiment was that off-the-shelf abstraction refinement is *not* a good method for deriving heuristic functions. An intuitive explanation is that in off-the-shelf abstraction refinement, the abstraction is tailored to capture a lot of information about one particular error path; other regions of the state space unrelated to that path are abstracted coarsely. When used as a heuristic function, such an abstraction yields precise estimates for states near the error path, but imprecise – overly optimistic – estimates otherwise. This can have the unwanted effect that states unrelated to the error path obtain lower heuristic estimates, and are preferred in the search. In addition, using off-the-shelf abstraction refinement, we have insufficient control to be able to tune the balance between heuristic quality and heuristic cost.

In this paper, while being inspired by ARMC, we do not use ARMC off-the-shelf, because we want to experiment with different methods of doing abstraction refinement in the context of heuristic generation, to find a method is more suitable for defining useful heuristic functions. Let us briefly explain the strategies we tried. The error state in our benchmarks is given by a formula $(loc(p_1) = \ell_1) \wedge (loc(p_2) = \ell_2)$, stating that process p_1 is in location ℓ_1 and p_2 is ℓ_2. The simplest method we tried is to use an initial abstraction consisting of the predicates $loc(p_1) = \ell_1$, $loc(p_2) = \ell_2$, so that the abstraction could always distinguish an error state from a non-error state. Alternatively, we generated two abstractions based on initial predicates $loc(p_1) = \ell_1$ and $loc(p_2) = \ell_2$ kept separate. Somewhat surprisingly, the latter turned out to be better, and can compete with other heuristics we use for comparison. To overcome the focus of the abstraction refinement on one particular path, we then tried to base each refinement step on *several paths*, rather than just a single path. The most surprising result for us was that this had no positive impact. We learnt that the way predicates are added based on an abstract path sometimes implies that the refinement loop terminates with an extremely coarse abstraction, and yet there is no "incentive" to refine this abstraction. Moreover, we learnt that this is not a question of choosing the right paths. To tackle this problem, we used initial abstractions based on "random" predicates as additional "seed" for the abstraction refinement. The results are generally unstable; sometimes they are extremely good.

Our overall experiments suggest that abstraction refinement is useful for *selecting* predicates from a certain repertoire so that the set obtained is informative enough yet small enough not to pose a prohibitive computational overhead; in this respect the present approach is an advance over [16]. We had also hoped that abstraction refinement can, compared to other ways of generating predicates, significantly enhance the repertoire itself; but, at least in our benchmarks, this does not seem to be the case. It remains to be seen if and how the situation changes in the context of DMC in other formalisms (or even just other benchmarks), and in the context of AI search problems. As such, our work provides only a first exploration of a much larger research topic.

This paper is organised as follows. In the next section, we introduce timed automata. In Sec. 3, we explain predicate abstraction for heuristic generation. In Sec. 4, we explain how predicates are generated by refinement based on an error path in ARMC, and how this approach is adapted for generating heuristic functions. In Sec. 5 we report on experiments, in Sec. 6 we discuss related work, and in Sec. 7 we conclude.

2   Timed Automata in Uppaal

We introduce timed automata [1] here following the terminology of UPPAAL [4], which is an integrated tool environment for modelling, simulation and verification of real-time systems. We restrict to the features that we actually consider in our benchmarks and implementation.

A **timed automaton** is a finite (ω-)automaton enhanced with real-valued variables called **clocks** and integer variables. Instead of the usual word *state*

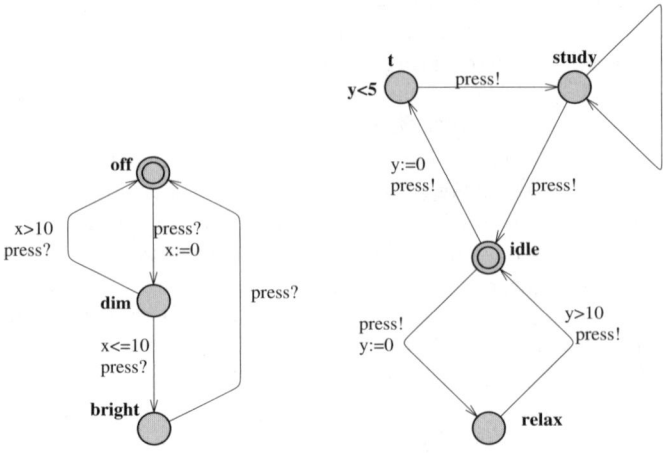

Fig. 1. A system composed of two processes

we speak of a **location** of a timed automaton, since a **state** in our parlance consists of a location together with a value for each variable of the automaton. One location is marked as **initial**.

Locations can be connected by directed **edges**. An edge can be labelled with a **clock** (resp. **integer**) **guard**, which is a conjunction of conditions of the form $x \bowtie c$ or $x - y \bowtie c$ (resp. $c \bowtie 0$), where x, y are clocks and c is an expression using natural constants and integer variables, and $\bowtie \in \{<, \leq, =, \geq, >\}$. An edge can also be labelled with one or several **effects**, which are assignments to an integer variable or resets of a clock variable to 0. A location can be labelled with an **invariant**, which is of the same form as a guard and states a condition that must hold while the automaton remains in this location. One usually requires that clock invariants are downwards closed, i.e., $\bowtie \in \{<, \leq\}$.

An automaton as described so far is called a **process**; several processes can be composed to a network of automata, called **system**, as follows: a **state** is characterised by a location for each of its processes and a value for each of its variables. An edge may be labelled by a synchronisation label $ch?$ or $ch!$ where ch is a symbol called **channel**. If one process has an edge labelled $ch?$ and another process has an edge labelled $ch!$, then the two must be taken simultaneously to obtain a *transition*. An edge of a process that has no synchronisation label can be taken alone; this is called a τ-*transition*.

Figure 1 shows an example. The process on the left-hand side models a lamp switch and the process on the right-hand side models the lamp user. We are dealing here with a widespread design of lamps where pressing the button twice "quickly" causes the light to be bright, whereas pressing it once causes the light to be dimmed if it was off before, and switches the light off otherwise. We illustrate some of the above concepts: x and y are clocks, **off** is a location (marked as initial by the double circle), x > 10 is a guard, x := 0 is an effect, **y** < **5** is an invariant of location **t**, and 'press' is a channel.

A **run** or **path** is defined in an intuitive way (see [1,4,5] for a formal definition): the system starts in its initial state, some time passes (during which all clocks increase at the same speed, and all relevant location invariants must hold), then a transition allowed by the guards is made (which takes no time) and its effects are applied, reaching a new state, and so forth. Here is a run for the lamp example (**L** and **U** stand for the "lamp" and "user" process, respectively):

$$(\mathbf{L}.\text{off}, \mathbf{U}.\text{idle}, x = 0, y = 0) \to (\mathbf{L}.\text{off}, \mathbf{U}.\text{idle}, x = 31, y = 31) \xrightarrow{\text{press}}$$
$$(\mathbf{L}.\text{dim}, \mathbf{U}.\text{t}, x = 0, y = 0) \to (\mathbf{L}.\text{dim}, \mathbf{U}.\text{t}, x = 2, y = 2) \xrightarrow{\text{press}}$$
$$(\mathbf{L}.\text{bright}, \mathbf{U}.\text{study}, x = 2, y = 2)$$

The **state space** $\mathcal{S}$ is the directed graph where the nodes are all states, and the edges are the transitions. The set of **error** or **target** states which are undesirable are given by a formula ϕ, specifying a condition on the locations and variables.

3   Predicate Abstraction for Heuristic Generation

In this section we recall our previous work [16]; we explain technically how heuristics for UPPAAL are computed based on predicate abstraction.

A **predicate** is a logic formula that "talks" about the system. We consider three kinds of predicates: **location** predicates $loc(proc) = \ell$ stating that process $proc$ is in location ℓ; and **integer**, resp. **clock** predicates, defined like guards, see Sec. 2.

A vector $\mathcal{P} = (p_1, \ldots, p_m)$ of predicates defines a **predicate abstraction**; e.g. $\mathcal{P} = (loc(1) = 3, x > 2, y = 0)$. We sometimes regard $\mathcal{P}$ as a **set**. When $|\mathcal{P}| = m$, we call a vector in $\{\mathsf{T}, \mathsf{U}, \mathsf{F}\}^m$ an **abstract state** or **TUF-vector** for $\mathcal{P}$. Here, $\mathsf{T}, \mathsf{U}, \mathsf{F}$ stand for *true*, *unknown*, and *false*. We usually assume that $\mathcal{P}$ is clear from the context.

Viewing a state s as a valuation of the system variables, we use the notation $s \models \psi$ to say that the formula ψ is true under s, and $\phi \models \psi$ means that ψ is true under every valuation under which ϕ is true.

Given a concrete state s, i.e., a vector consisting of a location for each process and a value for each variable, the **abstraction** of s is a vector $\mathbf{b} = (b_1, \ldots, b_m) \in \{\mathsf{T}, \mathsf{F}\}^m$ where $b_i = \mathsf{T}$ if $s \models p_i$ and $b_i = \mathsf{F}$ if $s \models \neg p_i$. E.g. if $s = (loc(1) = 2, loc(2) = 4, x = 2.3, y = 4.7)$ and $\mathcal{P}$ is as above, then the abstraction of s is FTF.

For an abstract state $\mathbf{b}$, we denote by $[\mathbf{b}]$ the **concretisation** of $\mathbf{b}$, i.e., $[\mathbf{b}] = \{s \mid \text{for all } i \in [1..m], s \models p_i \text{ if } b_i = \mathsf{T}, s \models \neg p_i \text{ if } b_i = \mathsf{F}\}$. For $\mathbf{b}, \mathbf{b}' \in \{\mathsf{T}, \mathsf{U}, \mathsf{F}\}^m$, we say that $\mathbf{b}'$ **subsumes** $\mathbf{b}$ if $[\mathbf{b}'] \supseteq [\mathbf{b}]$, which is the case iff $\mathbf{b}'$ is obtained from $\mathbf{b}$ by replacing zero or more occurrences of T or F by U. The **abstract state space** for $\mathcal{P}$, denoted $[\mathcal{S}]^{\mathcal{P}}$, is the directed graph where the nodes are all TUF-vectors for $\mathcal{P}$, and there is an edge from $\mathbf{b}_1$ to $\mathbf{b}_2$ iff there exist $s_1 \in [\mathbf{b}_1]$ and $s_2 \in [\mathbf{b}_2]$ so that there is an edge from s_1 to s_2 in $\mathcal{S}$ (see Sec. 2). Note that $[\mathcal{S}]^{\mathcal{P}}$ is an *over*-approximation of $\mathcal{S}$, i.e., every concrete path corresponds to an abstract path but not necessarily vice versa. This can be seen as follows: suppose we have four concrete states s_1, s_2, s_2', s_3 such that $s_1 \rightarrow s_2$ and $s_2' \rightarrow s_3$ hold in $\mathcal{S}$ but $s_1 \rightarrow s_2'$ and $s_2 \rightarrow s_3$ do not hold in $\mathcal{S}$, and $[s_2] = [s_2']$; then we have $[s_1] \rightarrow [s_2] \rightarrow [s_3]$ in $[\mathcal{S}]^{\mathcal{P}}$ although s_3 might not be reachable from s_1 is $\mathcal{S}$.

Given an error condition ϕ as in Sec. 2, the **abstract error state** is defined as the TUF-vector $\mathbf{b} = (b_1, \ldots, b_m)$ where $b_i = \mathsf{T}$ if $\phi \models p_i$, and $b_i = \mathsf{F}$ if $\phi \models \neg p_i$, and $b_i = \mathsf{U}$ otherwise. Note that ϕ might not uniquely determine the value of each predicate p_i. In addition, we obtain a precision loss due to the fact that we consider the predicates in isolation. E.g., it might be the case that $\phi \models (p_1 \wedge p_2 \wedge p_3) \vee (p_1 \wedge \neg p_2 \wedge \neg p_3)$, so that we should have *two* abstract error states TTT and TFF, but instead, we just take *the* abstract error state TUU. This merging is referred to as *Cartesian abstraction* [3].

The abstract state space is computed starting from the abstract error state and computing its abstract predecessors to obtain the first *layer*; then all predecessors of those states give the second layer, and so forth. Whenever a state is computed that is subsumed by a state computed earlier, then the new state will be ignored. This computation is called *regression*.

Computing the predecessor of an abstract state $\mathbf{b}$ is a logical deduction task. To compute the predecessor of $\mathbf{b}$ obtained by applying (backward) some edge (pair) t, we construct a formula using the variables occurring in $\mathcal{P}$ and in the guards, effects, and invariants of (the sources and targets of) t, where we prime $(')$ the variables to denote their value in the target location; the unprimed variants correspond to the source location. First, $\mathbf{b}$ translates into $\psi_{\mathbf{b}} = \bigwedge_{b_i=\mathsf{T}} p_i' \wedge \bigwedge_{b_i=\mathsf{F}} \neg p_i'$, where p_i' denotes the result of priming each variable in p_i. Secondly, t translates into a formula ψ_t that expresses the effect of applying t, by relating the values of the variables in the sources and targets. E.g. if t has an effect $i := i + 1$ then one of the conjuncts of ψ_t will be $i' = i + 1$.

The exact method of determining all the abstract predecessor states of $\mathbf{b}$ would be as follows: we enumerate all abstract states $\mathbf{a} \in \{\mathsf{T}, \mathsf{F}\}^m$, build a formula $\psi_{\mathbf{a}} = \bigwedge_{a_i=\mathsf{T}} p_i \wedge \bigwedge_{a_i=\mathsf{F}} \neg p_i$ in analogy to $\psi_{\mathbf{b}}$ but with unprimed variables, and check if $\psi_{\mathbf{b}} \wedge \psi_t \wedge \psi_{\mathbf{a}}$ is satisfiable. If yes, then there is an assignment to the variables, corresponding to concrete states in $[\mathbf{a}]$ and $[\mathbf{b}]$, respectively, with a transition between these concrete states, and hence $\mathbf{a}$ is an abstract predecessor state of $\mathbf{b}$.

However, the method described in the previous paragraph would be too inefficient because we would have to enumerate 2^m abstract states. Instead, we again apply Cartesian abstraction: we compute just *one* abstract predecessor state $\mathbf{a}$ of $\mathbf{b}$ w.r.t. t by taking each predicate p_i *in isolation*: if p_i is implied by $\psi_{\mathbf{b}} \wedge \psi_t$, then $a_i = \mathsf{T}$; if $\neg p_i$ is implied by $\psi_{\mathbf{b}} \wedge \psi_t$, then $a_i = \mathsf{F}$; otherwise $a_i = \mathsf{U}$. For checking the implications we use the solver ICS [13].

Since we compute the abstract state space $[\mathcal{S}]^{\mathcal{P}}$ backwards starting from the error state, we obtain the distance of each abstract state from the abstract error state for free. This information is stored in a so-called *pattern database*, which is implemented as a certain tree data structure [15] supporting efficient subsumption tests. The pattern database is the basis for defining the heuristic value of a concrete UPPAAL search state s. Essentially, the lookup of a heuristic

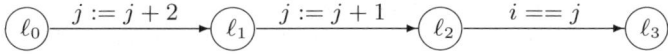

Fig. 2. Predicate Generation in ARMC

value for a concrete UPPAAL search state s works as follows: the abstraction of s is computed; call it $\mathbf{b}$; now consider all $\mathbf{c}$ in the pattern database that subsume $\mathbf{b}$; among those, take the one whose (precomputed) distance to the abstract error state is minimal; this distance is the heuristic value of s (see [16] for more details).

We (and others before us [12,17]) have experienced that combining several simple abstractions is often better than having one complicated abstraction. Thus we usually have several sets of abstraction predicates and thus abstract spaces and "raw" heuristic functions. The latter can be combined by taking, for each concrete search state, the maximum or the sum.[1] We refer to this as *MAX option, SUM option*, resp.

4   Abstraction Refinement

When predicate abstraction refinement is used for verification, one successively refines an abstraction by adding predicates in order to exclude spurious error paths. But which predicates? We explain here how the *abstraction refinement model checker (ARMC)* [23] answers this question, since we generate predicates in the same way. We immediately jump to a timed automata setting. So the aim is to verify a timed automaton, i.e. to show that a certain error location ℓ_{err} is unreachable.

A *predicate* is of the form $e_1 \bowtie e_2$ where e_1, e_2 are expressions involving integer variables and $\bowtie \in \{=, \leq, <, \geq, >\}$. Each location ℓ is associated with a set of predicates $\mathcal{P}_\ell$, and an abstract state is a pair $(\ell, \mathbf{a})$ where $\mathbf{a} \in \{\mathsf{T}, \mathsf{U}\}^{|\mathcal{P}_\ell|}$. Note that in the verification context [23], one only distinguishes *true* and *unknown*.

The abstraction refinement loop starts with an initial abstraction where $\mathcal{P}_\ell = \emptyset$ for all ℓ. We now explain how one iteration of the loop works. Assume that we have a current abstraction, i.e., a $\mathcal{P}_\ell$ for each ℓ. We compute an abstract error path $\ell_0 \to \ldots \to \ell_n = \ell_{\mathsf{err}}$, i.e. a path from the initial location to ℓ_{err}. By treating $\ell_0 \to \ldots \to \ell_n$ backward, we generate new predicate sets $\mathcal{P}'_{\ell_0}, \ldots, \mathcal{P}'_{\ell_n}$ as follows: $\mathcal{P}'_{\ell_n} := \mathcal{P}_{\ell_n}$; if $\mathcal{P}'_{\ell_{i+1}}$ is already computed, and $\ell_i \to \ell_{i+1}$ has guard $g_1 \wedge \ldots \wedge g_r$ and assignments $x_1 := e_1, \ldots, x_k := e_k$, then $\mathcal{P}_{\ell_i} = (\{g_1, \ldots, g_r\} \cup \mathcal{P}'_{\ell_{i+1}})[x_k \mapsto e_k, \ldots, x_1 \mapsto e_1] \cup \mathcal{P}_{\ell_i}$ (the notation $[x \mapsto e]$ denotes the replacement of x by e).

In Fig. 2 we illustrate a fragment of an error path. Here, $i == j$ is a guard. Starting with $\mathcal{P}_{\ell_i} = \emptyset$ for $i \in [0..3]$ we obtain $\mathcal{P}'_{\ell_3} = \emptyset$, $\mathcal{P}'_{\ell_2} = \{i = j\}$, $\mathcal{P}'_{\ell_1} = \{i = j+1\}$ and $\mathcal{P}'_{\ell_0} = \{i = j+3\}$. Each $\mathcal{P}'_\ell$ corresponds to the *weakest precondition* of $i = j$ w.r.t. the subsequent updates, i.e. it expresses exactly the condition under which $\ell_2 \to \ell_3$ can be taken. If ℓ_0 is the initial location of the automaton and

---

[1] The issue of *admissibility* is discussed in [16].

we assume that variables are initialised to 0, then $\mathcal{P}'_{\ell_0}, \mathcal{P}'_{\ell_1}, \mathcal{P}'_{\ell_2}, \mathcal{P}'_{\ell_3}$ are sufficient to exclude this spurious error path (fragment), i.e., this error path will not be computed again.

We adopt the method of generating predicates just described. Yet there are some differences between ARMC and our setting. Unlike ARMC, our abstract states represent location information only to the extent that there are location predicates. Therefore, our abstract paths can be spurious for location reasons, i.e., we could have a transition $\ell_0 \to \ell_1$ followed by a transition $\ell'_1 \to \ell_2$ where $\ell_1 \neq \ell'_1$, because the abstraction cannot distinguish ℓ_1 from ℓ'_1. One could of course change this, but our experiments suggest that abstractions preserving all location information lead to abstract state spaces that are much too expensive to compute. Therefore, we do not have a different predicate set *per location*, but an abstraction is given by one global predicate set.

More importantly, as explained in the introduction, our aim is not to exclude all spurious error paths (verification), but to characterise a sufficiently large environment of the error state with sufficient precision to provide a good heuristic.[2] Therefore, instead of basing one refinement step on one path from the initial to the error state, we can base one refinement step on *arbitrarily many* paths starting from an *arbitrary state* and leading to the error state.

We present the core of our abstraction refinement algorithm: the generation of new predicates based on a single abstract path. Given a set of predicates $\mathcal{P}$ and an abstract path $t_1, \ldots, t_n$ leading to the abstract error state, we refine $\mathcal{P}$ as shown in Fig. 3. To simplify the presentation, we only show the case of a synchronised transition. We denote by $edge!(t)$, $edge?(t)$ the two edges of t, and by $targ(d)$, $src(d)$ the target and source locations, and by $proc(d)$ the process of an edge d.

The algorithm processes the edge(pair)s of the abstract path backward. The most relevant difference to ARMC is that the abstract path may be spurious for location reasons. We maintain information about the current location of each process in $curloc$. Whenever $targ(edge!(t_i))$ is different from $curloc(proc(edge!(t_i)))$ (or analogously for $edge?$), we have detected that $t_1, \ldots, t_n$ is spurious for location reasons. We then add a location predicate that will exclude the abstract path in the next iteration, and stop the processing of the edge(pair)s (see lines marked "⌈").

The algorithm must be embedded in one or several refinement loops, to generate one or several abstractions (see end of Sec. 3). Now there are three questions:

- What should the initial abstraction(s) be?
- How many and which abstract paths should be chosen for the refinement?
- When should the refinement loop stop?

We have tried many possible approaches to answering these questions, of which we present some in Sections 5.2 to 5.4, after explaining the setup for our experiments.

---

[2] Whether or not a heuristic is good is measured here, as usual, by considering the size of the explored state space (see Sec. 5).

procedure *refine_path*(Predicates $\mathcal{P}$, Path $(t_1, \ldots, t_n)$)
  foreach process p **do**
    $curloc(p) := unknown$ **od**
  for $i := n$ **to** 1 **do**
  ⎡ **if** $curloc(proc(edge!(t_i))) \neq unknown \wedge targ(edge!(t_i)) \neq curloc(proc(edge!(t_i)))$
  ⎢ $\mathcal{P} := \mathcal{P} \cup \{loc(proc(edge!(t_i))) = curloc(proc(edge!(t_i)))\}$ **break fi**
  ⎣ $curloc(proc(edge!(t_i))) := src(edge!(t_i))$
  ⎡ **if** $curloc(proc(edge?(t_i))) \neq unknown \wedge targ(edge?(t_i)) \neq curloc(proc(edge?(t_i)))$
  ⎢ $\mathcal{P} := \mathcal{P} \cup \{loc(proc(edge?(t_i))) = curloc(proc(edge?(t_i)))\}$ **break fi**
  ⎣ $curloc(proc(edge?(t_i))) := src(edge?(t_i))$
    foreach invariant g of $targ(edge!(t_i)), targ(edge?(t_i))$ **do**
      $\mathcal{P} := \mathcal{P} \cup \{g\}$ **od**
    foreach assignment $i := e$ of $edge!(t_i), edge?(t_i)$ in reverse order **do**
      $\mathcal{P} := \mathcal{P}[i \mapsto e] \cup \mathcal{P}$ **od**
    foreach guard g of $edge!(t_i), edge?(t_i)$ and
    foreach invariant g of $src(edge!(t_i)), src(edge?(t_i))$ **do**
      $\mathcal{P} := \mathcal{P} \cup \{g\}$ **od**
  od
  return $\mathcal{P}$

Fig. 3. Refining an abstraction based on a path $t_1, \ldots, t_n$

5 Experiments

Our benchmarks come from two industrial case studies [9,18]. Since we are dealing with error detection, i.e., falsification, our examples had an error injected.

Examples "Mi" and "Ni", $i = 1, \ldots, 4$, come from a study called "Mutual Exclusion". This study models a real-time protocol to ensure mutual exclusion of states in a distributed system via asynchronous communication [9]. An error was injected by increasing an upper time bound. Examples "Ci", $i = 2, \ldots, 9$, are a case study called "Single-tracked Line Segment" coming from an industrial project partner of the UniForM-project [18]. The problem is to design a distributed real-time controller for a segment of tracks where trams share a piece of track. The controller was modelled in terms of PLC-automata (*PLC* stands for *programmable logic controllers*) [9,18] and translated into timed automata. We injected an error by manipulating a delay such that the asynchronous communication between some automata is faulty. The given set of PLC-automata had eight input variables and we constructed eight models with decreasing size by abstracting more and more of these inputs. The numbering of the benchmarks is ad hoc, but the benchmarks become bigger with increasing i.

Concerning "Ci", we observed that the model checking could be dramatically simplified by a slight modification of the benchmarks, namely to reduce the number of times a certain loop edge can be taken. This issue is completely orthogonal to the topic of this paper, but we mention the fact that we used the modified benchmarks for the sake of comparison with other works [10,16,19,20].

We performed DMC using UPPAAL. We used *greedy best-first search* [20], i.e., the search queue is a priority queue over the value of the heuristic function. The

Table 1. M1-M4, N1-N4: search space size | heuristic computing time | user time

	M1	M2	M3	M4
h^L	5656|n.a.|**0.1**	30743|n.a.|**0.3**	**18431**|n.a.|**0.2**	122973|n.a.|1.3
h^U	*14679*|n.a.|**0.2**	*68407*|n.a.|0.9	75976|n.a.|0.9	*233378*|n.a.|2.8
syn 5000/10/SUM	*23257*|0.3|0.6	*84475*|0.4|1.5	92548|0.4|1.6	*311049*|0.6|4.7
syn 5000/10/MAX	*23744*|0.3|0.6	*102042*|0.4|1.7	98715|0.4|1.7	*399114*|0.6|5.6
syn 20000/20/SM	*12780*|1.7|*1.7*	34947|10.7|*10.7*	55098|10.8|10.8	139875|15.1|*15.1*
1abs 5000/10	*20188*|0.7|0.8	39369|0.3|0.7	64522|0.3|1.0	110240|0.3|1.6
2abs 5000/10/SUM	*14955*|0.7|0.7	17753|0.5|**0.6**	86316|0.4|1.4	110240|0.3|1.5
2abs 5000/10/MAX	3769|0.6|0.6	**7637**|0.5|**0.5**	119108|0.4|1.7	**32034**|0.3|**0.5**
seed 100/10/SUM	*18566*|0.6|0.7	29253|0.5|0.8	64671|0.5|1.3	110240|0.5|1.8
seed 100/10/MAX	**1050**|0.5|0.5	**3921**|0.6|**0.6**	*5514784*|0.5|*97.6*	**32034**|0.5|**0.8**
seed 5000/10/SUM	*14955*|1.7|*1.7*	17753|1.3|1.3	86316|1.0|2.0	110240|0.7|2.0
seed 5000/10/MAX	3769|1.7|*1.7*	**7637**|1.3|1.3	119096|1.0|2.4	**32034**|0.7|**0.9**

	N1	N2	N3	N4
h^L	16335|n.a.|**0.5**	*88537*|n.a.|2.5	**28889**|n.a.|**0.6**	226698|n.a.|**5.0**
h^U	*25577*|n.a.|**0.8**	*132711*|n.a.|3.9	*143969*|n.a.|4.2	*747210*|n.a.|20.0
syn 5000/10/SUM	*36030*|0.3|*1.8*	*178333*|0.5|6.9	*196535*|0.4|7.7	*983344*|0.6|*37.4*
syn 5000/10/MAX	*31589*|0.3|*1.3*	*163001*|0.4|5.6	*207665*|0.5|7.5	*1255213*|0.6|*47.1*
syn 20000/20/SM	17357|1.7|*2.1*	63596|10.8|*12.0*	96202|10.6|*12.4*	445359|15.0|*29.0*
1abs 5000/10	*31042*|0.7|*1.8*	*91367*|0.3|3.2	*135906*|0.3|4.9	353609|0.3|12.5
2abs 5000/10/SUM	17584|0.7|*1.2*	38216|0.5|**1.6**	*157491*|0.4|5.5	353609|0.3|12.4
2abs 5000/10/MAX	4031|0.7|**0.7**	**18914**|0.5|**1.0**	*242012*|0.4|*8.7*	**119802**|0.3|**3.9**
seed 100/10/SUM	*27364*|0.6|*1.4*	71411|0.6|2.9	*132538*|0.5|5.0	353609|0.5|13.0
seed 100/10/MAX	**1209**|0.5|**0.5**	**15920**|0.6|**1.0**	117276|0.6|4.5	**119802**|0.5|**4.3**
seed 5000/10/SUM	17584|1.7|*2.0*	38216|1.3|2.3	*157491*|1.0|*6.2*	353609|0.7|13.0
seed 5000/10/MAX	4031|1.6|*1.6*	**18914**|1.3|**1.7**	*241968*|1.0|*9.3*	**119802**|0.7|**4.4**

interface to UPPAAL is the one introduced in [19].[3] For the experiments, we used a machine with two Intel Xeon processors running at 3.02 GHz with 6 GB RAM.

We present results for six kinds of heuristics here. First, we have heuristics h^L and h^U, which are based on a heuristic method from AI planning [20]. Second, we have heuristic "syn" based on extracting abstraction predicates from the guards of a system [16]. Third, we have a heuristic based on refinement of a single error path with initial predicate set $\{loc(p_1) = \ell_1, loc(p_2) = \ell_2\}$ ("1abs"), and fourth, a heuristic based on two abstractions obtained by having two initial predicate sets $\{loc(p_1) = \ell_1\}, \{loc(p_2) = \ell_2\}$ ("2abs"). Fifth, we have a method where refinement is based on several abstract paths (Table 3), and finally, a method where we use initial predicate sets that contain "random" predicates as additional "seed" for the abstraction refinement.

The entries in Tables 1 and 2 are of the form $a|b|c$. Here, a is the size of the search space explored by UPPAAL, i.e., the number of explored states (not to be confused with the size of the abstract state space!). The second figure b is the total time in seconds taken for precomputing the heuristic, and c is the total user time for the UPPAAL model checking as measured by the Linux command `time`, including the precomputation time b. Note that in some cases b is equal

---

[3] The UPPAAL source code was provided to our group by Gerd Behrmann.

Table 2. C2-C9: search space size | heuristic computing time | user time

	C2			C3			C4			C5		
h^L	**4059**	n.a.	**0.2**	3253	n.a.	**0.2**	**2683**	n.a.	**0.2**	87342	n.a.	*6.5*
h^U	5629	n.a.	**0.4**	4756	n.a.	**0.3**	3471	n.a.	**0.2**	19598	n.a.	1.2
syn 5000/10/SUM	**2866**	3.3	3.3	**2691**	3.8	3.8	3941	5.3	5.3	*68077*	5.9	*6.0*
syn 5000/10/MAX	**2421**	3.7	3.7	**2360**	3.8	3.8	**1621**	5.3	5.3	518	5.9	*5.9*
syn 20000/20/SUM	9938	8.5	*8.5*	5446	9.2	*9.2*	*11061*	13.4	*13.4*	timeout		
syn 20000/20/MAX	*18085*	8.2	*8.2*	9506	8.8	*8.8*	21712	13.0	*13.0*	timeout		
1abs 5000/10	*28303*	1.3	1.3	*13458*	1.4	1.4	*11836*	1.6	1.6	**378**	2.0	2.0
2abs 5000/10/SUM	7382	1.4	1.4	**2866**	1.5	1.5	**2679**	1.8	1.8	**258**	2.0	2.0
2abs 5000/10/MAX	5616	1.4	1.4	**3612**	1.4	1.4	3376	1.7	1.7	**299**	2.0	2.0
seed 100/10/SUM	5154	0.5	0.5	4793	0.6	0.6	4002	0.8	0.8	657	0.5	**0.5**
seed 100/10/MAX	7011	0.6	0.6	**4196**	0.6	0.6	3512	0.8	0.8	797	0.5	**0.5**
seed 5000/10/SUM	6849	5.7	*5.7*	**3496**	5.9	*5.9*	3140	6.6	6.6	583	7.8	*7.8*
seed 5000/10/MAX	5612	6.0	*6.0*	**3608**	6.0	*6.0*	3374	6.7	6.7	304	7.8	*7.8*

	C6			C7			C8			C9		
h^L	*16284*	n.a.	1.3	*79769*	n.a.	6.2	37202	n.a.	2.6	134489	n.a.	**9.1**
h^U	9327	n.a.	**0.5**	46193	n.a.	**2.6**	**6569**	n.a.	**0.5**	127924	n.a.	11.0
syn 5000/10/SUM	*13518*	6.7	6.7	*71916*	7.1	*7.1*	61871	10.4	*10.4*	156445	14.5	15.0
syn 5000/10/MAX	**1514**	6.3	6.3	17534	7.6	7.6	39158	11.2	*11.2*	146810	15.8	16.7
syn 20000/20/SUM	6176	14.1	*14.1*	32290	15.4	*15.4*	30394	18.3	*18.3*	**31280**	25.8	*25.8*
syn 20000/20/MAX	**863**	13.8	*13.8*	**9603**	16.4	*16.4*	19682	19.9	*19.9*	**22176**	27.9	*27.9*
1abs 5000/10	*16346*	2.0	2.0	*102611*	2.1	**2.7**	*329298*	2.2	5.2	*1637759*	1.9	*19.1*
2abs 5000/10/SUM	3127	2.2	2.2	31584	2.3	**2.4**	106065	2.8	3.9	451610	3.2	8.8
2abs 5000/10/MAX	3549	2.1	2.1	31676	2.3	**2.3**	103416	2.8	3.6	359530	3.2	**7.4**
seed 100/10/SUM	*18711*	0.6	**0.8**	*110878*	0.7	**1.9**	*333488*	0.6	4.5	*1623070*	0.7	*20.0*
seed 100/10/MAX	*20583*	0.6	**0.8**	*119415*	0.7	**2.0**	*340927*	0.7	4.6	*1637147*	0.7	*20.3*
seed 5000/10/SUM	*20250*	8.0	*8.0*	*118830*	8.1	*8.1*	*290987*	10.0	*11.8*	*1270802*	12.0	*30.0*
seed 5000/10/MAX	3539	7.6	7.6	31610	7.9	7.9	103140	9.3	9.3	358171	11.3	**14.7**

to c because the time for the actual Uppaal model checking is negligible. We have highlighted the best and the worst figures. For each example, those figures within factor 2 of the best figure are in **boldface**, and those within factor 2 of the worst are in *italics*.

5.1   Other Heuristics Used for Comparison

On the one hand, we used two heuristics introduced in [20], which are among the best heuristics for these benchmarks [19]. There, a heuristic method from AI planning is adapted, based on a notion of "monotonicity" where it is assumed that a state variable accumulates, rather than changes, its values. In Tables 1 and 2 and in [20], there are two heuristics referred to as h^L (which states in which layer of the *relaxed transition graph* a state can be found, and is a strongly underestimating heuristic) and h^U (which gives an actual path in the abstract system, and may be overestimating). Since h^L and h^U are computed on-the-fly, there is no heuristic precomputation.

Concerning the runtime, h^L and h^U are very often among the best by far. Concerning the size of the explored state space, they are more often among the worst than among the best. The heuristics are relatively expensive to compute *per state* which shows for N3, C5, C9, but the fact that the runtime is so small whenever the size of the explored search space is small exhibits the advantage of on-the-fly computation: in contrast, for heuristics based on predicate abstraction and pattern databases, it could happen that a heuristic is very good but expensive to compute because the abstract state space is big.

On the other hand, we compared with a kind of abstraction we developed previously [16], where the repertoire of predicates consists of all guards and invariants that textually occur in the system definition, together with all possible location predicates. Since taking one abstraction based on all these predicates is much too inefficient to compute, we only take the predicates of one single process, generate an abstract state space, and see if the number of states or the number of layers exceeds certain thresholds. If yes, we take the current predicate set for defining one pattern database and start generating another one based on another process. Otherwise, we continue to add the predicates coming from another process to the current abstraction. Typically we end up with two or three abstractions this way. The results are referred to as "syn" for "syntax-based".

A notation such as "5000/10/SUM", used not only for "syn" but also for other heuristics, means that the threshold on the number of states (resp., layers) is 5000 (resp., 10), and that we use the SUM option (see Sec. 3). The figures for "syn 20000/20/MAX" and "syn 20000/20/SUM" are identical in Table 1 because only one (or only one non-trivial) abstraction was generated, which is why we write "SM".

For M and N, the results are never among the best and often among the worst. For C, the explored state space size is sometimes among the best (note in particular C9), but often among the worst as far as the runtimes are concerned, as computing the heuristic is so expensive. The problem with "syn" is that composing predicate sets along process boundaries as described above is a very coarse approach: it can happen that we have a predicate set that is very small and yields a heuristic that is fast to compute but not very good, and then adding the predicates from another process immediately results in an abstraction that might be good but is extremely expensive to compute.[4] In contrast, with our abstraction refinement the differences between subsequent abstractions will typically be much smaller so that the balance between heuristic quality and heuristic computation time can be better tuned.

5.2   Using the (Joint or Separate) Target Locations as Initial Predicates

In our benchmarks the error condition is given by a formula of the form $(loc(p_1) = \ell_1) \wedge (loc(p_2) = \ell_2)$, i.e., the error state consists of process p_1 being in ℓ_1 and p_2 being in ℓ_2 simultaneously. The simplest setup we tried is the following: the initial abstraction consists of the two location predicates for the two target locations.[5]

---

[4] This problem also occurs when we use off-the-shelf abstraction refinement [16].

[5] Note that having two processes involved in the target condition does not mean that the whole system consists of just these two processes.

The abstraction can thus definitely distinguish a target state from a non-target state, which in our intuition is a good basis for a heuristic function. In each step, the refinement is based on a single abstract path of maximal length in the current abstract space. The results for this strategy are marked in Tables 1 and 2 with "1abs".

As a termination criterion for the refinement, we used thresholds on the size of the abstract state space and on the number of layers as in Sec. 5.1. Whenever one of them is exceeded, then the current abstraction will be the last one generated in this refinement loop. The thresholds were chosen to pose a sensible limit on the computational resources spent in building the abstractions.

Although it seems intuitively reasonable to have an initial abstraction that contains location predicates for both target locations, on the other hand one may also argue that it is good to combine several abstractions, and a simple way of doing this is to have two abstractions, each based on the initial predicate set $\{loc(p_i) = \ell_i\}$ for $i = 1, 2$. Everything else is as before. The results are marked in the tables with "2abs".

Concerning the size of the explored state space, "2abs" is better than "1abs" on most examples. This suggests that, *ceteris paribus*, the argument that having several different heuristics is better than having just one outweighs the argument that a good heuristic should at least capture the difference between a target state and a non-target state. Therefore, in the investigation of other aspects of the design space presented in the sequel, we decided to base the initial abstractions on the two targets kept separate.

Concerning the total runtime, "1abs" is sometimes negligibly better than "2abs" because we only have to compute one abstract space instead of two.

Now compare "2abs" to the other heuristics. The results are never extraordinarily bad: in the few cases where the results are among the worst, they are "in good company". The results are often among the best, but in none of these cases are they dramatically better than the corresponding result for "seed", see Sec. 5.4. Compared to "syn", the balance between heuristic quality and heuristic computation time can be better tuned because the differences between subsequent abstractions are typically small.

5.3   Abstractions Based on Several Paths

In this setup, each iteration of the refinement loop is based on refining *several* paths, each as shown in Fig. 3. We generated two abstractions, each based on the initial predicate set $\{loc(p_i) = \ell_i\}$ for $i = 1, 2$.

For each target, the refinement loop works as follows: given the current abstract space, we select several paths for doing refinement — selecting *all* paths would be too expensive, selecting just one path might result in too few predicates being added in the refinement step. Moreover, the longer the abstract path the more predicates will be added due to this path. Therefore our intuition was that the number and quality of the predicates added are strongly correlated to the length of the abstract paths one chooses, and so we decided that all abstract paths should all have the same length l, which is thus a parameter of

Table 3. Refinement based on q paths of length l, setting 5000/10/SUM

$l \rightarrow$	$\frac{w}{1}$	$\frac{w}{2}$	$\frac{w}{3}$	$\frac{w}{4}$	$\frac{w}{1}$	$\frac{w}{2}$	$\frac{w}{3}$	$\frac{w}{4}$	$\frac{w}{1}$	$\frac{w}{2}$	$\frac{w}{3}$	$\frac{w}{4}$	$\frac{w}{1}$	$\frac{w}{2}$	$\frac{w}{3}$	$\frac{w}{4}$
$\downarrow q$	M1				M2				M3				M4			
1,2,4,8	14955		22162		17753		38234		86316		61252		110240		110240	
	N1				N2				N3				N4			
1,2,4,8	17584		30269		38216		69276		157491		145018		353609		353609	

$l \rightarrow$	$\frac{w}{1}$	$\frac{w}{2}$	$\frac{w}{3}$	$\frac{w}{4}$	$\frac{w}{1}$	$\frac{w}{2}$	$\frac{w}{3}$	$\frac{w}{4}$	$\frac{w}{1}$	$\frac{w}{2}$	$\frac{w}{3}$	$\frac{w}{4}$
$\downarrow q$	C2				C5				C8			
1	7382	13653	23389	23389	258	258	522	522	106065	293694	308413	308413
2,4,8	7382	12500	12500	12500	258	258	258	258	106065	288112	288112	288112
	C3				C6				C9			
1	2866	5208	9634	9634	3127	14707	15925	15925	451610	1412455	1560656	1560656
2,4,8	2866	4819	4819	4819	3127	12922	12922	12922	451610	1413494	1413494	1413494
	C4				C7							
1	2679	4989	8587	8587	31584	92322	98028	98028				
2,4,8	2679	4600	4600	4600	31584	86465	86465	86465				

the method. Technically, in an ad hoc random way one selects up to q states in the abstract state space such that there is an abstract path of length l from such a state to the error state. Then one refines the current abstraction based on these paths.

In Table 3, we show the explored state space size depending on q and l. Here w is the number of layers of the current abstract state space, e.g., $l = \frac{w}{2}$ means that the refinement is based on abstract paths whose length is half the maximal length of any path in the current abstract state space. We set l to a minimum of 3 to avoid some extremely short paths. Note that the results for $l = \frac{w}{1}$, $q = 1$ are necessarily identical to those of "2abs 5000/10/SUM".

The parameter q has little influence on the number of explored states. I.e., it does not seem to matter which or how many of the paths are chosen for the refinement. This is a bit surprising, and contrary to our intuition [16] that off-the-shelf abstraction refinement is too much focused on a single path, which should be bad because it leads to abstractions that are fine in some regions and coarse in others. In contrast, the parameter l is important. If l is too small, then the refinement will not "take off", i.e., it will converge very quickly generating very few predicates (with M3 and N3 as exceptions).

We analysed some of the predicate sets generated for our benchmarks more closely. Our observations suggest the following thesis: it is not the case that the above strategy could lead to many very different predicate sets, depending on how the parameters are chosen. Rather, for reasonably chosen parameters, an abstraction refinement based on one of the target locations will converge to a certain predicate set. This convergence can happen very early and the predicate set can be very small. This motivates the method described next, adding additional "seeds" for the abstraction. We go back to taking $q = 1$ and l maximal, as in Sec. 5.2.

5.4   Generating Several Abstractions Based on "Random Seeds"

Using the setups above, we observed that our refinement sometimes reaches a fixpoint extremely early, way before any "artificial" termination criterion (see Sec. 5.1) applies. If the final transition of the abstract path is $\ell \rightarrow \ell'$ and the initial abstraction is just the predicate $loc = \ell'$, then the abstract space will have two states T and F, and the refinement will not add any predicates. Generally, if the abstract path consists of location-wise consistent edges and either there are no integer guards/invariants or they have already been added, then the refinement stops, and this can happen very early, so that the abstraction is extremely coarse.

Our idea to overcome this phenomenon is to insert a "random" location predicate as an additional "seed" for the abstraction refinement, i.e., to use a slightly finer initial abstraction. As a first naïve realisation of this, we generated abstractions by refinement based on each pair $(loc = \ell_0, loc = \ell)$ where ℓ_0 is a target location and ℓ any other location, for any process. This will give dozens of abstract spaces for our examples, so we had to find ways of generating fewer abstractions yet sufficiently many interesting ones. After observing that many generated spaces are extremely similar, we pruned spaces that are likely to be similar to previously generated spaces, as follows: firstly, if for a refinement based on some seed predicate, the generated abstract space in the first refinement iteration consists of abstract states where the seed predicate is always U, then we deem the seed predicate to be useless and abort the refinement based on it. Secondly, we take at most one location predicate per system process as seed, that is to say, we consider the location predicates of each process in turn, but once we have successfully generated an abstraction for the current location predicate, we disregard all remaining location predicates of the current process. With this approach, we typically obtained between four and six abstractions.

The results are marked in Tables 1 and 2 with the word "seed". The results are very unstable, sometimes extremely good, sometimes extremely bad. An improvement of the approach could be to allow for random restarts, that is to say, whenever the error search is taking too long, one might abort the search and compute a new heuristic function, obtained by modifying some of the parameters. This is in loose analogy to random restarts in propositional satisfiability solving [21]. Alternatively, one could have several searches running in parallel, based on several abstractions obtained by choosing the parameters in different ways.

For the M and N examples, the search space sizes are sometimes the same for "100/10" and "5000/10". Also, some search space sizes are identical to the respective values for "2abs". Of course, we do not believe that this is a pure coincidence, but rather, that it is due to the fact that the underlying abstractions are similar. While inspection confirms this to some extent, it is not obvious that the abstractions should be so *extremely* similar, but we do not consider this to be a particularly important issue.

6   Related Work

Using pattern database heuristics for DMC has been proposed in [25]. The systems considered are finite-state transition systems, where each state consists of an assignment of values from a finite domain to the state variables. In a next step, it is assumed that a state can be encoded as a bitvector. Unlike in our work, the bits are not interpreted as logical formulas that "talk about" system states, and predicate abstraction is not even mentioned. The encoding of states as bitvectors is no abstraction, in the sense of information loss; it is only in the next step that a pattern database abstraction is defined by ignoring some of the bits. Note that there is no abstraction *refinement* in that work.

Another work by the same authors [24] does consider refinement, however it is not the abstractions that are refined, but the abstract error paths themselves are refined, removing those that are spurious.

In [12], pattern database heuristics are also used for DMC. Refinement is not considered. It is observed that combining several pattern databases is useful.

In [10], DMC of timed automata is considered. The heuristic function is based on an abstraction that merges locations until there are at most N locations left, where N is a parameter. The heuristic function is read off the overall merged automaton. This approach does not involve predicate abstraction or refinement.

We have already mentioned another approach to DMC, which we used for comparison because it is among the best for our benchmarks [20]. Several heuristic functions including [10,20] have been joined in the tool UPPAAL/DMC [19].

In our own previous work [16], we have presented a first implementation of predicate abstraction for DMC of timed automata, including one approach where the abstraction was generated using refinement. Unlike in the work presented here, in the implementation we actually used the tool ARMC [23]. The setup of the refinement process differs substantially from the one of this paper — most importantly, in [16] we have a preprocessing of the original system splitting it into several subsets of its processes, similarly as described for "syn". The motivation for implementing the refinement process ourselves instead of relying on ARMC is that we wanted to cater for the aspects that are different in our scenario, as discussed in Sec. 4.

7   Discussion

In this paper, we have presented various methods of setting up a predicate abstraction refinement loop for the purpose of generating heuristic functions for DMC.

We found that generating predicates by collecting guards along abstract paths is useful for generating reasonably small and good abstractions (Sec. 5.2), in contrast to the syntax-based abstractions [16] that tend to be too big ("syn"). So the main benefit is that abstraction refinement selects good predicates from a repertoire.

Moreover, we hoped that abstraction refinement enlarges the repertoire of predicates, as in Fig. 2, where the predicate $i = j + 3$ cannot be read off the system syntax. We have looked into this, and it seems to be of hardly any significance. For our benchmarks it happens very rarely (though not never!) that a predicate is generated that is not contained as a guard or invariant in the system. Thus for these benchmarks, generating predicates by updating guards and invariants is overly subtle and complicated.

Basing the refinement loop on several, not necessarily error paths rather than just one path did not have the positive impact of adding more predicates that we hoped (Sec. 5.3). As we explained in Sec. 5.4, this is mostly due to the fact that the refinement can reach a fixpoint at a very early point: the abstract paths, even though extremely short, do not give rise to the addition of any further predicates.

The idea of adding seeds (Sec. 5.4) provides a remedy to this problem. The idea can be varied in many ways, of which we discussed some. It can yield very good results, but the results are quite unpredictable, and we still hope to enhance abstraction refinement using some technique which systematically improves on the method of Sec. 5.2.

In fact, suppose there is a more stable solution to the problem of early convergence, consistently obtaining reasonably good results. Then this solution might provide the key to boosting the performance of our initial idea, basing the refinement on several paths rather than just one path. This is a promising issue to be explored in further work.

In summary, while the application of abstraction refinement for the intelligent creation of heuristic functions is an exciting idea, making this idea work in practice is non-trivial and involves several subtle issues. A variety of these issues has been identified and investigated in our work. It remains to be seen in future work how the prevailing difficulties can be overcome. In particular, it may be that some of the issues disappear or are less critical in other search problems. Hence investigating the method in other contexts – other DMC formalisms or AI problems – is important.

Acknowledgements. This work was partly supported by the German Research Council (DFG) as part of the Transregional Collaborative Research Center "Automatic Verification and Analysis of Complex Systems" (SFB TR14/AVACS). We would like to thank Henning Dierks, Sebastian Kupferschmid, Bernhard Nebel, Andreas Podelski, and Martin Wehrle for useful discussions and help with the implementation. We could also like to thank the anonymous reviewers of this paper for their useful comments.

References

1. Alur, R., Dill, D.L.: A theory of timed automata. Theoretical Computer Science 126(2), 183–235 (1994)
2. Ball, T., Podelski, A., Rajamani, S.K.: Completeness of abstraction refinement for software model checking. In: Katoen, J.-P., Stevens, P. (eds.) TACAS 2002. LNCS, vol. 2280. Springer, Heidelberg (2002)

3. Ball, T., Podelski, A., Rajamani, S.K.: Boolean and Cartesian abstraction for model checking C programs. International Journal on Software Tools for Technology Transfer 5(1), 49–58 (2003)

4. Behrmann, G., David, A., Larsen, K.G.: A tutorial on Uppaal. In: Bernardo, M., Corradini, F. (eds.) SFM-RT 2004. LNCS, vol. 3185, pp. 200–236. Springer, Heidelberg (2004)

5. Bengtsson, J., Yi, W.: Timed automata: Semantics, algorithms and tools. In: Desel, J., Reisig, W., Rozenberg, G. (eds.) Lectures on Concurrency and Petri Nets. LNCS, vol. 3098, pp. 87–124. Springer, Heidelberg (2004)

6. Clarke, E., Gupta, A., Strichman, O.: SAT-based counterexample-guided abstraction refinement. IEEE Transactions on Computer Aided Design 23(7), 1113–1123 (2004)

7. Cousot, P., Cousot, R.: Abstract interpretation: a unified lattice model for static analysis of programs by construction or approximation of fixpoints. In: Proceedings of the 4th ACM Symposium on Principles of Programming Languages, pp. 238–252 (1977)

8. Culberson, J.C., Schaeffer, J.: Pattern databases. Computational Intelligence 14(3), 318–334 (1998)

9. Dierks, H.: Comparing model checking and logical reasoning for real-time systems. Formal Aspects of Computing 16(2), 104–120 (2004)

10. Dräger, K., Finkbeiner, B., Podelski, A.: Directed model checking with distance-preserving abstractions. In: Valmari, A. (ed.) SPIN 2006. LNCS, vol. 3925, pp. 19–34. Springer, Heidelberg (2006)

11. Edelkamp, S., Leue, S., Lluch-Lafuente, A.: Directed explicit-state model checking in the validation of communication protocols. International Journal on Software Tools for Technology 5(2-3), 247–267 (2004)

12. Edelkamp, S., Lluch-Lafuente, A.: Abstraction in directed model checking. In: Proceedings of the ICAPS Workshop on Connecting Planning Theory with Practice, pp. 7–13 (2004)

13. Filliâtre, J.-C., Owre, S., Rueß, H., Shankar, N.: ICS: Integrated canonizer and solver. In: Berry, G., Comon, H., Finkel, A. (eds.) CAV 2001. LNCS, vol. 2102, pp. 246–249. Springer, Heidelberg (2001)

14. Graf, S., Saïdi, H.: Construction of abstract state graphs with PVS. In: Grumberg, O. (ed.) CAV 1997. LNCS, vol. 1254, pp. 72–83. Springer, Heidelberg (1997)

15. Hoffmann, J., Koehler, J.: A new method to index and query sets. In: Dean, T. (ed.) Proceedings of the 16th International Joint Conference on Artificial Intelligence, pp. 462–467. Morgan Kaufmann, San Francisco (1999)

16. Hoffmann, J., Smaus, J.-G., Rybalchenko, A., Kupferschmid, S., Podelski, A.: Using predicate abstraction to generate heuristic functions in UPPAAL. In: Edelkamp, S., Lomuscio, A. (eds.) MoChArt IV. LNCS, vol. 4428, pp. 51–66. Springer, Heidelberg (2007)

17. Korf, R.E.: Finding optimal solutions to Rubik's Cube using pattern databases. In: Proceedings of the 14th National Conference on Artificial Intelligence and 9th Innovative Applications of Artificial Intelligence Conference, pp. 700–705. MIT Press, Cambridge (1997)

18. Krieg-Brückner, B., Peleska, J., Olderog, E.-R., Baer, A.: The UniForM workbench, a universal development environment for formal methods. In: Woodcock, J.C.P., Davies, J., Wing, J.M. (eds.) FM 1999. LNCS, vol. 1709, pp. 1186–1205. Springer, Heidelberg (1999)

19. Kupferschmid, S., Dräger, K., Hoffmann, J., Finkbeiner, B., Dierks, H., Podelski, A., Behrmann, G.: UPPAAL/DMC – Abstraction-based heuristics for directed model checking. In: Grumberg, O., Huth, M. (eds.) TACAS 2007. LNCS, vol. 4424, pp. 679–682. Springer, Heidelberg (2007)
20. Kupferschmid, S., Hoffmann, J., Dierks, H., Behrmann, G.: Adapting an AI planning heuristic for directed model checking. In: Valmari, A. (ed.) SPIN 2006. LNCS, vol. 3925, pp. 35–52. Springer, Heidelberg (2006)
21. Moskewicz, M.W., Madigan, C.F., Zhao, Y., Zhang, L., Malik, S.: Engineering an efficient SAT solver. In: Proceedings of the 38th Design Automation Conference, pp. 530–535. ACM Press, New York (2001)
22. Pearl, J.: Heuristic. Addison-Wesley, Reading (1985)
23. Podelski, A., Rybalchenko, A.: ARMC: The logical choice for software model checking with abstraction refinement. In: Hanus, M. (ed.) PADL 2007. LNCS, vol. 4354, pp. 245–259. Springer, Heidelberg (2007)
24. Qian, K., Nymeyer, A.: Abstraction-based model checking using heuristical refinement. In: Wang, F. (ed.) ATVA 2004. LNCS, vol. 3299, pp. 165–178. Springer, Heidelberg (2004)
25. Qian, K., Nymeyer, A.: Guided invariant model checking based on abstraction and symbolic pattern databases. In: Jensen, K., Podelski, A. (eds.) TACAS 2004. LNCS, vol. 2988, pp. 497–511. Springer, Heidelberg (2004)

Model Checking Strategic Equilibria

Nicolas Troquard, Wiebe van der Hoek, and Michael Wooldridge

Department of Computer Science, University of Liverpool, UK

Abstract. Solutions concepts are a fundamental tool for the analysis of game-like systems, and as a consequence, much effort has been devoted to the problem of characterising solution concepts using logic. However, one problem is that, to characterise solution concepts such as Nash equilibrium, it seems necessary to refer to strategies in the object language, which tends to complicate the object language. We propose a logic in which we can formulate important properties of games (and in particular pure-strategy solution concepts) without recourse to naming strategies in the object language. The idea is that instead of using predicates which state that a particular collection of strategies forms a solution, we define formulae of the logic that are true at a state if and only if this state constitutes a particular equilibrium outcome. We demonstrate the logic by model checking equilibria of strategic games.

1 Introduction

Game theory [18] has come to be seen as a topic of major importance for computer science, since it focuses on the study of protocols from an economic perspective. *Social software* [20] aims to give social procedures a theory analogous to the formal theories for computer algorithms, e.g., program correctness or analysis of programs. One aspect of *game logics* [23] is to study those theories with logical tools. We can distinguish two complementary families of formalism: dynamic logics (action, time), and logics of mental states (epistemic, preferences).

Games of interaction and their solutions. A game is a description of the protocol of interaction between players and their preferences. A solution concept describes what may be the solutions (or outcomes) in some class of game.

To describe the different models of interaction, the solutions and their properties, game theory makes use of the language of mathematics which is merely set theory and plain English. One objective of game logics is to build purely logical formal languages that are able to talk about social procedures and games in particular. Some obvious merits would be to obtain unambiguous formalisations for the domain of social procedures, and the opportunity to apply formal methods of computer science to game-like systems.

Game theory is concerned with identifying sensible solutions for a particular class of game. Our present task is to propose a framework in which we can reason about them.

Model checking game solutions. The interest of the computer science community in the *agent paradigm* for software architecture is dramatically increasing, and game theory is one of the most successfully applied theories of agent interaction in computer science.

D. Peled and M. Wooldridge (Eds.): MOCHART 2008, LNAI 5348, pp. 166–188, 2009.

As a consequence, it is not hard to argue in favour of formal methods for verifying social procedures as they are fundamental for the validation of such complex systems.

Model checking is one of these methods for hardware or software verification. A problem of model checking can be formally stated as follows: given a property (or logical formula) φ, a model $\mathcal{M}$, return the set of states S such that $s \in S$ iff φ is true at the state s in M.

One important aspect that one should have in mind when designing methods for model checking is then to provide a language of specification that will facilitate the work of the user. In this paper, we attach a particular importance to the simplicity of the syntax of our logic for the very purpose of characterising properties of games.

Action abstraction. Typically in game logics, the characterisation of solution concepts is achieved by defining predicates of the form $SC((s_i)_N)$, stating that the particular strategy profile $(s_i)_N$ is an equilibrium with respect to the solution concept SC^1 (for example take SC as Nash equilibrium). In such predicate definitions, strategies or actions are parameters, and so we must have a way of referring to these in the logic's object language. Propositional Dynamic Logic [14] is a natural candidate. However when this principle is integrated to logics of ability and agency like Alternating-time Temporal Logic [1], Coalition Logic [22] or STIT theories [5], there is a paradigmatic issue. Indeed, the agenda of reasoning about solution concepts seems to make it necessary to reify strategies in the object language — yet one of the putative advantages of temporal-based logics such as ATL is to abstract away from strategies and actions.

But let us take a step back, and ask the question: are explicit names of actions necessary for the logical characterisation of solution concepts? In this note, we shall provide evidence for a negative answer. For the time being a motivational question is: what would we gain by abstracting actions away?

For model checking solution concepts we would like to give as input (1) a game, and (2) a *general* formulation of a solution concept, and obtain as output the set of outcomes that verify it. For the existing logics able to express game equilibria, model checking possible approaches to verifying solution concepts are somewhat limited because the modeller first has to choose an action profile $(s_i)_N$ and then check whether the game satisfies $SC((s_i)_N)$. Either the hard work is done by the designer, in selecting the action profile, or we need to provide to the model checker a large formula containing as many disjunctions as the model to be tested has strategy profiles. This leads to a formula exponentially large w.r.t. to the number of strategies. As we shall see, our definitions of solution concept are not subject to this drawback. We thus can characterise important properties of game in a more succinct manner. This is also desirable since the complexity of model checking typically depends on the size of the input formula.

Naturally, abstraction of action names is not a solution to every problem in social software. For a completely different perspective, see [24] in which the author considers strategies to be "the unsung heroes of game theory". However, we show in what follows that without relying on explicit actions, we are able to give a general logical formulation

---

[1] We call N the *grand coalition*, the coalition containing every players. A *strategy profile* is a combination of one strategy for every player of the grand coalition.

SC for most solution concepts in strategic games. As a consequence, we can check in a very natural manner where the equilibria are in a game.

Outline. This article aims at providing a language for characterising properties of games, which is expressive, easy to manipulate, unambiguous, and in this sense particularly suitable for a designer of interaction protocols in need of a tool for model checking their game theoretic properties. We first introduce some concepts from game theory and some solution concepts. Next, we present our logic and characterise the solution concepts in logic. We continue with examples. We conclude with an informal discussion and perspectives.

2   Some Notions from Game Theory

In this section, we review the basics of game theory in strategic games.

2.1   Strategic Games

Definition 1 (strategic game form). *A strategic game form is a tuple* $\langle N, (A_i) \rangle$ *where:*

- *N is a finite set of* players *(or agents);*
- A_i *is a nonempty set of* actions *for each player* $i \in N$.

A strategic game form is sometimes called the *mechanism*. It specifies the agents taking part in the game and the actions available to them. Next, we need preferences, which will give the players the incentive for taking an action.

Definition 2 (preference relation). *A preference relation* $\succeq$ *over S is a total, transitive and reflexive binary relation over S.*

We can now see a strategic game as basically the composition of a strategic game form with a collection of preference relations (one for every agent).

Definition 3 (strategic game). *A strategic game is a tuple* $\langle N, (A_i), (\succeq_i) \rangle$ *where* $\langle N, (A_i) \rangle$ *is a strategic game form, and for each player* $i \in N$, $\succeq_i$ *is a preference relation over* $A = \times_{j \in N} A_j$.

We refer to a collection $(a_j)_{j \in N}$, consisting of one action for every agent in N, as an *action profile.* Given an action profile a, we denote by a_i the action of the player i, and by a_{-i} the action profile of the coalition $N \setminus \{i\}$. We write a_C for the *coalitional actions* that are members of $A_C = \times_{j \in C} A_j$ for any $C \subseteq N$.

Strategic games are models of interaction in which each player chooses an action simultaneously and independently. It is convenient to see the elements of A as the outcomes of the game, resulting from an action profile. There are three ingredients that are characteristic of *game theoretic* interactions in strategic games: (i) agents are independent, in the sense that every player i can freely decide which action in A_i to play whatever the other agents choose – all combinations of agents' choice are compatible; (ii) not only those combinations are compatible, but they also lead to a unique outcome (here formally represented by the action profile itself); and (iii) the preferences $\succeq_i$ are

	a_2	b_2
a_1	$1, 1$	$2, 0$
b_1	$0, 2$	$0, 0$

Fig. 1. An example of 2-player strategic game

over the possible outcomes A, which gives the game theoretic flavour: players must take into account the preferences of others in order to determine how to achieve the best outcome for themselves.

In 2-player games, it is convenient to represent a strategic game as a matrix of utilities (or payoffs). In the game shown in Figure 1, player 1 is the row player and player 2 is the column player. The entries (x, y) of the matrix represent the payoffs of agents for a particular outcome — x is the payoff for the row player, while y is the payoff for the column player. The preferences are easily derived. For example $(a_1, a_2) \succeq_1 (b_1, a_2)$, $(a_1, a_2) \succeq_2 (a_1, b_2)$ but $(a_1, a_2) \not\succeq_1 (a_1, b_2)$, and $(b_1, b_2) \succeq_2 (a_1, b_2)$ and $(a_1, b_2) \succeq_2 (b_1, b_2)$.

2.2   Game Equilibria

Next, we define some important solution concepts in *pure strategies*. Those are definitions of very standard notions of game theory. We refer the reader to [18]. We will later demonstrate the ability of our logic to represent properties of strategic games and game equilibria in particular. In order to show how fine-grained the logic is, we will study several variants of equilibria, namely two sorts of Pareto optimality, three sorts of dominance, two sorts of Nash equilibria and the concept of the core.

Definition 4 (Pareto optimality). *An action profile a^* is a* weak Pareto optimum *if there is no action profile strictly preferred over a^* by every agent. a^* is a* strong Pareto optimum *if there is no action profile considered at least as good as a^* by every agent and strictly preferred by at least one agent.*

Definition 5 (dominance equilibria). *a^* is a* very weakly dominant *action profile if for every player i and action a_{-i}, i considers (a_i^*, a_{-i}) at least as good as (a_i', a_{-i}) for every a_i'. a^* is a* weakly dominant *action profile if for every agent i, one preference is strict for at least one action a_i'. a^* is a* strictly dominant *action profile if all preferences are strict.*

Definition 6 (Nash equilibrium). *An action profile $a^* \in A$ is a* Nash equilibrium *iff for every player $i \in N$ and for all $a_i \in A_i$, i considers (a_{-i}^*, a_i^*) at least as good as (a_{-i}^*, a_i).*

To conclude this collection of solution concepts, we will also show interest in cooperative games via the study of strong Nash equilibrium and the core of strategic games.

Definition 7 (strong Nash equilibrium). *An action profile a^* is a* strong Nash equilibrium *of a strategic game iff there is no coalition $C \subset N$ and no strategy a_C such that (a_C, a_{-C}^*) is considered strictly better than a^* by every players of C.*

Definition 8 ((weak) core membership). *An action profile a^* is* dominated *in a strategic game iff there is a coalition $C \subset N$ and a strategy a_C such that for all a_{-C}, every $i \in C$ strictly prefers (a_C, a_{-C}) over a^*. a^* is in the (weak)* core *of the game if it is not* dominated.

This last definitions hold for a *coalitional game without transferable utilities*. That is, players can form coalitions, but cannot redistribute the sum of the payoffs among the individuals of the coalition.

3   A Hybrid Logic of Choice and Preferences

We now introduce a logic that will allow us to capture game theoretic solution concepts such as those above, without recourse to naming strategies/actions in the object language.

At the heart of the models we use *Kripke frames*: we assume a set of states and binary relations over them. We will think of a state as an action profile. For any coalition J, an equivalence relations R_J will cluster together the states that J cannot differentiate by one of its choices. The main task is to constrain the frames $\langle S, (R_J) \rangle$ such that they are a correct conceptualisation of strategic game forms. We will also have a preference relation P_i for every agent i. This logic is a hybrid logic [3], and in what follows, we pre-suppose some familiarity with this class of formalisms.

3.1   Language and Semantics

Let us assume $Agt = \{0, 1 \ldots n\}$ a nonempty finite set of *agents*, $Prop = \{p_1, p_2 \ldots\}$ a countable set of *propositions*, $Nom = \{i_1, i_2 \ldots\}$ a countable set of *nominals* and $WVar = \{x_1, x_2 \ldots\}$ a countable set of *state variables*. $Prop, Nom, WVar$ are pairwise disjoint. We call $Symb = Nom \cup WVar$ the set of *state symbols*. The set of atoms is then denoted $Atm = Prop \cup Symb$.

The syntax of HLCP is defined by the BNF

$$\varphi ::= \top \mid a \mid \neg\varphi \mid \varphi \vee \varphi \mid [J]\varphi \mid [\preceq_i]\varphi \mid @_s\varphi \mid \downarrow x.\varphi$$

where $a \in Atm, x \in WVar, s \in Symb, i \in Agt$ and $J \subseteq Agt$ are terminal symbols. This is a multi-modal language of the hybrid logic with @ and $\downarrow$ (from now on $\mathcal{H}(@, \downarrow)$).

As usual, the remaining Boolean connectives are defined by abbreviations, and $\langle J \rangle\varphi =_{def} \neg[J]\neg\varphi$. Analogously, $\langle \preceq_i \rangle\varphi =_{def} \neg[\preceq_i]\neg\varphi$. In the object language, we denote by $\bar{J}$ the complement of J w.r.t. Agt.

The intended reading of $[J]\varphi$ is "group J chooses such that φ whatever other agents do" or "the current choices of agents in J ensure that φ". $\langle J \rangle\varphi$ is "J by its current choice does not rule out φ as a possible outcome." In particular, because the empty coalition cannot make any choice (or more precisely has a unique vacuous choice), $[\emptyset]\varphi$ can be read as "φ cannot be avoided" and $\langle \emptyset \rangle\varphi$ reads "φ is a possible outcome". $\langle \preceq_i \rangle\varphi$ means that at the current state, i prefers φ or is indifferent. $@_s\varphi$ means that φ is true at the state labelled s. $\downarrow x.\varphi$ labels the current state with the state variable x. Then it allows further explicit reference to the state by using x as an atom in the formula in the scope of the operator.

Definition 9 (HLCP model). *A model for HLCP is a tuple* $\langle Agt, \mathcal{P}rop, \mathcal{N}om, \mathcal{W}Var, S,$
$(R_J), (P_i), \pi \rangle$ *where:*

- Agt, $\mathcal{P}rop$, $\mathcal{N}om$ *and* $\mathcal{W}Var$ *are as before;*
- *S is a set of states;*
- *every* R_J *is an* equivalence relation *over S such that:*
    1. $R_{J_1 \cup J_2} \subseteq R_{J_1}$;
    2. $R_{J_1} \cap R_{J_2} \subseteq R_{J_1 \cup J_2}$;
    3. $R_{\emptyset} \subseteq R_J \circ R_{Agt \setminus J}$;
    4. $R_{Agt} = Id$;
- *every* P_i *is a total, transitive relation over S;*
- $\pi : S \longrightarrow 2^{\mathcal{P}rop \cup \mathcal{N}om}$ *is a valuation function where* $\pi^{-1}(i)$ *is a singleton for every* $i \in \mathcal{N}om$.

An assignment, *g, is a mapping from Symb into S. We define* g_s^x *as* $g_s^x(x) = s$ *and* $g_s^x(x) = g(y)$ *for* $x \neq y$.

The definition of valuation function of our models is conceptually important here.

The fact that the valuation of a nominal is a singleton reflects the main aspect of hybrid logic. A nominal uniquely characterises a state in the Kripke model and can thus can be understood as the name of a state.

R_J represents the choices of J. We can see it as a representation of the power of J in the game. $R_{\emptyset}$ represents the choice of the empty coalition. Since the empty coalition is assumed to have only one ubiquitous choice, $R_{\emptyset}$ is the relation over the possible outcomes. (1.) means that adding agents to a coalition makes it at least as effective. (2.) means that a coalition is not more effective than the combination of its parts. (3.) says that an outcome is possible only if one can reach it by two successive moves along two relations of choice of two complementary coalitions. This is intended to reflect the independence of agents. (4.) means that the grand coalition is maximally effective: if an outcome is possible then the grand coalition can choose it deterministically.

An example of a *malformed* HLCP (pre-)model with two players is given in Figure 2. $R_{Agt} = R_{\{0,1\}}$ relation is represented by dashed lines. $R_{\emptyset} = R_{\{0\}} \circ R_{\{1\}}$ relation groups the outcomes of a strategic game together. At s, the constraint (2.) on R is not satisfied. At t, the constraint (4.) on R is not satisfied. An example of HLCP (pre-)model with two players is represented in Figure 3.

Truth values are given by:

- $\mathcal{M}, g, s \models p$ iff $p \in \pi(s)$, for $p \in \mathcal{P}rop$
- $\mathcal{M}, g, s \models t$ iff $g(t) = s$, for $t \in Symb$
- $\mathcal{M}, g, s \models @_t\varphi$ iff $\mathcal{M}, g, g(t) \models \varphi$, where $t \in Symb$
- $\mathcal{M}, g, s \models \downarrow x.\varphi$ iff $\mathcal{M}, g_s^x, s \models \varphi$
- $\mathcal{M}, g, s \models [J]\varphi$ iff for all $s' \in R_J(s)$, $\mathcal{M}, g, s' \models \varphi$
- $\mathcal{M}, g, s \models [\preceq_i]\varphi$ iff for all $s' \in P_i(s)$, $\mathcal{M}, g, s' \models \varphi$

and as usual for classical connectives. We also adopt the conventional definitions of satisfiability and validity: an HLCP formula φ is *satisfiable* iff there exists a pointed model $\mathcal{M}, g, s$ such that $\mathcal{M}, g, s \models \varphi$ and φ is *valid* iff for every pointed model $\mathcal{M}, g, s$ we have $\mathcal{M}, g, s \models \varphi$.

We shall write $\mathcal{M}, s \models \varphi$ when it is the case that $\mathcal{M}, g, s \models \varphi$ for any mapping g.

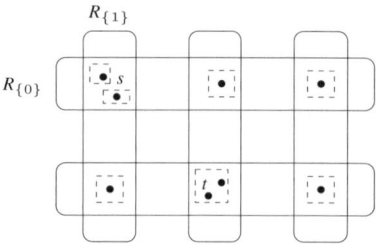
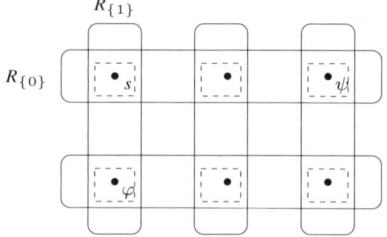

Fig. 2. Dashed lines represent R_{Agt} relations. This is *not* an HLCP model.

Fig. 3. An example of HLCP pre-model. Preferences are not represented.

3.2   Some Intuitions about the Logic

The frames of HLCP models are the frames we expect for studying strategic games. Definition 9 item 3 defines the powers of the empty coalition and reflects the independence of agents. A state is considered possible if it can be reached via the relation $R_\emptyset$. A state is possible only if it is compatible with the choices of complementary coalitions. From items 2 and 4, the pointwise intersections of agents' classes of choice are singletons: $\bigcap_{i \in Agt} R_{\{i\}}(s) = \{s\}$ for every s. Hence, possible states map directly to action profiles. We explain this in more detail now.

Actions and choices explained.   Given a coalition J, and two states s and s' in S, $s \in R_J(s')$ means that s and s' are two possible outcomes of a same choice of J. By definition (Definition 9 item 2), a choice of a coalition is the intersection of the choices of its individual members. Hence $s \in R_J(s')$ means that s and s' are in a same choice of every agent in J. To put it another way, no agent in J can choose (resp. dismiss) s without choosing (resp. dismissing) s'.

The operator $\langle J \rangle$ allows to quantify over possible states, given that the actions of the agents out of J are fixed. Equivalently, keeping in mind the analogy of states as action profiles, it makes it possible to quantify over actions of J. For example, $\langle \overline{\{i\}} \rangle$ quantifies over i's actions. $\langle \overline{J} \rangle \varphi$ can be read "the action of the agents that are not in J been maintained, there is an action of J such that φ".

In the model of Figure 3 with $Agt = \{0, 1\}$, at state s, player 1 can unilaterally change its current choice such that ψ holds: $\mathcal{M}, s \models \langle \overline{\{1\}} \rangle \psi$, or equivalently $\mathcal{M}, s \models \langle \{0\} \rangle \psi$, meaning that player 0 allows ψ. Analogously player 1 allows φ: $\mathcal{M}, s \models \langle \{1\} \rangle \varphi$. Hence player 0 can change its choice such that φ holds: $\mathcal{M}, s \models \langle \{0\} \rangle \varphi$.

The action component of the logic is largely inspired by the weaker Chellas's STIT logic [15]. The logic limited to individuals has been axiomatised by Xu [5, Chap. 17] and studied further in [4]. [9] proposes a group version of the logic. With HLCP, in order to fit with strategic games, the only difference with the original logic is a further constraint that says that the grand coalition can deterministically choose the outcome of the game.

Then, like STIT, HLCP has obvious links with multi-agent epistemic logic [11] and multi-dimensional logics over equivalence relations [17]. It may indeed be helpful to think about a choice relation as an epistemic relation. In epistemic logics, $[i]\varphi$ would read "i knows that φ". For a coalition J, $[J]$ is similar to the *distributed knowledge* operator of epistemic logic, usually written D_J. Let us make a quick observation and also emphasise that for the action component, we could have used cylindric modal logic [27] or logics of propositional control [26,13]. In these logics, a formula of the form $\Diamond_J\varphi$ reads the agents in J can change their choice such that φ holds. It trivially corresponds in HLCP to the formula $\langle \overline{J} \rangle \varphi$ meaning that the agents out of J allow for φ.

About the hybridisation. Intuitively, $\downarrow x.\varphi$ assigns the name of the current state to the variable x, and it can be reused in the scope of the binder as a propositional letter. The authors of [2] compare the role of the binder $\downarrow$ to the Reichenbachian *generalised present tense*. They write:

> It enables us to "store" an evaluation point, thereby making it possible to insist later that certain events happened at *that* time, or that certain other events must be viewed from that particular perspective. This is precisely the kind of expressive power we need to encode Reichenbach's ideas.

We argue that this ability to fix an 'evaluation point', viz. an action profile in our setting, and looking at alternatives from that perspective, is also precisely what we need to encode most game equilibria.

We can already take advantage of the power of hybrid logic for defining strict preferences which will be useful later.

Definition 10 (strict preferences). *The* strict preference *of i for an alternative where φ holds is defined by:*

$$\langle \prec_i \rangle \varphi =_{def} \downarrow x.\langle \preceq_i \rangle (\varphi \wedge \neg \langle \preceq_i \rangle x)$$

Note that the expressive power of hybrid logic makes it possible to characterise in the object language some features of models in a way that is not possible in conventional modal logic. For instance, the ability to grasp the intersection of relations was a key trigger for the modern era of hybrid logic [21]. This leads us to the axiomatic characterisation of HLCP.

3.3   Axiomatisation

x will be used as a meta-variable over the set of state variables $WVar$; s, t and u will be meta-variables over the set of state symbols $Symb$; and $\square$ is any modality from $\{[J] \mid J \subseteq Agt\} \cup \{[\preceq_i] \mid i \in Agt\}$.

There exist several presentations of the axiomatics of the basic hybrid logic with @ and $\downarrow$ (hereafter $\mathbb{K}_{\mathcal{H}(@,\downarrow)}$) [7,6,3]. We use one given in [6] which unlike the others we can find in the literature, does not have recourse to unorthodox rules, viz. rules of inference that apply under syntactic constraints. We show it in Figure 4. note that a substitution replaces uniformly (1) proposition variable by arbitrary formulae and (2) nominals by other nominals.

The principles are sound and axiomatise completely $\mathbb{K}_{\mathcal{H}(@,\downarrow)}$ when the operators symbolised by $\square$ are normal modalities over arbitrary frames (i.e., K-modalities). We now need to give the principles that will ensure that the modalities of the form

axioms:	
(CT)	enough classical tautologies
$(K_\Box)$	$\Box(p \to q) \to (\Box p \to \Box q)$
$(K_@)$	$@_s(p \to q) \to (@_s p \to @_s q)$
$(\text{selfdual}_@)$	$@_s p \leftrightarrow \neg @_s \neg p$
$(\text{ref}_@)$	$@_s s$
(agree)	$@_t @_s p \leftrightarrow @_s p$
(intro)	$s \to (p \leftrightarrow @_s p)$
(back)	$\neg \Box \neg @_s \varphi \to @_s \varphi$
(DA)	$@_s(\downarrow x.\varphi \leftrightarrow \varphi[x/s])$
$(\text{name}_\downarrow)$	$\downarrow x.(x \to \varphi) \to \varphi$, provided that x does not occur in φ
$(\text{BG}_\downarrow)$	$@_s \Box \downarrow x.@_s \neg \Box \neg x$
rules:	
(MP)	From $\vdash \varphi$ and $\vdash \varphi \to \psi$ infer $\vdash \psi$
(subst)	From $\vdash \varphi$ infer $\vdash \varphi^\sigma$, for σ a substitution
$(\text{nec}_@)$	From $\vdash \varphi$ infer $\vdash @_s \varphi$
$(\text{nec}_\downarrow)$	From $\vdash \varphi$ infer $\vdash \downarrow x.\varphi$
$(\text{nec}_\Box)$	From $\vdash \varphi$ infer $\vdash \Box\varphi$

Fig. 4. An axiomatisation of $\mathbb{K}_{\mathcal{H}(@, \downarrow)}$

$[\preceq_i]$ represent a relation of preference and the collection of modalities of the form $[J]$ represent a strategic game form.

We say a formula is *pure* if it contains no propositional variables (but may contain nominals). We obtain the full axiomatisation of HLCP by adding the pure axiom schemata listed in Figure 5. It is easy to check that these principles are sound. An important theorem of hybrid logic states that if Σ is a set of pure $\mathcal{H}(@, \downarrow)$ formulae, then $\mathbb{K}_{\mathcal{H}(@, \downarrow)} + \Sigma$ is complete for the class of frames on which each formula of Σ is valid [7, Th. 4.11]. Proving the completeness of the inference system is thus straightforward.

We try to give intuitive readings of the axioms of Figure 5. $(T_{[J]})$ means that if s is the state at hand, everyone has accepted it. $(5_{[J]})$ means that for every coalition J, if J accepts s then J refuse not to accept it. (mon) expresses the fact that if a group accepts s then its parts accept s also. (inter) means that if some parts accept s then the coalition composed of these parts accepts s too. (elim) means that if an outcome is acceptable

$(T_{[J]})$	$s \to \langle J \rangle s$
$(5_{[J]})$	$\langle J \rangle s \to [J]\langle J \rangle s$
(mon)	$\langle J_1 \cup J_2 \rangle s \to \langle J_1 \rangle s$
(inter)	$\langle J_1 \rangle s \wedge \langle J_2 \rangle s \to \langle J_1 \cup J_2 \rangle s$
$(\text{elim}_{[\emptyset]})$	$\langle \emptyset \rangle s \to \langle J \rangle \langle \overline{J} \rangle s$
$(\det_{[Agt]})$	$\langle Agt \rangle s \to s$
$(4_{[\preceq_i]})$	$\langle \preceq_i \rangle \langle \preceq_i \rangle s \to \langle \preceq_i \rangle s$
(total)	$s \wedge \langle \emptyset \rangle t \to \langle \preceq_i \rangle t \vee @_t \langle \preceq_i \rangle s$

Fig. 5. Principles added to the axiomatisation of $\mathbb{K}_{\mathcal{H}(@, \downarrow)}$, completing the axiomatisation of HLCP

then a coalition always accepts that its complementary coalition could accept s too. (det) captures the fact that if the grand coalition accepts s then s is the outcome. $(4_{[\preceq_i]})$ and (total) are intuitively the transitivity and connectedness of preferences.

Proposition 1 (completeness). *HLCP is complete with respect to the class of HLCP models.*

PROOF. By applying the Standard Translation (ST) for hybrid logic, we can check that the pure axioms in the last tabular correspond to the constraints we imposed on the frames. The correspondence is pretty clear for who is familiar with the ST for hybrid logic. (Or modal logic: just recall that a nominal is true exactly at one state.) For the example, we nevertheless give the translation for (inter) and (total). (The subscript t is a state symbol that does not occur in the formula being translated.)

– (inter) corresponds to the constraint $R_{J_1} \cap R_{J_2} \subseteq R_{J_1 \cup J_2}$:
  1. $ST_t(\langle J_1 \rangle s \wedge \langle J_2 \rangle s \rightarrow \langle J_1 \cup J_2 \rangle s)$.
  2. $ST_t(\langle J_1 \rangle s) \wedge ST_t(\langle J_2 \rangle s) \rightarrow ST_t(\langle J_1 \cup J_2 \rangle s)$
  3. $\exists y_1.(R_{J_1}(t, y_1) \wedge ST_{y_1}(s)) \wedge \exists y_1.(R_{J_2}(t, y_2) \wedge ST_{y_2}(s)) \rightarrow$
     $\qquad \exists y_1.(R_{J_1 \cup J_2}(t, y_3) \wedge ST_{y_3}(s))$
  4. $\exists y_1.(R_{J_1}(t, y_1) \wedge (y_1 = s)) \wedge \exists y_1.(R_{J_2}(t, y_2) \wedge (y_2 = s)) \rightarrow$
     $\qquad \exists y_1.(R_{J_1 \cup J_2}(t, y_3) \wedge (y_3 = s))$
  5. $R_{J_1}(t, s) \wedge R_{J_2}(t, s) \rightarrow R_{J_1 \cup J_2}(t, s)$
– (total) corresponds to the constraint "P_i is total":
  1. $ST_u(s \wedge \langle \emptyset \rangle t \rightarrow \langle \preceq_i \rangle t \vee @_t \langle \preceq_i \rangle s)$
  2. $ST_u(s) \wedge ST_u(\langle \emptyset \rangle t) \rightarrow ST_u(\langle \preceq_i \rangle t) \vee ST_u(@_t \langle \preceq_i \rangle s)$
  3. $(u = s) \wedge \exists y_1.(R_\emptyset(u, y_1) \wedge ST_{y_1}(t)) \rightarrow$
     $\qquad \exists y_2.(P_i(u, y_2) \wedge ST_{y_2}(t)) \vee \exists y_3.(P_i(t, y_3) \wedge ST_{y_3}(s))$
  4. $(u = s) \wedge \exists y_1.(R_\emptyset(u, y_1) \wedge (y_1 = t)) \rightarrow$
     $\qquad \exists y_2.(P_i(u, y_2) \wedge (y_2 = t)) \vee \exists y_3.(P_i(t, y_3) \wedge (y_3 = s))$
  5. $R_\emptyset(s, t) \rightarrow P_i(s, t) \vee P_i(t, s)$

HLCP only consists in a set of pure axiom schemata added to the axiomatisation of $\mathbb{K}_{\mathcal{H}(@, \downarrow)}$. Hence, the result follows as a corollary of [7, Th. 4.11]. ∎

4 Application to Game Analysis

In the introduction to the paper, we promised that we would formalise solution concepts without using names for actions. In this section, we make good on that promise. We show how it is possible to characterise a number of solution concepts using the logic.

4.1 Relating Strategic Games and HLCP Models

We here guarantee that HLCP models are an adequate conceptualisation of strategic games. With this aim, we relate strategic games $G = \langle N, (A_i), (\succeq_i) \rangle$ with the models of HLCP. Let us first introduce a hybrid version of strategic games.

Definition 11 (hybrid game model). *A hybrid game model is a tuple* $\langle N, (A_i), (\succeq_i),$ *$\mathcal{P}rop, \mathcal{N}om, \mathcal{W}Var, v\rangle$ where $\langle N, (A_i), (\succeq_i)\rangle$ is a strategic game, $\mathcal{P}rop, \mathcal{N}om$ and $\mathcal{W}Var$ are as in Definition 9, and v maps elements from $\times_{i \in N} A_i$ to $2^{\mathcal{P}rop \cup \mathcal{N}om}$.*

Hybrid game models are strategic games with propositions and a function of interpretation, to which we add the standard 'hybrid machinery'. They are sufficiently rich to give a semantics to the language of HLCP. Truth values of HLCP formulae over hybrid game models are defined recursively as follows.

Definition 12 (truth values in hybrid game models). *Let a hybrid game model* $\mathcal{M}_G = \langle N, (A_i), (\succeq_i), \mathcal{P}rop, \mathcal{N}om, \mathcal{W}Var, v\rangle$ *and* g, *is a mapping from* $\mathcal{S}ymb$ *into* A *as in Definition 9.*

- $\mathcal{M}_G, g, a \models_{sg} p$ *iff* $p \in \pi(a)$, *for* $p \in \mathcal{P}rop$
- $\mathcal{M}_G, g, a \models_{sg} t$ *iff* $g(t) = a$, *for* $t \in \mathcal{S}ymb$
- $\mathcal{M}_G, g, a \models_{sg} @_t \varphi$ *iff* $\mathcal{M}_G, g, g(t) \models_{sg} \varphi$, *where* $t \in \mathcal{S}ymb$
- $\mathcal{M}_G, g, a \models_{sg} \downarrow x. \varphi$ *iff* $\mathcal{M}_G, g_a^x, a \models_{sg} \varphi$
- $\mathcal{M}_G, g, a \models_{sg} [J] \varphi$ *iff for every* $a'_{-J} \in \times_{j \in N \setminus J} A_j$ *we have* $\mathcal{M}_G, g, (a_J, a'_{-J}) \models_{sg} \varphi$
- $\mathcal{M}_G, g, a \models_{sg} [\preceq_i] \varphi$ *iff for every* $a' \succeq_i a$ *we have* $\mathcal{M}_G, g, a' \models_{sg} \varphi$

and as usual for classical connectives.

We say a HLCP formula φ is *sg-satisfiable* iff there exists a pointed hybrid game model $\mathcal{M}_G, g, a$ such that $\mathcal{M}_G, g, a \models_{sg} \varphi$ and φ is *sg-valid* iff for every pointed hybrid game model $\mathcal{M}_G, g, a$ we have $\mathcal{M}_G, g, a \models_{sg} \varphi$.

From a hybrid game model we obtain a corresponding HLCP model as follows.

Definition 13 (from hybrid game models to HLCP models). *We say an HLCP model* $\langle \mathcal{A}gt, \mathcal{P}rop, \mathcal{N}om, \mathcal{W}Var, S, (R_J), (P_i), \pi\rangle$ *corresponds to a hybrid game model* $\langle N, (A_i), (\succeq_i), \mathcal{P}rop, \mathcal{N}om, \mathcal{W}Var, v\rangle$ *if:*

- $\mathcal{A}gt = N$;
- $S = \times_{i \in N} A_i$;
- $(a_J, a_{-J}) R_J (a_J, a'_{-J})$;
- $a' \in P_i(a)$ *iff* $a' \succeq_i a$;
- $\pi = v$.

It was already clear that we conceive a state in HLCP as an action profile. Two action profiles are in the same class of choice of J if agents in J do the same action in both profiles; preferences are immediate.

The other way round, we could construct a hybrid game model corresponding to an HLCP model. We just give it for clarification but will not make use of it.

Definition 14 (from HLCP models to hybrid games models). *We say that a hybrid game model* $\langle N, (A_i), (\succeq_i), \mathcal{P}rop, \mathcal{N}om, \mathcal{W}Var, v\rangle$ *corresponds to an HLCP model* $\langle \mathcal{A}gt, \mathcal{P}rop, \mathcal{N}om, \mathcal{W}Var, S, (R_J), (P_i), \pi\rangle$ *if:*

- $N = \mathcal{A}gt$;
- $A_i = S|_{\equiv R_{\{i\}}} = \{|s|_{\equiv R_{\{i\}}} : s \in S\}$;

$-\ (|s_0|_{\equiv R_{\{0\}}}, \dots |s_k|_{\equiv R_{\{k\}}}) \succeq_i (|s'_0|_{\equiv R_{\{0\}}}, \dots |s'_k|_{\equiv R_{\{k\}}})$ *iff* $y \in P_i(x)$, *where* $k = Card(\mathcal{A}gt) - 1$, $x \in \bigcap_{i \in \mathcal{A}gt} |s'_i|_{\equiv R_{\{i\}}}$ *and* $y \in \bigcap_{i \in \mathcal{A}gt} |s_i|_{\equiv R_{\{i\}}};$

$-\ v = \pi.$

The notation makes it perhaps less self explanatory than the previous definition. It identifies the set of actions of an agent i with the set of classes in the equivalence relation of choice $R_{\{i\}}$. An action profile is then captured by a tuple of such classes of choice, one for every agent. As a consequence of the items 2 and 4 of Definition 9, the classes of choice in a tuple intersect in exactly one state: thus, x and y in the definition above are uniquely determined. The preferences in the strategic game model are then derived from the relation P_i applied to this state.

4.2   Equilibria in HLCP Models

Our next task is to adapt the previous definitions of equilibria in the context of HLCP models. We also state their correspondence with the game theoretic definitions.

Definition 15. *Given an* HLCP *model* $\mathcal{M}$ *and a state* s^* *in* $\mathcal{M}$, s^* *is weakly Pareto optimal iff there is no* $s \in R_\emptyset(s^*)$ *such that* $s \in P_i(s^*)$ *and* $s^* \notin P_i(s)$ *for every i in* $\mathcal{A}gt$. s^* *is strongly Pareto optimal iff there is no* $s \in R_\emptyset(s^*)$ *such that* $s \in P_i(s^*)$ *for every i in* $\mathcal{A}gt$, *and there is a j such that* $s^* \notin P_j(s)$.

Definition 16. *Given an* HLCP *model* $\mathcal{M}$ *and a state* s^* *in* $\mathcal{M}$, s^* *is*

1. very weakly dominant *iff for all i in* $\mathcal{A}gt$ *and for all* $s \in R_i(s^*)$, *we have that for all* $s' \in R_{\mathcal{A}gt \setminus \{i\}}(s)$, $s \in P_i(s')$;
2. weakly dominant *iff for all i in* $\mathcal{A}gt$ *and for all* $s \in R_i(s^*)$, *we have that for all* $s' \in R_{\mathcal{A}gt \setminus \{i\}}(s)$, $s \in P_i(s')$ *and there is a* $s'' \in R_{\mathcal{A}gt \setminus \{i\}}(s)$ *such that* $s'' \notin P_i(s)$;
3. strictly dominant *iff for all i in* $\mathcal{A}gt$ *and for all* $s \in R_i(s^*)$, *we have that for all* $s' \in R_{\mathcal{A}gt \setminus \{i\}}(s)$, $s \in P_i(s')$ *and* $s' \notin P_i(s)$.

Definition 17. *Given an* HLCP *model* $\mathcal{M}$ *and a state* s^* *in* $\mathcal{M}$, s^* *is*

1. Nash equilibrium *iff for all i in* $\mathcal{A}gt$, *for all s in* $R_{\mathcal{A}gt \setminus \{i\}}(s^*)$ *we have* $s \in P_i(s^*)$;
2. strong Nash equilibrium *iff for all* $J \subset \mathcal{A}gt$ *and* $s \in R_{\mathcal{A}gt \setminus J}(s^*)$ *there is an i in J such that* $s^* \in P_i(s)$.

Definition 18. *Given an* HLCP *model* $\mathcal{M}$ *and a state* s^* *in* $\mathcal{M}$, s^* *is in the weak* core *iff for all* $J \subset \mathcal{A}gt$ *and* $s \in R_{\mathcal{A}gt \setminus J}(s^*)$ *there is an i in J and an* $s' \in R_J$ *such that* $s^* \in P_i(s')$.

These definitions are adequate with the definition of game theory. This is stated by the next proposition.

Proposition 2. *Let SC be a solution concept among weakly Pareto optimal, strongly Pareto optimal, very weakly dominant, weakly dominant, strictly dominant, Nash equilibrium, strong Nash equilibrium and core. Given a hybrid strategic game* $\mathcal{M}_G$ *and a corresponding* HLCP *model* $\mathcal{M}$, *an action profile of* $\mathcal{M}_G$ *is SC iff it is an SC in* $\mathcal{M}$.

We will rely next on the definitions in terms of relational models introduced in this section for implementing the solution concepts in the language of HLCP.

4.3   Implementation of Equilibria in HLCP

This section provides 'constant predicates' characterising that a state is a particular solution concept. To put it another way, we give context-free definitions of solution concepts in the language of HLCP. We start by defining predicates for *best response* (weak and strict) that will be instrumental in the definition of Nash equilibrium and dominance equilibria next. As an illustration, we also characterise the concept of *never best response*.

WBR_i is intended to read "i plays a weak best response to other agents choice in the current state" by what could be reworded as "the other agents choose that i considers the current state at least as good". Formally,

$$WBR_i =_{def} \downarrow x.[\overline{\{i\}}]\langle \preceq_i \rangle x$$

We see how "binding" the current state to the variable x permits us to use it such that $[\overline{\{i\}}]x$ exactly quantifies over the alternatives allowed by the current choice of the other agents (agents in $Agt \setminus \{i\}$) at the state recorded in x. Since the grand coalition is deterministic, i itself is the 'final chooser'. i plays its best response if in every alternative allowed by the other agents' current choice, i would consider its current choice at least as good.

The notion of strict best response is obtained by replacing the weak preference modality by the strict one, and since $[\overline{\{i\}}]$ is reflexive, we need to use a conditional such that the current state (obviously not strictly preferred) is not compared.[2]

$$SBR_i =_{def} \downarrow x.[\overline{\{i\}}](\neg x \rightarrow \langle \prec_i \rangle x)$$

We can use WBR_i and SBR_i as the building blocks for defining more complex notions. Before focusing on several equilibria, we can see for example that the notion of a choice that is never a best response is intuitively captured in our language, using an agentive formula stating that i chooses that it does not play a weak best response (whatever other agents do):

$$NBR_i =_{def} [i]\neg WBR_i$$

The current choice of an agent i is never a best response if i chooses that it does not play a best response (whatever other agents do). A choice that is never a best response (or equivalently which is always dominated) are often worth considering in game theory because a rational player will never use such a choice.

In the remaining of this section, we give the characterisation of every solution concept defined previously.

Pareto optimality. A state is a *weak Pareto optimum* if there is no other state that makes every agent better off.

$$WPO =_{def} \downarrow x.[\emptyset] \bigvee_{i \in Agt} \langle \preceq_i \rangle x$$

---

[2] Note that this is perfectly uniform with the weak case since, due to the reflexivity of $[\preceq_i]$ we have $WBR_i \leftrightarrow \downarrow x.[\overline{\{i\}}](\neg x \rightarrow \langle \preceq_i \rangle x)$.

A state labelled x is a strong Pareto optimum if there is no state y that is considered by every agent at least as good as x and which is strictly preferred by at least one agent. We can formulate this as:

$$SPO =_{def} \downarrow x.[\emptyset](\downarrow y.(@_x \bigwedge_{i \in Agt} \langle \preceq_i \rangle y) \rightarrow (\bigwedge_{i \in Agt} \langle \preceq_i \rangle x))$$

Contrarily to *WPO*, *SPO* is a fairly complicated formula obtained directly from the definition and without much simplification. The next proposition states that these formalisations are correct.

Proposition 3. *Given an* HLCP *model* $\mathcal{M}$ *and a state s in* $\mathcal{M}$, s^* *is weakly Pareto optimal iff* $\mathcal{M}, s^* \models WPO$. *It is strongly Pareto optimal iff* $\mathcal{M}, s^* \models SPO$

PROOF. From Definition 15, for *WPO* we obtain $\downarrow x. \neg \langle \emptyset \rangle [\downarrow y. \bigwedge_{i \in Agt} ((@_x \langle \preceq_i \rangle y) \wedge \neg \langle \preceq_i \rangle x)]$. We simplify this by the observation that, from (total), $s \wedge \langle \emptyset \rangle t \wedge \neg \langle \preceq_i \rangle t \rightarrow @_t \langle \preceq_i \rangle s$ is a theorem of HLCP. *SPO* is straightforward from the definition with minor rewriting. ∎

We omit the proofs for the other equilibria. They all consist in translating the definitions of Section 4.2 and rewriting the formulation.

Dominance equilibria. We define *very weak dominance*, *weak dominance* and *strict dominance*. Our definitions of dominance largely make use of the concept of best response.

An agent is currently playing a *very weakly dominant* strategy if this is its (weak) best response whatever what the other agents play. It should be clear now that we just have to formalise it via an agentive formula stating that "i chooses that it plays its best response whatever other agents do". Thus we characterise a state where i plays a very weakly dominant strategy by the formula $[i]WBR_i$. We then capture a very weak dominance equilibrium by:

$$VWSD =_{def} \bigwedge_{i \in Agt} [i]WBR_i$$

Weak dominance imposes the strategy to be the strict best response to at least one of the possible combination of choice of the other agents, and this is the only difference with weak dominance. This is formalised by $\langle i \rangle SBR_i$. Thus, we characterise a state where i plays a weakly dominant strategy by the formula $[i]WBR_i \wedge \langle i \rangle SBR_i$, and we capture a weak dominance equilibrium by

$$WSD =_{def} \bigwedge_{i \in Agt} [i]WBR_i \wedge \langle i \rangle SBR_i$$

Strict dominance is intuitively along the same line as very weak dominance, substituting the weak best response by the strict one (or the weak preference modality by a strict one). We characterise a strict dominance equilibrium by

$$SSD =_{def} \bigwedge_{i \in Agt} [i]SBR_i$$

Proposition 4. *Given an* HLCP *model* $\mathcal{M}$ *and a state* s^* *in* $\mathcal{M}$, s^* *is*

1. *very weakly dominant iff* $\mathcal{M}, s^* \models VWSD$;
2. *weakly dominant iff* $\mathcal{M}, s^* \models WSD$;
3. *strictly dominant iff* $\mathcal{M}, s^* \models SSD$.

It is routine to check that strict strategy dominance implies weak strategy dominance which in turn implies very weak strategy dominance.

Proposition 5. $\vdash SSD \rightarrow WSD$ *and* $\vdash WSD \rightarrow VWSD$

Nash equilibria. A state being a Nash equilibrium is simply defined by:

$$NE =_{def} \bigwedge_{i \in \mathcal{A}gt} WBR_i$$

A state is a Nash equilibrium if every agent uses its best response to the choice of the other agents. Remarkably, [25] proposed a similar definition along the pattern $\bigwedge_i D_{\mathcal{A}gt \setminus \{i\}} \langle \preceq_i \rangle x$ within an epistemic language. (Recall our quick comparison in Section 3.2 between epistemic logic and our logic of choice.)

A state is a strong Nash equilibrium of the game if there is no coalition J that can change its choice and lead to a state considered strictly better by every members of J.

$$SNE =_{def} \downarrow x. \bigwedge_{J \subset \mathcal{A}gt} [\overline{J}] (\bigvee_{i \in J} \langle \preceq_i \rangle x)$$

Proposition 6. *Given an* HLCP *model* $\mathcal{M}$ *and a state* s^* *in* $\mathcal{M}$, s^* *is a*

1. *Nash equilibrium iff* $\mathcal{M}, s^* \models NE$.
2. *strong Nash equilibrium iff* $\mathcal{M}, s^* \models SNE$.

The next proposition is straightforward.

Proposition 7. $\vdash SNE \rightarrow NE$

Core. The use of HLCP is not restricted to non-cooperative games. We have already characterised strong Nash equilibrium. It is also easy to capture the concept of *core* of a cooperative strategic game without transferable payoff. We did not do so in our definition in Section 4.2, but as we did for Definition 8 we can start by giving the characterisation of an undominated state. A straightforward translation would be $DOM =_{def} \downarrow x. \langle \overline{J} \rangle \bigvee_{J \subset \mathcal{A}gt} [J] \bigwedge_{i \in J} \downarrow y. @_x \langle \prec_i \rangle y$.

INCR is simply the negation of *DOM*. Up to equivalence (in particular because of (total), (agree), and modal distributivity/contraction) we obtain:

$$INCR =_{def} \downarrow x. \bigwedge_{J \subset \mathcal{A}gt} [\overline{J}] \langle J \rangle \bigvee_{i \in J} \langle \preceq_i \rangle x$$

Proposition 8. *Given an* HLCP *model* $\mathcal{M}$ *and a state* s^* *in* $\mathcal{M}$, s^* *is in the (weak) core iff* $\mathcal{M}, s^* \models INCR$.

Note the difference with (or the resemblance to) strong Nash equilibrium. We clearly have the following.

Proposition 9. $\vdash SNE \rightarrow INCR$

On the succinctness of solution concept characterisations. As noted in the introduction, the number of strategies has no impact on the size of the characterisation of
solution concepts. In the case of cooperative equilibria, the size of the characterisation
depends on the number of coalitions, and is then exponential in the number of players.
However, for all solution concepts but strong Nash equilibrium and core membership,
the size of the formula is polynomial in the number of agents.

In summary, the syntax of **HLCP** allows to a designer to formalise important properties of games succinctly. This is a very desirable feature of a language when we are
interested in model checking. There are at least two reasons for that: (i) less efforts are
needed for the designer to write down a property to be tested, and (ii) the complexity of
model checking is usually function of the size of the input formula.

5   Model Checking

In order to verify properties of games, we can use the Hybrid Logic Model Checker
(HLMC) [10]. This is an implementation of the algorithms of [12], where model checking of hybrid fragment including binders is proved PSPACE-complete when the size of
the input formula is taken as parameter. (Model checking can be solved in polynomial
time if the size of the model is the parameter.) HLMC is given a model and a formula. The
output is the set of states in the model where the formula is satisfied, plus some statistics.

We present the model checking by means of two examples. This will allow us to
demonstrate the ability of our logic with a wide assortment of properties. We first focus
on solution concepts for which players are assumed to be individually rational. We
define Nash equilibrium, very weak dominance and strict dominance in the language
of HLMC (to be introduced). We also make explicit how an **HLCP** model is encoded.
In a second part, we make a move to solution concepts for team reasoners: players are
assume to be able to form coalitions. In the specification language of HLMC, we then
define strong Nash equilibrium, core membership and the 'composite equilibrium' of
Pareto optimal Nash equilibrium.

5.1   Equilibria of Individual Rationality

The language of HLMC for implementing the formulae to be tested matches with the
logical representation. For example, we use `[ag1]` for the $[\{1\}]$, `<pref2>` stands for
$\langle \preceq_2 \rangle$, `B  x` is the down-arrow binder $\downarrow x.$, `&` is the conjunction $\wedge$, `|` is the disjunction
$\vee$, `!` is the negation $\neg$. We propose three progressive examples.

A Nash equilibrium in a 2-agent game is characterised by:

```
B x (
( [ag2]( <pref1>(x) ) )
&
( [ag1]( <pref2>(x) ) )
)
```

A very weak dominant equilibrium in a 2-agent game is a slight modification of Nash
equilibrium:

```
[ag1] ( B x ( [ag2]( <pref1>(x) ) ) )
&
[ag2] ( B x ( [ag1]( <pref2>(x) ) ) )
```

A strict dominant equilibrium in a 2-agent game is obtained from the very weak dominant equilibrium, expanding the definition of strict preferences:

```
[ag1] ( B x ( [ag2](!x ->
    ( B y (<pref1>( (x) & !<pref1>(y))) ) ) ))
&
[ag2] ( B x ( [ag1](!x ->
    ( B y (<pref2>( (x) & !<pref2>(y))) ) ) ))
```

The game of Figure 1 can be represented in the language of HLMC. It is the translation of the following definition of $\mathcal{M} = \langle Agt, \mathcal{P}rop, \mathcal{N}om, \mathcal{W}Var, S, (R_J), (P_i), \pi \rangle$ where:

- $Agt = \{1, 2\}$;
- $\mathcal{P}rop = \emptyset$;
- $\mathcal{N}om = \{i_0, i_1, i_2, i_3\}$;
- $\mathcal{W}Var = \{x, y\}$;
- $S = \{s_0, s_1, s_2, s_3\}$;
- $R_\emptyset = \{(s, s') \mid s \in S, s' \in S\}$;
- $R_{\{1\}} = \{(s_0, s_1), (s_2, s_3)\}^*$, where $*$ is the equivalence closure;
- $R_{\{2\}} = \{(s_0, s_2), (s_1, s_3)\}^*$, where $*$ is the equivalence closure;
- $R_{Agt} = \{(s, s) \mid s \in S\}$;
- $P_1 = \{(s_0, s_1), (s_2, s_0), (s_2, s_1), (s_2, s_3), (s_3, s_0), (s_3, s_1), (s_3, s_2)\}^*$, where $*$ is the reflexive closure;
- $P_2 = \{(s_0, s_3), (s_1, s_0), (s_1, s_2), (s_1, s_3), (s_3, s_0), (s_3, s_1), (s_3, s_2)\}^*$, where $*$ is the reflexive closure;
- $\pi(s_0) = \{i_0\}, \pi(s_1) = \{i_1\}, \pi(s_2) = \{i_2\}, \pi(s_3) = \{i_3\}$.

We give in Appendix the XML script which is the representation of this model. The following is a resume of the model generated by HLMC. Note that we did not give the relations of choice for the grand coalition and the empty coalition. The former is simply obtained as the identity relation, the latter is the composition of the relations of the two individual agents.

```
Kripke structure: XML
    Worlds: s0 (0), s1 (1), s2 (2), s3 (3)
    Modalities:
        ag1 (0) = <s0, s0> <s0, s1> <s1, s0> <s1, s1> <s2, s2> <s2, s3>
        <s3, s2> <s3, s3>
        ag2 (1) = <s0, s0> <s0, s2> <s1, s1> <s1, s3> <s2, s0> <s2, s2>
        <s3, s1> <s3, s3>
        pref1 (2) = <s0, s0> <s0, s1> <s1, s1> <s2, s0> <s2, s1> <s2, s2>
        <s2, s3> <s3, s0> <s3, s1> <s3, s2> <s3, s3>
        pref2 (3) = <s0, s0> <s0, s3> <s1, s0> <s1, s1> <s1, s2> <s1, s3>
        <s2, s2> <s3, s0> <s3, s1> <s3, s2> <s3, s3>
    Propositional symbols:
    Nominals:
        i0 (0) = s0
        i1 (1) = s1
        i2 (2) = s2
        i3 (3) = s3
```

formula	result	RT (in sec)	# recursive calls	# modal calls	# binder calls	max. nesting
NE	$\{s_0\}$	0.0000	45	16	1	7
WSD	$\{s_0\}$	0.0000	49	18	2	10
SSD	$\{s_0\}$	0.0000	273	74	10	17

Fig. 6. Experimental results on non-cooperative solution concepts

Once the game encoded, we can verify that in all cases we obtain the expected output, that is, that the state s_0 corresponding to the action profile (a_1, a_2) is the only equilibrium of the three sorts tested.

We can now test some properties of this game. The result of the model checking in HLMC consists in giving the states satisfying the input formula and some statistics that we give such that the reader can have a grasp on the difference of resources needed for model checking the various properties. Figure 6 presents the results of model checking Nash equilibrium, weak strategy dominance and strict strategy dominance against the the previous model.

5.2   Equilibria for Teams

It must be clear that the expressive power of HLCP is not limited the basic properties of games. The language is precise enough for specifying numbers of properties that one would like to verify. For instance, we can elaborate on equilibria that are desirable from the point of view of team reasoning.

On Figure 7, we have represented a strategic game involving three player. There are two Nash equilibria, (b_1, b_2, a_3) and (a_1, a_2, b_3), that are also strong Nash equilibria. Then, they are also in the core, which also contains (a_1, b_2, b_3). Perhaps a better solution of this game when players reason as a team is the concept of Pareto optimal Nash equilibrium. In this case (b_1, b_2, a_3) is the only solution.

We are now going to verify these statements with HLMC.

The internal representation of the corresponding model in HLMC is the following:

```
Kripke structure: XML
        Worlds: s0 (0), s1 (1), s2 (2), s3 (3), s4 (4), s5 (5), s6 (6), s7 (7)
        Modalities:
                ag1 (0) = <s0, s0> <s0, s1> <s0, s4> <s0, s5> <s1, s0> <s1, s1>
<s1, s4> <s1, s5> <s2, s2> <s2, s3> <s2, s6> <s2, s7> <s3, s2> <s3, s3> <s3, s6>
<s3, s7> <s4, s0> <s4, s1> <s4, s4> <s4, s5> <s5, s0> <s5, s1> <s5, s4> <s5, s5>
<s6, s2> <s6, s3> <s6, s6> <s6, s7> <s7, s2> <s7, s3> <s7, s6> <s7, s7>
                ag2 (1) = <s0, s0> <s0, s2> <s0, s4> <s0, s6> <s1, s1> <s1, s3>
<s1, s5> <s1, s7> <s2, s0> <s2, s2> <s2, s4> <s2, s6> <s3, s1> <s3, s3> <s3, s5>
<s3, s7> <s4, s0> <s4, s2> <s4, s4> <s4, s6> <s5, s1> <s5, s3> <s5, s5> <s5, s7>
<s6, s0> <s6, s2> <s6, s4> <s6, s6> <s7, s1> <s7, s3> <s7, s5> <s7, s7>
                ag3 (2) = <s0, s0> <s0, s1> <s0, s2> <s0, s3> <s1, s0> <s1, s1>
```

$a_3.$

	a_2	b_2
a_1	$1, 0, -5$ (s_0)	$-5, -5, 0$ (s_1)
b_1	$-5, -5, 0$ (s_2)	$0, 0, 10$ (s_3)

$b_3.$

	a_2	b_2
a_1	$-1, -1, 5$ (s_4)	$5, -5, 0$ (s_5)
b_1	$-5, -5, 0$ (s_6)	$-2, -2, 0$ (s_7)

Fig. 7. A 3-player strategic game. Player 1 chooses rows, player 2 chooses columns and player 3 chooses matrices.

```
<s1, s2> <s1, s3> <s2, s0> <s2, s1> <s2, s2> <s2, s3> <s3, s0> <s3, s1> <s3, s2>
<s3, s3> <s4, s4> <s4, s5> <s4, s6> <s4, s7> <s5, s4> <s5, s5> <s5, s6> <s5, s7>
<s6, s4> <s6, s5> <s6, s6> <s6, s7> <s7, s4> <s7, s5> <s7, s6> <s7, s7>
              ag12 (3) = <s0, s0> <s0, s4> <s1, s1> <s1, s5> <s2, s2> <s2, s6>
<s3, s3> <s3, s7> <s4, s0> <s4, s4> <s5, s1> <s5, s5> <s6, s2> <s6, s6> <s7, s3>
<s7, s7>
              ag13 (4) = <s0, s0> <s0, s1> <s1, s0> <s1, s1> <s2, s2> <s2, s3>
<s3, s2> <s3, s3> <s4, s4> <s4, s5> <s5, s4> <s5, s5> <s6, s6> <s6, s7> <s7, s6>
<s7, s7>
              ag23 (5) = <s0, s0> <s0, s2> <s1, s1> <s1, s3> <s2, s0> <s2, s2>
<s3, s1> <s3, s3> <s4, s4> <s4, s6> <s5, s5> <s5, s7> <s6, s4> <s6, s6> <s7, s5>
<s7, s7>
              pref1 (6) = <s0, s0> <s0, s5> <s1, s0> <s1, s1> <s1, s2> <s1, s3>
<s1, s4> <s1, s5> <s1, s6> <s1, s7> <s2, s0> <s2, s1> <s2, s2> <s2, s3> <s2, s4>
<s2, s5> <s2, s6> <s2, s7> <s3, s0> <s3, s3> <s3, s5> <s4, s0> <s4, s3> <s4, s4>
<s4, s5> <s5, s5> <s5, s0> <s5, s6> <s5, s1> <s6, s2> <s6, s3> <s6, s4> <s6, s5> <s6, s6>
<s6, s7> <s7, s1> <s7, s3> <s7, s4> <s7, s5> <s7, s7>
              pref2 (7) = <s0, s0> <s0, s3> <s1, s0> <s1, s1> <s1, s2> <s1, s3>
<s1, s4> <s1, s5> <s1, s6> <s1, s7> <s2, s0> <s2, s1> <s2, s2> <s2, s3> <s2, s4>
<s2, s5> <s2, s6> <s2, s7> <s3, s0> <s3, s3> <s4, s0> <s4, s3> <s4, s4> <s5, s0>
<s5, s1> <s5, s2> <s5, s3> <s5, s4> <s5, s5> <s5, s6> <s5, s7> <s6, s0> <s6, s1>
<s6, s2> <s6, s3> <s6, s4> <s6, s5> <s6, s6> <s6, s7> <s7, s0> <s7, s3> <s7, s4>
<s7, s7>
              pref3 (8) = <s0, s0> <s0, s1> <s0, s2> <s0, s3> <s0, s4> <s0, s5>
<s0, s6> <s0, s7> <s1, s1> <s1, s2> <s1, s3> <s1, s4> <s1, s5> <s1, s6> <s1, s7>
<s2, s1> <s2, s2> <s2, s3> <s2, s4> <s2, s5> <s2, s6> <s2, s7> <s3, s3> <s4, s3>
<s4, s4> <s5, s1> <s5, s2> <s5, s3> <s5, s4> <s5, s5> <s5, s6> <s5, s7> <s6, s1>
<s6, s2> <s6, s3> <s6, s4> <s6, s5> <s6, s6> <s6, s7> <s7, s1> <s7, s2> <s7, s3>
<s7, s4> <s7, s5> <s7, s6> <s7, s7>
        Propositional symbols:
        Nominals:
              i0 (0) = s0
              i1 (1) = s1
              i2 (2) = s2
              i3 (3) = s3
              i4 (4) = s4
              i5 (5) = s5
              i6 (6) = s6
              i7 (7) = s7
```

We need to define the solution concepts that are relevant for this game. For three agents, Pareto optimal Nash equilibrium can be implemented in HLMC as follows:

```
B x (
  ( [ag23]( <pref1>(x) ) )
  &
  ( [ag13]( <pref2>(x) ) )
  &
  ( [ag12]( <pref3>(x) ) )
  &
  [ag12] ([ag3] ( <pref1>(x) | <pref2>(x) | <pref3>(x) ))
)
```

Observe that we did not use the global modality $[\emptyset]$ in the last clause (corresponding to Pareto optimality). As a consequence of $(elim_{[\emptyset]})$, it is indeed definable from two modalities $[J_1]$ and $[J_2]$ when $J_1 \cap J_2 = \emptyset$. Hence, we do not have to specify the relation of choice for the empty coalition in the input model.

Strong Nash equilibrium can be implemented as follows in HLMC:

```
B x (
  ( [ag1]( <pref2>(x) | <pref3>(x)) )
  &
  ( [ag2]( <pref1>(x) | <pref3>(x)) )
  &
  ( [ag3]( <pref1>(x) | <pref2>(x)) )
```

formula	result	RT (in sec)	# recursive calls	# modal calls	# binder calls	max. nesting
NE	$\{s_3, s_4\}$	0.0000	137	48	1	8
$NE \wedge PO$	$\{s_3\}$	0.0000	289	88	1	14
SNE	$\{s_3, s_4\}$	0.0100	425	120	1	14
$INCR$	$\{s_3, s_4, s_5\}$	0.0200	473	168	1	15

Fig. 8. Experimental results on Nash equilibrium, weak Pareto Nash equilibrium and cooperative solution concepts

```
&
( [ag23]( <pref1>(x)) )
&
( [ag13]( <pref2>(x)) )
&
( [ag12]( <pref3>(x)) )
)
```

Finally core membership can be implemented as follows:

```
B x (
  ( [ag1] (<ag23> ( <pref2>(x) | <pref3>(x)) ))
  &
  ( [ag2] (<ag13> ( <pref1>(x) | <pref3>(x)) ))
  &
  ( [ag3] (<ag12> ( <pref1>(x) | <pref2>(x)) ))
  &
  ( [ag23] (<ag1> ( <pref1>(x)) ))
  &
  ( [ag13] (<ag2> ( <pref2>(x)) ))
  &
  ( [ag12] (<ag3> ( <pref3>(x)) ))
)
```

Note that a solution concept defined for k agents can be used for model checking games of less than k players. All we shall need to do is to model the choices of the extra players as the vacuous and dummy choice. That is, every extra player will have not more power that the empty coalition.

We can now verify that our quick analysis of the solutions in the example is correct. Figure 8 presents the results of model checking Nash equilibrium, Pareto Optimal Nash equilibrium, strong Nash equilibrium and core membership against the the previous model.

6   Discussion and Perspectives

It should be clear from what precedes that a logical language without action labels appears to be useful for model checking equilibrium in games. The main aspect is that when combined with the down arrow binder bringing the expressively of "here and now" in the object language, it allows general characterisations of equilibria. With the small exception of [25], and as far as we know, such an approach has not been followed elsewhere.

Adding epistemic reasoning. A theory of interaction cannot be complete without epistemic attitudes. Since the action component of HLCP is inspired by STIT logics, a natural extension is to integrate knowledge, as in [9]. This simply consists of adding straightforward epistemic relations over states to the models and the underlying knowledge operators to the language. As a result we have an expressive logic capable of strategic reasoning under uncertainty.

As an illustration, the infamous notion of *knowing a strategy* is not ambiguous. (See [16] for an account of the problem in logics of ability.) We can distinguish: "*for all* epistemically indistinguishable states, *there exists* a strategy of J that leads to ϕ", from "*there exists* a strategy σ of the coalition J such that *for all* states epistemically indistinguishable for J, σ leads to ϕ". The former is a $\forall$-$\exists$ schema of "knowing a strategy". It is in contrast to the latter sentence, which is a $\exists$-$\forall$ schema.

The need for succinct models. It is not difficult to see that modelling even small strategic games is almost unfeasible. The HLMC basic constructor is

```
<modality label="M">
         ...
    <acc-pair to-world-label="s1" from-world-label="s0"/>
         ...
</modality>
```

stating that the relation underlying the modality [M] has an edge from the state s0 to the state s1. Hence, given the language of HLMC the designer needs to specify *every* edge of every relation of the model.

Relations of choice. In the case of choice relations, every edges for reflexivity, transitivity and euclideanity must be specified. It is quite easy to see that we can encode choices efficiently. We could for instance use *ad hoc* constructors.

```
<choice-mod label="ag1">
        <equiv-class "s0 s1 s2">
</choice-mod>
```

would build all the edges to make $\{s_0, s_1, s_2\}$ an equivalence class representing a choice. Choice relations for coalitions can next be extrapolated from individual relations by intersection.

Relations of preferences. As the relations of preference are much less structured as the relations of choice, their case is also more problematic in practice. Given a game $\langle N, (A_i), (\succeq_i) \rangle$, a corresponding **HLCP** model $\langle \mathcal{A}gt, \mathcal{P}rop, \mathcal{N}om, \mathcal{W}Var, S, (R_J), (P_i), \pi \rangle$ will have $|S| = \prod_{i \in N} |A_i|$ states. Hence, only due to the totality of the preferences, for every agent i, $Card(P_i) \geq |S| + \frac{|S|(|S|-1)}{2}$. Then, for example, for any game of 3 players with 3 choices each, we need to specify at least 1134 edges of preference relation, and we still have to fix the transitivity!

From a practical point of view it means that HLMC is not optimal. It has to be associated with a piece of software taking a compact representation of the model in input and giving in output the XML script readable by HLMC. Such a 'black-box' can take inspiration from the research in compact representation of games. See for example [19, Sect. 2.5] for a short survey.

Acknowledgement

This research is funded by the EPSRC grant EP/E061397/1 *Logic for Automated Mechanism Design and Analysis (LAMDA)*. We are grateful to the reviewers and participants of LOFT'08 and EUMAS'08.

References

1. Alur, R., Henzinger, T.A., Kupferman, O.: Alternating-time temporal logic. Journal of the ACM 49, 672–713 (2002)
2. Areces, C., Blackburn, P., Marx, M.: Hybrid logics: Characterization, interpolation and complexity. Journal of Symbolic Logic 66, 977–1010 (2001)
3. Areces, C., ten Cate, B.: Hybrid Logics. In: Handbook of Modal Logic. Blackburn, et al. [?], vol. 3, pp. 821–868 (2006)
4. Balbiani, P., Herzig, A., Troquard, N.: Alternative axiomatics and complexity of deliberative STIT theories. Journal of Philosophical Logic 37(4), 387–406 (2008)
5. Belnap, N., Perloff, M., Xu, M.: Facing the future: agents and choices in our indeterminist world. Oxford (2001)
6. Blackburn, P., ten Cate, B.: Pure extensions, proof rules, and hybrid axiomatics. Studia Logica 84, 277–322 (2006)
7. Blackburn, P., Tzakova, M.: Hybrid languages and temporal logic. Logic Journal of the IGPL 7(1), 27–54 (1999); Revised Version of MPI-I-98-2-006
8. Blackburn, P., van Benthem, J.F.A.K., Wolter, F. (eds.): Handbook of Modal Logic. Studies in Logic and Practical Reasoning, vol. 3. Elsevier Science Inc., New York (2006)
9. Broersen, J., Herzig, A., Troquard, N.: Normal simulation of coalition logic and an epistemic extension. In: Proceedings of TARK 2007, Brussels, Belgium. ACM DL, New York (2007)
10. Dragone, L.: Hybrid logic model checker (2005),
    http://www.luigidragone.com/hlmc/
11. Fagin, R., Halpern, J.Y., Moses, Y., Vardi, M.Y.: Reasoning about knowledge. The MIT Press, Cambridge (1995)
12. Franceschet, M., de Rijke, M.: Model checking hybrid logics (with an application to semistructured data). Jounal of Applied Logic 4, 279–304 (2006)
13. Gerbrandy, J.: Logics of propositional control. In: AAMAS 2006: Proceedings of the fifth international joint conference on Autonomous agents and multiagent systems, pp. 193–200. ACM Press, New York (2006)
14. Harel, D., Kozen, D., Tiuryn, J.: Dynamic Logic. MIT Press, Cambridge (2000)
15. Horty, J.F., Belnap Jr., N.D.: The deliberative STIT: A study of action, omission, and obligation. Journal of Philosophical Logic 24(6), 583–644 (1995)
16. Jamroga, A., van der Hoek, W.: Agents that know how to play. Fundamenta Informaticae 62(2-3), 185–219 (2004)
17. Kurucz, A.: Combining modal logics. In: Handbook of Modal Logic. Blackburn et al. [?], vol. 3, pp. 869–924 (2006)
18. Osborne, M.J., Rubinstein, A.: A Course in Game Theory. The MIT Press, Cambridge (1994)
19. Papadimitriou, C.: The complexity of finding Nash equilibria. In: Algorithmic Game Theory, pp. 29–51. Cambridge University Press, Cambridge (2007)
20. Parikh, R.: Social software. Synthese 132(3), 187–211 (2002)
21. Passy, S., Tinchev, T.: An essay in combinatory dynamic logic. Information and Computation 93, 263–332 (1991)

22. Pauly, M.: A modal logic for coalitional power in games. Journal of Logic and Computation 12(1), 149–166 (2002)
23. van Benthem, J.: Open problems in logic and games. In: Artëmov, S.N., Barringer, H., d'Avila Garcez, A.S., Lamb, L.C., Woods, J. (eds.) We Will Show Them! Essays in Honour of Dov Gabbay, vol. 1, pp. 229–264. King's College Publications, London (2005)
24. van Benthem, J.: In praise of strategies. In: van Eijck, J., Verbrugge, R. (eds.) Discourses on Social Software. Texts in Logic and Games. Amsterdam University Press (2009)
25. van Benthem, J., van Otterloo, S., Roy, O.: Preference Logic, Conditionals, and Solution Concepts in Games. In: Lagerlund, H., Lindström, S., Sliwinski, R. (eds.) Modality Matters, pp. 61–76. University of Uppsala (2006)
26. van der Hoek, W., Wooldridge, M.: On the logic of cooperation and propositional control. Artificial Intelligence 164(1-2), 81–119 (2005)
27. Venema, Y.: Cylindric modal logic. Journal of Symbolic Logic 60(2), 591–623 (1995)

Appendix: Representation of the Example in HLMC

We give the XML script which is the representation of the model pictured in Figure 1.

We first define four states representing the set of strategy profiles of the game. Then we enumerate explicitly every edge of the relations underlying the choices of agent 1, the choices of agent 2, the preferences of agent 1 and the preferences of agent 2. Finally we assign one nominal to each state. Remark that we did not give the relations of choice for the grand coalition and the empty coalition.

```xml
<?xml version="1.0" encoding="UTF-8"?>
<!DOCTYPE hl-kripke-struct SYSTEM "hl-ks.dtd">
<hl-kripke-struct name="XML">
  <world label="s0"/>
  <world label="s1"/>
  <world label="s2"/>
  <world label="s3"/>

  <!-- s0 is NE, VWSD and SSD
    (s0)1,1    (s1)2,0
    (s2)0,2    (s3)0,0 -->

  <modality label="ag1">
    <acc-pair to-world-label="s0" from-world-label="s0"/>
    <acc-pair to-world-label="s1" from-world-label="s1"/>
    <acc-pair to-world-label="s2" from-world-label="s2"/>
    <acc-pair to-world-label="s3" from-world-label="s3"/>

    <acc-pair to-world-label="s0" from-world-label="s1"/>
    <acc-pair to-world-label="s1" from-world-label="s0"/>

    <acc-pair to-world-label="s2" from-world-label="s3"/>
    <acc-pair to-world-label="s3" from-world-label="s2"/>
  </modality>

  <modality label="ag2">
    <acc-pair to-world-label="s0" from-world-label="s0"/>
    <acc-pair to-world-label="s1" from-world-label="s1"/>
    <acc-pair to-world-label="s2" from-world-label="s2"/>
    <acc-pair to-world-label="s3" from-world-label="s3"/>

    <acc-pair to-world-label="s0" from-world-label="s2"/>
    <acc-pair to-world-label="s2" from-world-label="s0"/>
    <acc-pair to-world-label="s1" from-world-label="s3"/>
    <acc-pair to-world-label="s3" from-world-label="s1"/>
  </modality>

  <modality label="pref1">
    <acc-pair to-world-label="s0" from-world-label="s0"/>
    <acc-pair to-world-label="s1" from-world-label="s1"/>
    <acc-pair to-world-label="s2" from-world-label="s2"/>
    <acc-pair to-world-label="s3" from-world-label="s3"/>

    <acc-pair to-world-label="s1" from-world-label="s0"/>
    <acc-pair to-world-label="s0" from-world-label="s2"/>
    <acc-pair to-world-label="s1" from-world-label="s2"/>
    <acc-pair to-world-label="s3" from-world-label="s2"/>
    <acc-pair to-world-label="s0" from-world-label="s3"/>
    <acc-pair to-world-label="s1" from-world-label="s3"/>
    <acc-pair to-world-label="s2" from-world-label="s3"/>
  </modality>

  <modality label="pref2">
    <acc-pair to-world-label="s0" from-world-label="s0"/>
    <acc-pair to-world-label="s1" from-world-label="s1"/>
    <acc-pair to-world-label="s2" from-world-label="s2"/>
    <acc-pair to-world-label="s3" from-world-label="s3"/>

    <acc-pair to-world-label="s3" from-world-label="s0"/>
    <acc-pair to-world-label="s0" from-world-label="s1"/>
    <acc-pair to-world-label="s2" from-world-label="s1"/>
    <acc-pair to-world-label="s0" from-world-label="s3"/>
    <acc-pair to-world-label="s1" from-world-label="s3"/>
    <acc-pair to-world-label="s2" from-world-label="s3"/>
  </modality>

  <nominal label="i0" truth-assignment="s0"/>
  <nominal label="i1" truth-assignment="s1"/>
  <nominal label="i2" truth-assignment="s2"/>
  <nominal label="i3" truth-assignment="s3"/>
</hl-kripke-struct>
```

Author Index

Printing: Mercedes-Druck, Berlin
Binding: Stein+Lehmann, Berlin